Noteworthy

"Chamberlain instills in writers the confidence to fabricate their own distinctive brands of self-publishing success. His approach outlines the knowledge and teaches the skills necessary to take control ... develop and implement the plans and promotional programs necessary for success—even with sparse capital."

– Dan Poynter
Author, Self-Publisher

"An essential reference tool, *Creative Self-Publishing in the World Marketplace* earns the WordWeaving Award for Excellence."

– Review by Cindy Penn
Senior Editor, WordWeaving.com

http://www.gracepublishing.org/
The Grace Publishing Group
P.O. Box 3070
Fort Myers Beach, FL 33931
staff@gracepublishing.org

If you purchased this book without a cover, you should be aware that this book is stolen property. It was reported as "unsold and destroyed" to the publisher, and neither the author nor the publisher has received any payment for this "stripped book."

A GRACE BOOK: © 2004 by Marshall R. Chamberlain

All rights reserved. This book, or parts thereof, may not be reproduced in any form without permission.

Library of Congress Control Number: 2002-091278

ISBN: 0-9740982-0-5

Printed copies of this book are available through the publisher's vendor of record and bookstores worldwide.

See *Books in Print* for complete book and publisher information.

Manufactured in the United States of America.

First Edition: Winter 2004.

10 9 8 7 6 5 4 3 2 1

Book design by Marshall Chamberlain.
Book cover by Matt Pramschuffer, http://www.budgetmediadesign.com.

Creative Self-Publishing in the World Marketplace

The What, Why, How, When, and How Much

"It's an indispensable companion to *The Self-Publishing Manual*."
– Dan Poynter

Marshall Chamberlain

First Edition

The Grace Publishing Group
Fort Myers Beach, FL

This book is dedicated
to writers and authors all over the
world, of all genres and subjects, who
want to level the publishing playing field,
create their works, and get them directly in front
of the market in the most cost-effective manner.

It is further dedicated to recognition that
the concepts of epiphany, insight, and serendipity
are always operative, if our eyes and
minds remain open.

Acknowledgements

I particularly thank: Dan Poynter, Marilyn and Tom Ross, Barbara Gaughen, Ernest Weckbaugh, Mark Ortman, John Kremer, Patricia Fry, Danny O. Snow, Mary Embree, M. J. Rose, and Angela Adair-Hoy for their great books; the Publishers Marketing Association (PMA), Small Publishers Association of North America (SPAN), Small Publishers, Artists & Writers Network (SPAWN), *Publishers Weekly* magazine, and Midwest Book Review for their excellent publishing and writing resources, timely dissemination of relevant news, and support of industry networking.

Without encouragement from my mother, Rita S. Chamberlain, who reviewed the inadequate initial draft of my first fiction book five years ago, I never would have committed to the author journey. She simply said, "It's not very good now, but you can write." Considering she had lived with my father during his 45-year career as a respected Associated Press writer and editor, it was enough.

I also thank: Betzi Abram, consummate writer and teacher, for her caring and kind words of encouragement; Robin Chamberlain, my oldest daughter, and Ruben Colon, a Fort Myers author and officer of the Gulf Coast Writers Association, for their gifts of precious time in making poignant editing suggestions for the excerpt of my upcoming fiction book, which appears at the end of this manuscript. It always helps to see the trees clearly so you can prune the dead wood.

I'm indebted to Nancy Chase and Meg Price for adding their editing skills to the development of the book, helping me establish consistency, stay within acceptable bounds of grammatical correctness, and focus the message while still retaining a personal writing voice.

Nancy Chase is a writer, editor, and writing coach. When she isn't running her manuscript critique business, NovelMentor.com, she administers several online mailing lists for writers, produces a quarterly newsletter, and works on her own novels and poetry. She lives in Virginia. Contact her at NovelMentor@aol.com.

Margaret (Meg) Price is an author, writer, ghostwriter, editor, and workshop teacher. She is currently working on two novels and a collection of short stories, and lives with her husband in Cape Coral, Florida. Contact her at megprice@megprice.net.

Foreword

Authors, poets, journalists, scientists, academics, writers of fiction, nonfiction, science fiction, romance, mystery, anthologies, business, how-to books, research articles, monographs, textbooks, diaries—any kind of writing: You can publish yourself.

At its heart this book is a self-help tool, written by a real self-publisher who took the road less traveled and climbed all the way up the learning curve from start to finish—is it ever finished?

Marshall Chamberlain distills his knowledge and experience in an informal, down-to-earth manner. He shows committed writers how to clearly navigate the jungles of the publishing industry and take advantage of the New Book Model: Digital printing technology and high-tech communication services make it possible for writers to achieve their publication dreams.

Chamberlain's *case study approach* places a grid of self-publishing choices over the publishing field. It provides sources of information, suggestions and recommendations, and real examples of the decision-making process. He empowers writers to plot their own self-publishing courses, based on personal lifestyle preferences and the availability of time, energy, and financial resources. His approach outlines the knowledge and teaches the skills necessary to take control of key publishing functions, and develop and implement the plans and promotional programs necessary for self-publishing success—even with sparse capital.

Throughout his two-and-a-half year case study, Chamberlain confronts key questions, issues, potential problems, and risks that face self-publishers, and offers ways and means to help deal with them creatively and effectively. By defining the what, why, how, when, and how much in the self-publishing process, Chamberlain instills in writers the confidence to fabricate their own distinctive brands of self-publishing success. He's right when he says, "Anybody can self-publish if they have determination and fire in the belly."

By developing a robust index and table of contents, Chamberlain makes this book an invaluable, issues-and-answers resource as well as subject reference. It's an indispensable companion to *The Self-Publishing Manual*.

– Dan Poynter
Author, Publisher, Speaker

Warnings and Disclaimers

Without limiting the rights under copyright reserved above, no part of this book may be reproduced, stored in or introduced into a retrieval system, transmitted in any form, or by any means (electronic, mechanical, photocopying, recording, or otherwise), without the prior written permission of the owner.

The opinions and references cited in this book are meant to serve as guidelines, and are subject to becoming outdated at any time due to changing information and evolving market conditions. Furthermore, purchasers and readers are put on notice herein that the author presents personal opinions and self-publishing concepts that may or may not be universally accepted or have been tested in the marketplace. Many of the estimates and calculations made in the book are not represented as being accurate in all conditions, and some are presented only as approximations. Purchasers entering the business of self-publishing must use prudence in utilizing any suggested or intimated course of action appearing in this book.

The book is designed and sold with the purpose and understanding that the author and/or publisher(s) are not rendering legal, accounting, or other professional advice. Effort has been made to make the book as useful, complete, and accurate as possible; however, there may be mistakes both typographical and in content. Facts, other business information, and technology are changing from minute to minute.

The time estimates and activities cited here—some of which have been experienced in self-publishing this book and some of which are planned for the future by the author himself or in conjunction with contracted service providers—should be considered as generic. These estimates, actions, and activities may or may not be successfully employed, and are subject to change without notice.

The author and publishers shall incur no liability or responsibility to any person or entity with respect to any damage or loss allegedly caused, whether directly or indirectly, by the information contained in this book. Potential purchasers who do not agree with the above caveats in this disclaimer are directed not to purchase the book or utilize its information.

Table of Contents

Noteworthy I

Acknowledgements V

Foreword VI

Warnings and Disclaimers VII

Table of Contents VIII

Introduction 1
    CAN YOU BECOME A SELF-PUBLISHER? 1
    BOOK OVERVIEW 3
    LAST COMMENTS 4

CHAPTER I: Observations On Key Subject Areas 7
    A. PUBLISHERS AND AGENTS 7
    B. DISTRIBUTORS AND WHOLESALERS 9
        1. FINANCIAL RISKS 10
        2. SOME ECONOMIC PERSPECTIVES 11
        3. VALUABLE SERVICES 11
    C. PERSPECTIVE ON INTERNET PUBLISHING 12
        1. WHO ARE THESE INTERNET PUBLISHERS? 12
        2. WHAT ARE THE SERVICES AND COSTS, AND WHO
           MIGHT USE THEM? 13
        3. WHAT ABOUT THE RISKS AND REWARDS? 15
           TYING UP THE AUTHOR AND BOOK 16
           LIMITED PROFITS AND FIXED BOOK-PRINTING COST ... 17
           SHARING OF NET PROFITS 17
           SOME HIDDEN RISKS 18
    D. VIABLE SELF-PUBLISHING APPROACHES 19
        1. YOU DON'T NEED TO BE ON THE SHELF 20
        2. A PRACTICAL PUBLISHING APPROACH 21
        3. ALTERNATIVE PUBLISHING APPROACH 23
    E. THE INTERNET AND THE FUTURE OF PUBLISHING 25

CHAPTER II: Resources, Software and Equipment (Months 1-6) .. 27

A. GROUPS AND ASSOCIATIONS (Months 1-3) 28
B. REFERENCES AND INTERNET RESOURCE SITES
(MONTHS 1-3) 28
  1. BOOKS AND BOOKLETS 29
  2. PMA NEWSLETTER ARCHIVE 29
  3. INTERNET SITES 29
  4. LEGAL ASSISTANCE 31
  5. INTERNET SEARCH AID 31
C. SOFTWARE (MONTHS 1-3) 31
  1. MICROSOFT WORD 32
  2. MICROSOFT PUBLISHER 32
  3. ADOBE PAGEMAKER 6.5 32
  4. ADOBE ACROBAT 4.0+ 32
  5. ADOBE READER 33
  6. WINFAX PRO 10.0 33
  7. MICROSOFT OUTLOOK 33
  8. MICROSOFT FRONTPAGE 34
  9. MICROSOFT ACCESS 34
  10. QUICKBOOKS 34
  11. MICROSOFT EXCEL 35
  12. IMAGE-MANAGEMENT SOFTWARE 35
  13. ENCYCLOPEDIA BRITANNICA CD ROM 36
  14. BULK E-MAIL SOFTWARE 36
  15. LEARNING TO USE SOFTWARE 37
D. EQUIPMENT (Months 1-3) 38

CHAPTER III: Book Development (Months 1-24) 41

A. BOOK FIRST DRAFT (Months 1-6) 41
  1. GENERAL STORY FOLDER 41
  2. SCENIZING 42
  3. WRITING VOICE 42
  4. SCULPTING 43
B. AUTHOR EDITING (Months 7-18) 43
  1. FIRST EDIT (Months 7-12) 43
  2. SECOND EDIT (Months 7-12) 44
  3. FINAL EDIT (Months 13-18) 45
C. OUTSIDE EDITING (Months 13-24) 45
  1. SOURCES 46
  2. CONTACTING 47

3. SCREENING 48
4. FINAL SELECTION 48

CHAPTER IV: Promotional-List Compilation and Use (Months 1-24) 51

A. GENERAL MECHANICS 51
B. EXAMPLE OF LIST CREATION USING MICROSOFT ACCESS 52
C. IMPORTING LISTS FOR BROADCASTING 53
D. PURGING THE LISTS 54
E. LIST DESCRIPTIONS 55
   1. LIBRARIES 55
   2. BOOKSTORES 56
   3. MAJOR AUTHORS 57
   4. FILM PRODUCERS AND FILM AGENTS 57
   5. NATIONAL MAGAZINES FEATURING BOOKS 57
   6. NATIONAL, DAILY, AND WEEKLY NEWSPAPERS 57
   7. MAJOR PUBLISHERS 59
   8. LITERARY AGENTS 60
   9. TRADITIONAL BOOK REVIEWERS AND SYNDICATORS. 60
   10. INTERNET BOOK REVIEWERS 60
   11. CATALOGS 61
   12. BOOK CLUBS 61
   13. MAJOR PAPERBACK PUBLISHERS 62
   14. MAJOR DISTRIBUTORS 62
   15. MAJOR WHOLESALERS 62
   16. FOREIGN RIGHTS PUBLISHERS 62
   17. ALTERNATIVE NEWSPAPERS 63
   18. NATIONAL CHAIN BOOKSTORES 63
   19. NATIONAL INDEPENDENT BOOKSTORES 63
   20. PRINT NEWSLETTERS THAT REVIEW BOOKS 63
   21. INTERNET LISTSERVS AND GROUPS 64
      LISTSERVS 64
      GROUPS AND CLUBS 65
      ORGANIZING MEMBERSHIPS FOR SENDING E-MAILS ... 66
   22. POTENTIAL INDIVIDUAL BUYERS 67
      ADDING GROUP AND LISTSERV MEMBERS 67
      USING THE LIST IN BROADCAST E-MAIL 68
   23. BOOK-RELATED ORGANIZATIONS 68

ORGANIZING KEY ELEMENTS OF INFORMATION 69
ADDING TO THE POTENTIAL INDIVIDUAL BUYERS LIST 70
SOME COMPILING SUGGESTIONS 70
24. BOOK PRESENTATION AND AUTHOR POSTING SITES 71
25. OPT-IN E-MAIL LISTS 72
26. BULK E-MAIL LISTS 72
27. RADIO AND TV PROGRAMS FEATURING BOOKS 73
28. NICHE LISTS 73
29. SUPER MAJOR REVIEWERS 74

CHAPTER V: Communications Systems (Months 25-27) 77

A. LOGO, BUSINESS HEADER AND SIGNATURE 77
B. BUSINESS CARDS 78
C. CHARGE-CARD SERVICES PROVIDER 79
D. TELEPHONE-SERVICES PROVIDER 82
E. LONG-DISTANCE TELEPHONE-SERVICES PROVIDER 83
F. TOLL-FREE, IN-BOUND TELEPHONE NUMBER 84
G. FAX-NUMBER SERVICES PROVIDER 85
H. INTERNET-SERVICE PROVIDERS 86
I. E-MAIL SERVICE PROVIDERS 88

CHAPTER VI: Book Production (Months 25-27) 91

A. BOOK FINAL EDITING AND PROOFING PROCESS (Months 25-27) 91
B. BOOK-PRODUCTION MECHANICS (Months 25-27) 92
  1. SELECTION OF PRINTER(S) FOR YOUR VARIOUS NEEDS 92
    GENERAL SOURCES 92
    GALLEY-BOOK 93
    TRADE PAPERBACK 93
    HARDBACK 94
  2. BOOK FORMATTING 94
    BOOK DRAFTING AND STYLES IN THE WORD PROCESSOR 95
    PAGINATION, HEADERS AND FOOTERS 96
    TABLE OF CONTENTS 98
    INDEXING 99
  3. BOOK COVER CREATION 101

TEMPLATE AND CUSTOM COVERS FROM PRINTERS .. 102
DESIGNING A COVER FROM SCRATCH 102
UTILIZING OUTSIDE DESIGNER SERVICES 103
4. CREATING PDF DOCUMENTS AND E-BOOKS 103
   ADOBE PAGEMAKER 6.5 104
   ADOBE ACROBAT 4.0+ 104
   E-BOOK COVERS 104
   PDF E-BOOKS 105
   OTHER USEFUL PDF APPLICATIONS 106
5. GALLEY COVER PREPARATION 107
   FRONT COVER KEY INFORMATION 107
   BACK COVER INFORMATION 108
   SPINE INFORMATION 109
6. E-BOOKS FOR HANDHELD DEVICES 109
7. E-BOOK INTERNET SALES SITES 110
8. E-BOOKS ON CDS 111
9. SEND GALLEY TO THE PRINTER (Month 27) 112

CHAPTER VII: Developing the Business Website (Months 25-27) 115

A. PURPOSE AND GENERAL ORGANIZATION 116
B. EXAMINE WEBSITES OF AUTHORS AND SELF-
PUBLISHERS 117
C. WEBSITE SOFTWARE 117
D. HOSTING SERVICES 118
E. CREATION MECHANICS 120
   1. MASTER PAGE 120
   2. HYPERLINKS AND PAGE CONSISTENCY 121
   3. CONTROL FORMS 122
      OPTION BUTTON EXAMPLE 122
      SINGLE-LINE TEXT BOX EXAMPLE 123
      COMMAND BUTTON EXAMPLE 123
      CHECK AND LIST-BOX EXAMPLES 123
      ORDER FORM EXAMPLE 123
      SPECIAL-PURPOSE FORM EXAMPLE 124
   4. ORIGINATION OF MASTER CONTENT FILES 125
F. MAJOR PAGES 125
   1. HOME 126
   2. MEDIA ROOM 127

3. LIBRARY ROOM 127
4. BOOKSTORE ROOM 128
5. READER ROOM 129
6. BUSINESS ROOM 130
7. RADIO AND TV ROOM 131
8. AUTHORS AND BOOKS 132
   BOOK PRESENTATION AND CONTENT 132
   MEDIA KIT AND CONTENT 133
   MEDIA KIT MASTER PDF FILE 136
   ACTIVITY CALENDAR 137
9. BUSINESS SERVICES 137
   THE AFFILIATE AUTHOR PROGRAM 138
   SELF-PUBLISHING WORKSHOPS 138
   OTHER SERVICES I OFFER 139
10. NEWSLETTER 139
11. INTERNET CLUB 139
12. BUSINESS LINKS 140
13. FREQUENTLY ASKED QUESTIONS 140
14. CONTACT US 141
15. POLICIES 141
G. TESTING AND UPLOADING THE WEBSITE 141
H. SEARCH-ENGINE REGISTRATIONS 143
I. DEVELOPING KEYWORDS 145
H. REGISTERING KEYWORDS 145

CHAPTER VIII: Phase I Promotion (Months 28-29) 147

A. BUSINESS-CONTACT FILE SYSTEM 147
B. BOOKS AND BOOK-RELATED PRODUCTS FOR SALE (Months 28-29) 148
   1. REGISTERED, AUTOGRAPHED, COLLECTOR'S EDITION 148
   2. PDF E-BOOK 148
   3. AUTOGRAPHED BOOKS 149
   4. OTHER PRODUCTS 149
C. PROMOTIONS TO GENERATE ADVANCE SALES (Months 28-29) 150
   1. MASTER PROMOTION LOG 150
   2. FIRST SALES OFFERS TO LIBRARIES 150

3. FIRST SALES OFFERS TO INDIVIDUAL POTENTIAL BUYERS 151
4. FIRST ANNOUNCEMENTS TO ORGANIZATIONS 152
5. FIRST INTERNET ANNOUNCEMENTS 153
6. SUBMIT THE BOOK PRESENTATION TO AMAZON.COM 153
7. SUBMIT TO SPECIALTY INTERNET SITES 153
D. POST AND PROMOTE YOUR BUSINESS ACTIVITIES (Months 28-29) 154
   1. POSTING 154
   2. PROMOTING 155
E. PARTICIPATION IN PMA CO-OP MARKETING PROGRAMS (Months 28-29) 155
F. GALLEY-BOOK REVIEW PROMOTION (Months 28-29) 156
   1. PREPARE AND DELIVER GALLEY REVIEW INVITATIONS 157
      THE PROCEDURE 157
      DRAFTING 157
      CONTENT 158
      E-MAILING 159
      FAXING 161
   2. COMPILING THE GALLEY-BOOK REVIEW LIST 162
   3. TELEPHONE FOLLOW-UP PROGRAM 162
      AUTOMATIC DELIVERIES LIST 163
      LOCAL MARKET AREA 163
      MOVERS AND SHAKERS 163
      MAJOR AUTHORS AND EXPERTS 163
      MAJOR PUBLISHERS 164
      OTHER MAJOR ORGANIZATIONS 164
   4. TELEPHONE TECHNIQUES 164
      GRAB ATTENTION 165
      DEVELOP A 30-SECOND TELL-AND-SELL 165
      SIGN OFF QUICKLY 166
      RAPPORT WITH REVIEWER ASSISTANTS 166
      FOLLOW-UP NOTES 167
   5. GALLEY-BOOK REVIEW PRESENTATION 167
      DELIVERING THE GALLEY PRESENTATION 168
      CONTENTS 168
         COVER LETTER 168
         GENERAL INFORMATION BROCHURE 169

PHOTOGRAPHS 170
PACKAGING MATERIALS AND CONSTRUCTION 170
FORMAT COSTS AND DELIVERY 170
HARD COPY 171
COMPUTER FILES AS ATTACHMENTS TO E-MAIL OR
POSTED AT YOUR WEBSITE 171
CD-R DISCS 172
6. TELEPHONE FOLLOW-UP TO GALLEY-BOOK
DELIVERIES 173
G. BOOK REGISTRATIONS AND LISTINGS (Months 28-29) ... 173
1. ISBN AND SAN 173
2. BAR CODE 174
3. ABI AND *BOOKS IN PRINT* 175
4. LIBRARY OF CONGRESS CATALOG CARD NUMBER 176
5. *PUBLISHERS DIRECTORY* 177
6. *SMALL PRESS RECORD OF BOOKS IN PRINT* 177
7. *PUBLISHERS TRADE LIST ANNUAL* 177
8. *PUBLISHERS, DISTRIBUTORS AND WHOLESALERS OF
THE UNITED STATES* 178
9. *PUBLISHERS' INTERNATIONAL ISBN DIRECTORY* 178
10. *ABA BOOK BUYER'S HANDBOOK* 178
11. *LITERARY MARKET PLACE* 178
12. *CONTEMPORARY AUTHORS* 178
13. *POLICIES OF PUBLISHERS: A HANDBOOK FOR ORDER
LIBRARIANS* 178

CHAPTER IX: Phase II Promotion (Months 30-31) 179

A. SECOND SALES OFFERS TO INDIVIDUAL POTENTIAL
BUYER LISTS (Month 30) 179
B. SECOND SALES OFFERS TO LIBRARIES (Month 30) 180
C. FINAL BOOK EDIT, ORDERING AND RECEIVING BOOKS
(Months 30-31) 180
D. REVIEW-BOOK PROMOTION (Months 30-31) 182
1. SENDING REVIEW-BOOK INVITATIONS 182
REVIEWER LISTS 182
CONTENT OF THE E-MAIL AND FAX INVITATIONS 183
POSTAL-MAILER 184
2. COMPILE THE REVIEW-BOOK LIST 185

3. TELEPHONE FOLLOW-UP PROGRAM TO INVITATIONS 185
4. PREPARING THE REVIEW-BOOK PRESENTATION 186
   MATERIALS and DESIGN 186
   CONTENT 187
      BOOK 187
      REVIEW SLIP 187
      COVER LETTER 188
      GENERAL INFORMATION BROCHURE 188
      PREPUBLICATION REVIEW SHEET 188
      REVIEW-BOOK REPLY CARD 189
      LONG-FORM DRAFT OF A GENERIC BOOK-REVIEW ARTICLE 190
      PHOTOGRAPHS 190
5. COSTS OF THE REVIEW-BOOK PRESENTATION AND DELIVERY 190
   USING HARD COPY 190
   USING CD-RS 191
   USING PDF FILES ON YOUR WEBSITE 192
   FLEXIBLE ALTERNATIVES 192
6. SPREADING OUT BOOK REVIEWS 192
E. POST THE BOOK FOR SALE AT THE MAJOR ONLINE BOOKSTORES (Months 30-31) 192
   1. SALES PRESENTATION 193
   2. ORDERS 193
   3. COSTS AND PROFITS 194
   4. OTHER VALUES 194
   5. E-BOOKS 195
F. SET UP YOUR FULFILLMENT SYSTEM AND FILL ORDERS (MonthS 30-31) 196
   1. INITIAL ORDER HANDLING 196
   2. INVOICE CREATION AND ORDER PROCESSING 197
   3. RECORD KEEPING 199
   4. RECEIVING AND STORING BOOKS 200
   5. PACKAGING 200
   6. FINISHING AND LABELING PACKAGES 201
   7. SHIPPING 202

CHAPTER X: Continuing Creative Promotional Plan 203

A. SUMMARY OF MAJOR PROMOTIONS TO DATE 203
B. TOWARD NON-SPAM STANDARDS FOR E-MAIL
COMMUNICATIONS 204
   1. USE RICH TEXT FORMAT 205
   2. IDENTIFY THE SENDER 205
   3. BULK E-MAIL SOFTWARE OR A SERVICES PROVIDER 205
   4. SUBJECT LINE 206
   5. FIRST THREE LINES 206
   6. BODY OF THE E-MAIL 207
   7. CLOSING AND ATTRIBUTION-SIGNATURE 209
   8. ACTION FOR REMOVAL 209
   9. CITE CURRENT LAW 209
C. DESIGNING A LONG-TERM PROMOTION STRATEGY 210
   1. CORE ADVICE 210
   2. DATABASES 210
   3. PROMOTIONAL AND ADVERTISING PIECES 211
      BUSINESS CARDS 211
      BOOKMARKS 211
      POSTCARDS 212
D. DEFINING PROGRAMS IN THE PROMOTION PLAN 212
   1. PRINT-MEDIA PROGRAM 213
      PERIODIC COMMUNICATIONS 213
      MEDIA APPROACH IDEAS 213
      POSTAL-MAIL MINI-MEDIA KIT TEST 214
   2. TELEPHONE FOLLOW-UP PROGRAM 215
   3. RADIO AND TV PROGRAM 216
      CREATE CONNECTIONS TO YOUR EXPERTISE 216
      A SUGGESTED PROMOTIONAL APPROACH 217
         THE QUERY 217
         GENERIC INTERVIEW 218
         EXAMPLE APPROACH 219
         TELEPHONE FOLLOW-UP 219
      SOURCES FOR STRATEGIES 220
   4. PMA CO-OP MARKETING PROGRAMS 220
      PROGRAMS, COSTS AND DELIVERY 221
   5. PERSONAL PROGRAM 221
      WORKSHOPS 222
      CLASSES AND COACHING 224
      CONSULTING SERVICES 224

SPEAKING AND PARTICIPATING AT EVENTS 225
ATTENDING EVENTS 226
   EVENT SCHEDULING SOURCES 227
   PREMIERE WRITER AND PUBLISHING EVENTS 228
6. INTERNET TESTING PROGRAM 228
TESTING OPT-IN E-MAIL LISTS 228
TESTING BULK E-MAIL LISTS 229
7. DIRECT SALES PROGRAM 229
SALES OFFERS TO LIBRARIES 230
SALES OFFERS TO BOOKSTORES 231
SALES OFFERS TO POTENTIAL INDIVIDUAL BUYERS .. 232
   EXAMPLE GIVEAWAYS 232
   DELIVERING COMMUNICATIONS TO INDIVIDUALS ... 233
SALES OFFERS TO BOOK-RELATED ORGANIZATIONS 234
   THE INVITATION/OFFER 234
   AN EXAMPLE 234
SALES TO NONTRADITIONAL MARKETS 235
   GENERAL MARKETS 236
   PREMIUM SALES 236
   PREMIUM IDEAS 237
8. INTERNET ADVERTISING PROGRAM 237
RECIPROCAL LINKS AND DIRECTORY REGISTRATIONS
.... 238
AFFILIATE/ASSOCIATE PROGRAMS 238
POSTING ARTICLES 238
NEWS DISSEMINATION 239
9. FOREIGN RIGHTS PROGRAM 240
E. ASSISTANCE AND SUPPORT TO WRITERS AND READERS
.... 240
   ARTICLES 241
   INTERNET CLUB 241
   CHAT ROOM 242
   NEWSLETTER 242

Postscript 245

   YOU CAN MAKE A LIVING SELLING BOOKS 245
   REORGANIZE WITH INCREASING SALES 246
   DON'T LET SUCCESS CHANGE YOUR MODUS OPERANDI. 247
   TALK THE TALK AND WALK THE WALK 247

XIX

NOTE	248
Index	249
Synopsis and Excerpt	267
Synopsis	269
Excerpt of Chapter I: Coming Home	271
About the Author	279
Rapid Book-Order Form*	281

XX

Introduction

CAN YOU BECOME A SELF-PUBLISHER?

I designed this book to be of significant value to authors and self-publishers across the breadth of the literary world, from writers of professional papers, research-journal articles, poetry, fiction and nonfiction books, to small publishers of books, journals, magazines, and newsletters. But I tell you up front, acquiring the tools and aptitudes of creative self-publishing should be viewed as an investment of time, like a PhD program with a required dissertation. Becoming a successful self-publisher takes commitment, concentration, and dedication. It's a bold adventure.

But if you sincerely want your shot in this day and age of print on demand (POD), print quantity needed (PQN), the Internet, and magical computer-software and communications capabilities, you can have it. I did it with a net worth in the low three figures, waiting tables at night as my sole means of support, and acquiring only what I absolutely needed as I went along.

If you bring to the drawing board a disciplined and organized mind, commitment to seeing your work in print, and openness to subtle opportunity, you can level the publishing field of play.

Becoming a successful self-publisher requires that you become a competent author as well as a publisher. Becoming a publisher calls for understanding and controlling most of the major functions in the publishing puzzle. Specifically, I mean: writing, editing, distribution, business and risk management, order fulfillment, bookkeeping, rights negotiation, document formatting, marketing and promotional planning, illustrating, website creation, speaking, photography, event planning, teacher and workshop facilitation, agenting, and even motion-picture collaborator. Okay, maybe not that. The only thing you can't do yourself is manufacture books.

You must perform these publishing functions yourself or, if your time, energy, and capital resources allow, contract as many as you are comfortable with to outside service providers. If you have the financial resources to use outside professional help, becoming a savvy self-publisher first will give you an understanding of the elements in the big picture, so you'll know exactly what to expect from your delegations of authority and responsibility.

Of course, if you become the consummate self-publisher, it will be like taking on the CEO's job in a publishing business; you will have zero time to write. A reasonable approach for authors who want to write and be published is to first invest the time and effort learning how to self-publish; then, win the freedom to continue a writing career by successfully self-publishing your book. Along the way, networking and promoting will open many doors of opportunity, and you should be able to farm out time-consuming functions to outside service providers or possibly incorporate your business with working partners. A major publishing house might even discover you. Who knows?

Having desire, business sense, total commitment to the writing craft, and willingness to step up and learn to take charge of the publishing functions is still not enough. It takes fire in the belly and a clear understanding that you are the only one who will make it all happen. A self-publisher cannot rely on serendipity. You can't count on luck to play a role, although if it occurs, you'll reap a windfall gain.

But wait a minute. Maybe it's not such a daunting journey. The road is certainly less traveled, but you and your book could join the likes of self-publishers cited by Dan Poynter and Danny O. Snow in their book, *U-Publish.com,* such as John Grisham and *A Time to Kill,* James

Introduction

Redfield with *The Celestine Prophecy, The Elements of Style* by William Strunk Jr. and E. B. White, *Dianetics* by L. Ron Hubbard, and Richard M. Nixon's *Real Peace*, to name only a few of the many legitimate, blockbusting bestsellers that were originally self-published. According to Poynter and Snow, even Mark Twain and Edgar Allen Poe were self-publishers.

BOOK OVERVIEW

This book is really a case study. It presents a two-and-a-half-year operating plan, based on experience, beginning six months prior to completion of a book's first draft. It ends by outlining concepts and cycles of continuing creative promotion after a book has been printed and made available for purchase at bookstores.

It's my purpose to make crystal clear that what you have to do to become a successful self-publisher can be accomplished with limited financial resources and minimum risk. I give you alternatives for how to get things done and how much it may cost, by creatively utilizing new technologies and developing the skills to perform the major functions of a publisher. I do not pretend to present all the options or means in accomplishing your objectives. Because I possessed limited financial resources during my journey, accomplishing objectives with common tools in hand and those within my grasp became the name of the game.

As the publishing playing field takes on shape and clarity, each self-publishing author will be faced with decisions of employing limited time, energy, and financial resources while defining how to reach his or her particular kind of success.

This book evolved from the business plan I began piecing together during the drafting and editing of my upcoming fiction book. I never set out to write a nonfiction how-to book. After two or three months of working on the business plan, I realized I had an opportunity to provide a worthy service by creating a map through the maze of publishing for authors with real determination. During the book's evolution, I developed several secondary objectives worth mentioning here:

- First, I wanted to create and publish this book using the concepts, principles, and planning it outlines.

- Second, as quickly as possible, I wanted to get the guts of the book into the hands of writers, editors, journalists, and researchers who would recognize value in early access. I accomplished this—a year in advance of traditional publication—by offering a working-paper version of a reasonably edited draft of the book for sale, formatted as a PDF (Portable Document Format, created by Adobe software) file.

- And third, I wanted to develop and implement a dynamic prerelease promotion that offered complimentary PDF e-book copies six months prior to the availability of the hard copy at bookstores, to invited writers, writer organizations and their staffs, and my favorite Internet writer's groups.

LAST COMMENTS

Learning how to write fiction and becoming an author: This is what I set out to do more than five years ago. But I discovered if I was going to get a shot at commercial success through the publication of my book, I had to become a self-publisher.

This book is not meant to be a literary work. I decided to write it as if you were here with me and I was talking to you. It's filled with information I hope will open your mind to the realities as well as the possibilities, while you develop your own brand of creative thinking and build your own self-publishing plan. It is based on my own work, climbing my mountains, being influenced by my individual biases and preferences, and operating in my own creative box.

The time frames inserted throughout the chapters and sections can be adjusted to your place in the writing scheme and position on the self-publishing learning curve, and altered to suit your abilities, resources, and goals. They reflect my actual experience, and I've included them because I thought they would be of value in the case-study approach I elected to use for the book.

At the end of the book, I've included an excerpt of my upcoming fiction book, *The Mountain and the Place of Knowledge,* the first of the Ancestor Series of sci-tech-mystery thrillers. Including an excerpt of upcoming writing at the end of a book is an effective promotional tool. It lets the market know you are for real and provides the opportunity to

its Advantage Program, it charges a new self-publishing author 55% of the cover price for the book presentation and sales facilitation on its website.

It's important for self-publishers to understand the risks and rewards of relationships with the traditional distributors and wholesalers. In general, I found the financial risks too great and the potential profits too lean to merit my participation in this inherently consignment-based business.

1. FINANCIAL RISKS

To effectively enter distributor/wholesaler relationships, you need the capital to support the traditional operations of the book trade. This means you pay up front for printing runs of your book that not only take care of your own promotional requirements, but also satisfy the stocking levels of bookstores. That could be thousands of books out there. Can you afford such a print run—around $10,000-$20,000?

What would happen if your book suddenly took off, and bookstores all over the world started to up their stocking levels? You could be talking $50,000-$100,000 for a second print run. You should be prepared for that possibility, so where would you get the capital? Banks won't make loans with bookstore orders as security, because bookstores don't pay for the books until they are sold.

Can you afford to finance the return of a capital investment over the time inherent in dealing with the layers of the consignment business?

If you borrow funds, you must add credit costs to the cost of financing the inventory held by consignees in the book trade. Are you prepared to absorb the cost of credit for 120+ days (from the time of sales at the bookstores, not from the delivery of the books to distributors or wholesalers), given the accepted scenario of payments from credit-stretching bookstores to wholesalers, then to your distributor, and finally to you?

What about the cost of returns? In the August 2001 *Publishers Marketing Association Newsletter*, some self-publishers experienced book returns of up to 30%. Each bookstore seemed to have its own determination of acceptable sales levels. Also, be aware that general industry experience shows that 10%-30% of returns will be damaged.

reacting to the ephemeral whims and false starts of a struggling industry. In the process, you'll absorb tremendous unnecessary frustration and waste gobs of precious time that you could have spent writing, taking control, and designing your own future.

Just as a side note, a traditionally designed, publishing hybrid seems to be evolving because of the Internet; check out http://www.publishamerica.com/. This website is around three years old (at the end of 2003). The company presents itself as offering full publishing contracts to authors through a submission and screening process, all online.

B. DISTRIBUTORS AND WHOLESALERS

For first-time authors, seeking a business relationship with a major distributor is virtually out of the question. Without proven writing success or celebrity status, distributors can't afford to be interested; they work for major publishers that commit their names and well-designed promotional plans to impact the book trade. Any effort a distributor puts forth with its sales force and catalogs must be supported by significant publisher commitments to promotion.

In a similar vein, the major wholesalers, Ingram Book Group and Baker & Taylor, don't usually develop business relationships directly with self-publishers; for example, at the time this book was published, Ingram had a policy of considering relationships only with publishers that had ten or more titles to offer. But it's worthwhile for self-publishers to be familiar with the basics of these relationships, most of which can be found at their websites, http://www.ingrambookgroup.com/ and http://www.btol.com/.

In return for around 65% of a book's cover price and an exclusive contract, a distributor will introduce your book to the book trade, including wholesalers, through catalogs and flyers that you will probably design. A distributor's real zeal for books under its control will necessarily focus on well-known authors. In any case, distributors, like wholesalers, don't promote your book. You do.

Wholesalers are nonexclusive order processors for the book trade. Many small and regional wholesale companies will work directly with small publishers and self-publishers at a cost of around 50%-55% of cover. Even Amazon.com could be considered a wholesaler; through

unproven commodities such as you or your book, even if you've produced a great book.

If a publisher did decide to take a chance, a one-in-a-million shot, it would probably make a minimum effort—perhaps a book-run of 5,000 and a budget of $25,000, with no book advance. You would do virtually all the promotion, and the publisher would stay with it for four to six months to see if the market bit. It would be a roll of the dice.

For example, a publisher might use its influence to garner positive reviews, create book displays, and use its name and distribution ties to generate introductory impact at bookstores. It might develop a special flyer for libraries—perhaps all in a test market. In this scenario, if book sales didn't take off, your books would be headed for *remaindersville,* and the work would probably be contractually tied up so you couldn't do anything with it yourself.

The only way to get serious attention from the publishing industry, if that's what you want, is to prove your book will sell. Then there's little risk to a publisher. You've broken the ice, proven you can promote, and shown your book will sell. Publishers may be more inclined to make a significant investment in such a book, based on confidence in using their resources to take it to much higher levels of publishing success.

In general, don't waste your time on agents either. The good ones are hard to interest for most of the same reasons as the publishers. These days, agents are forced to compete in an industry in chaos, protect hard-won turf, and adapt to changes in the publishing industry, such as decreasing advances and royalties to authors, consolidations in publishing organizations, publisher downsizing, business failures, and all facets of the book industry competing for more control of book manufacturing and distribution in response to recent developments in technology.

If you want an overview of how the author representative profession works, and an appreciation of the issues and problems, visit the website of the Association of Authors' Representatives at http://www.aar-online.org/.

If you fall into the trap of pursuing traditional avenues by seeking an agent and/or a publisher, you can tie up months, perhaps even years,

CHAPTER I: Observations On Key Subject Areas

For the most part, the sections of this chapter represent a summary of responses to questions I've fielded from workshops, classes, consulting, and conversations with writers and authors about important and confusing self-publishing subjects. In most cases, my comments center on areas of critical decision-making required early on by self-publishers. Admittedly, what is presented is colored by my bias and point of view. The subject areas include:

- Relationships with publishers and agents.
- Realities of dealing with distributors and wholesalers.
- Perspectives on Internet publishing.
- Viable self-publishing approaches.
- The Internet and the future of publishing.

A. PUBLISHERS AND AGENTS

The primary motivation for authors to consider self-publishing is the understanding and acceptance that the chance of interest in your book by a major publisher is almost nil. Publishers don't risk capital on

Introduction 5

drive further interest in your works to outlets you've prepared at your website.

Be inspired, encouraged, and empowered. Go with the flow. Good luck and best regards!

Marshall Chamberlain
Author, Publisher, Speaker

I've read that returns can be as low as 15%, but can you even afford that?

What about the industry trend of bookstores, wholesalers, and distributors abruptly winding up business and going bankrupt? Can you accept the risk of write-offs from those potential bad debts, or the time and opportunity costs of changing partners in midstream?

2. SOME ECONOMIC PERSPECTIVES

In my view, it's not prudent to take the open-ended risks of financing book-trade inventory to support distributor/wholesaler/bookstore consignment selling, especially in this unstable, evolving marketplace.

On the surface, just the bare economics of the printing process in relation to the costs of employing a distributor or wholesaler—without considering the costs of book creation and formatting, consignment credit, inventory maintenance, insurance, packing materials and shipment, returns, damaged books, bad debts, and capital to create and execute an effective promotional plan—are forbidding. For example, just for perspective, printing a quality, four-color trade paperback currently costs about $4 each, assuming a 300-page book, a run of 1,000 ($6 each for 200), setup costs, and shipping 1,000 miles. At a cover price of $18.95, and discounting 65% to a major distributor or 55% to a wholesaler, is what's left sufficient to cover the other real and potential costs and provide a reasonable profit? Not to my way of thinking.

3. VALUABLE SERVICES

On the other hand, distributors and wholesalers provide valuable services in taking orders, facilitating delivery, and processing payments from a variety of points-of-sale. Through name recognition, they bring credibility and efficiency to the ordering and handling process for booksellers and libraries. But viable avenues for effective and economical fulfillment now exist as alternative ways to provide these services.

If you are interested in a relationship with a major distributor, consider sending a galley-book, together with a completed application, to the Publishers Marketing Association's (PMA) Trade Distribution Acceptance Program. If you are a PMA member, the cost is $50. Go to the PMA's website, http://www.pma-online.org/, for information about the program and to complete an application.

C. PERSPECTIVE ON INTERNET PUBLISHING

Another example of a confusing but important decision-making area for the self-publisher is whether or not to contract with an Internet publisher as an outside services provider. The answer to that dilemma depends on decisions you make in defining the time, energy, and financial resources you are willing to commit to the self-publishing business, and the image you want to create for your business, your book, and yourself as an author.

1. WHO ARE THESE INTERNET PUBLISHERS?

For a prudent businessperson, gathering information on an investment opportunity is standard procedure; it's due diligence. But in the case of Internet publishers, I found it nearly impossible to obtain financial information, organizational charts, ownership information, business-position statements, thorough listings of references and advisors, or biographical background for staffs and owners. Seldom do their websites offer any form of communication other than e-mail, and the "About Us" information is usually cursory. I've sent well-thought-out e-mail letters to many of these Internet publishers. Some came back with tight, protective replies that didn't focus on answering my questions. Many sent canned responses, and some didn't reply at all. Only occasionally did an amiable, knowledgeable decision-maker return the inquiry or ask to be contacted directly by telephone.

In late 2001, I e-mailed a key person at one of the better-known Internet publishers, a recognized mover and shaker in the self-publishing world, to request a copy of the publishing agreement. I was told in the reply that people who ended up competing with them had copied the agreement, so they didn't give it out anymore in advance. Period. Another website of a well-known Internet publisher put browsers on notice by stating that if you were a jerk, not to waste their time.

Although this investigative process was disconcerting for me as an experienced businessperson, I do sense a trend toward more effective communications and professional business attitude surfacing within the evolving cream of the crop. Unfortunately, the larger, respected organizations that have entered the business with POD subsidiaries, for example, Ingram Book Group and Baker & Taylor, don't conduct business with self-publishers. But that may not be the case shortly down the pike as self-publishing continues its skyrocketing growth.

So, if Internet publishing ends up being the best route for you, then you will be stuck with the job of finding a comfort level with one or more of the many smaller Internet publishers that have worked hard over the last three to five years to gain respect and pull the necessary resources together to deliver consistent quality services to self-publishers. I found only a few I would consider, but since the state of Internet publishing is in such flux, constantly changing to maintain competitive advantage, I recommend authors do a fresh Internet search and scrutinize the Internet publishers themselves.

At this writing, *A Basic Guide to Fee Based Print on Demand Publishing Services*, a 25-page PDF e-book, was offered free by Dehanna Bailee at her website at http://dehanna.com/pod_guide.htm.

2. WHAT ARE THE SERVICES AND COSTS, AND WHO MIGHT USE THEM?

In general, most Internet publishers print books on demand and contract with and deliver nonreturnable books to the major wholesalers, who then fill orders from bookstores and libraries and provide record keeping for the Internet publishers. Online bookstores are usually serviced through the major wholesalers.

Some Internet publishers provide online bookstores at their websites to handle any direct sales from individuals or the book trade; in many cases, this is true whether book trade orders come from wholesalers or directly from bookstores. This is an advantage for the promotion-bound self-publisher, providing a central location to drive sales. If the Internet publisher acts as a fully integrated fulfillment center, the author can look forward to royalties in the neighborhood of 25%-35% of cover for sales to individuals and 10%-15% for book-trade sales.

Most Internet publishers don't offer fulfillment beyond dealing with wholesalers, but leave the author to set up his own if he wants to take advantage of potential profits from his promotional efforts with potential individual buyers and/or niche markets.

In this scenario, the self-publishing author has made the decision to relegate the majority of book-trade sales to his Internet publisher's wholesale relationships and reap a net profit of 8%-14% of cover. The next step would be to purchase books from the Internet publisher (this varies from about 18% over cost to as little as a 20% discount off cover), or contract with an outside printer (POD or traditional). Then the books would be delivered to the self-publisher's business for signings and fulfillment of orders driven to his website or received by fax or postal-mail. Alternatively, books could be delivered to a fulfillment-services provider, and all sales promotions would drive sales there. I found experienced fulfillment-services providers charging around 35% of cover for their complete 24/7 services on sales to individuals, and 20%-25% of cover for sales to the book trade.

The upfront costs charged by Internet publishers range from $99 to $1,500 for a basic publishing package. The package fees cover the out-of-pocket, setup, and initial administrative costs of the Internet publisher, and reflect the degree of assistance a self-publisher selects from the Internet publisher in designing and formatting the book.

Typically, Internet publishers offer many add-on services and products you can buy, such as marketing kits, custom cover designs and, in some cases, editing assistance. Cover designs, included as part of basic packages, will typically be limited to a selection of generic templates. Add-on editing assistance will not come close to the detailed plot- and character-developing advice required of good editing; it will more than likely fall into the category of mediocre proofreading. Remember, getting a book into the best shape for success in the marketplace is not the Internet publisher's responsibility.

Internet publishers set fixed charges for printing and delivering books that guarantee them a built-in profit on every book printed. In addition to this source of profit from a relationship with a self-publishing author, they usually are vested in from 35%-50% of the net profits from book sales after all costs—such as printing, discounts, shipping, handling, and charge-card processing—are charged against the book.

The services provided by Internet publishers are tailored into packages designed to satisfy a variety of author needs and objectives, for example, authors who might:

- Want their books broadly accessible to purchasers.
- Not place high priority on financial reward.
- Not want the hassle of storing books, taking orders, processing payments, shipping, and handling, but who do want to receive decent record keeping.
- Have produced books with limited sales potential.
- Want to get into print for personal satisfaction.
- Desire to keep books available on demand after promotion has ground to a halt and sales have diminished to some marginal level (assuming that rights come back to the author in a publishing contract, or that you are a successful self-publisher).
- Want to test a book without exclusive contracts and with relatively limited risks and affordable setup costs.

For the most part, self-publishing authors will have to convince the more professional Internet publishers that they are able and willing to promote their book. These publishers are in business to make a profit, and need to believe there's reasonable potential for the net-profit share in their contractual relationships to produce income. They are becoming more and more selective as to which authors and books they will accept into their publishing programs.

On the other hand, many Internet publishers will not turn down a well-put-together book. The fact is that they will most likely break even with the setup fees charged. Most Internet publishers will build in profit from the printing costs charged against any book sales, including sales to their author/partners, who in many cases are forced to purchase books to satisfy personal sales and the need for review copies.

3. WHAT ABOUT THE RISKS AND REWARDS?

For the author/writer who has taken the time to thoroughly learn the art and craft of self-publishing, and particularly for those whose objective is maximum commercial success, the services of a potential Internet publishing partner should be scrutinized for hidden risks. Even though most Internet publishers represent their services as economical packages for testing the market with limited financial risk, prudent self-publishers should be aware that:

- The relationship may hamstring an author if he wants to graduate quickly to another publishing relationship.
- The economics of the relationship are financially limiting.
- There may be more financial risk than meets the eye.
- The author and the book may be subtly identified with the stigma of vanity-press publishing.
- The relationship will not provide any of the effective marketing/promotional elements recognized as the heart of publishing success.

I briefly address the first three of these points below, relying on the information developed in this book to help guide committed authors in designing effective promotional plans.

TYING UP THE AUTHOR AND BOOK

If your self-publishing effort is successful, a traditional publishing opportunity could come your way, or you might decide you want to consolidate all the publishing functions into a working business to maximize profits and perhaps expand. Because one of the covenants of typical Internet publishing agreements is the ability to terminate the relationship with 90 days notice and without cause, one might think that to be a positive attribute. But the process of reorganization could cause a major loss of sales momentum and profits and require additional capital and time resources, because you'll need to:

- Redesign and redirect your promotional efforts to include the identity of new publishing and distribution components.
- Reregister the book with databases to provide new publisher/distribution/fulfillment information to the book trade so that sales can effectively take place.
- Reorganize your business and negotiate with new publishing, printing, and fulfillment partners.
- Edit and reformat a revised edition of the book to incorporate a new ISBN, additional acknowledgements, new publisher

credits, front and back cover alterations, and any back-page order-form changes.

LIMITED PROFITS AND FIXED BOOK-PRINTING COST

The covenants of contractual relationships with Internet publishers usually fix the profitability to an author for the life of the relationship, no matter how well a book sells. This limiting factor comes about because the Internet publisher charges a set printing price for every book without regard to the economics of volume printing. This is the nature of print-on-demand publishing enterprises. It's the principal reason most Internet publishers can stay in business, because they make a profit on every book they print.

Another limiting factor on author profits is the inability to make worthwhile net profits selling books directly at websites, at chosen fulfillment-services providers, out of the trunks of their cars, at signings, or at workshops, because most Internet publishers don't allow authors to purchase books at deep enough discounts.

Typically, authors pay the retail price, less a discount in the range of 10%-25% off cover price, to purchase books in small quantities, even books needed for review copies. Larger quantity discounts were available at one Internet publisher I checked out, going up to 70% off cover for an order over 1,000 copies. In addition, contracts typically don't include sales to authors in the net-profit-sharing arrangement.

SHARING OF NET PROFITS

Sharing the net profits from book sales with the author is usually a part of a contract with an Internet publisher. It provides a kicker. If lots of books are sold—and the Internet publisher hopes you will make this happen exclusively through your promotional efforts—the Internet publisher receives a fixed percentage of the net profits.

The definition of net profits is perhaps the most difficult information to glean from the outline of services and costs presented by most Internet publishers. Participation by Internet publishers in these net profits from book sales ranges from 0% to 70%, with 50% being common. The author receives the remainder. In the case of 0%, an Internet publisher is only interested in fixed profits from book manufacturing, so the price of printing is very high.

Net-profit sharing takes place after printing costs, discounts to wholesalers and online bookstores, and the costs of any payment processing, packaging, and shipping associated with direct sales or delivery to the book trade. Typically, discounts range from as little as 20% off cover price to some bookstores and libraries that purchase direct from the Internet publisher, to as much as 55% to online bookstores. However, it appears that the larger, experienced Internet publishers have negotiated around a 40% discount with the major wholesalers, who in turn supply the major online bookstores.

So, it's a tricky piece of discernment to figure out what's really happening here. The bottom line is that the more powerful Internet publishers have negotiated a 40% off cover outgoing discount for all book-trade transactions via the two big wholesalers, Ingram Book Group and Baker & Taylor. They have been able to do this because they command volume and they use the POD subsidiaries of these wholesalers to print the books of their client authors. In the process, some of the economic benefits are passed down to their client authors, and everybody can win—if that's the way an author chooses to go.

So, who gets what in a generic Internet publisher relationship? Let's assume a 300-page trade paperback, selling for $18.95. I have seen fixed costs of POD printing that range from $6.20 to over $10. So you can see why there's such a wide range in the sharing percentages of net profits between the Internet publisher and the author. The $10 Internet publisher is satisfied with a larger printing profit; it doesn't take any risks associated with anticipated book sales, and leaves all the potential profit to authors.

Based on the numbers supplied by one well-known Internet publisher, 8% of cover price was the estimate of an author's 50% sharing of net profits, considering book-trade sales made at a 40% discount. But the fine print indicated that deductions for payment-processing fees, packaging, and shipping were not included in the estimate. This is only one situation; it is mentioned here to further point out the need for due diligence by self-publishers in analyzing potential business partners.

SOME HIDDEN RISKS

Other vital considerations are:

- The potential business risks associated with mergers, acquisitions, and bankruptcies affecting Internet publishing. This includes the wholesalers and bookstores typically allowed common trade-payment terms by the Internet publishers.

- The risks associated with the changing business conditions of a maturing Internet, meaning the possibility of the bookselling business now so economically and effectively conducted by a plethora of players being turned upside down by regulation and/or new technology.

Admittedly, some exposure to risk must be accepted by any publishing effort, but the consequences could be devastating for the frugal self-publisher who places all his eggs in one basket. A poignant example is the brief, two-year life of ipublish.com, a POD business launched directly by Time Warner Books in 2001 that offered writers a potential publishing relationship. It ceased operations sometime in the first half of 2002. One can only imagine the consequences for the authors who had signed on—and this was the effort of a major publishing company.

Another potential hidden risk from Internet publishing relationships is a disconcerting contractual covenant found in many contracts that places the author in the position of accepting any change the Internet publisher might dictate in the definition of costs applied against book sales in deriving net profit. So, the author stands financially exposed to any addition or increase in charged costs made by an Internet publisher, with or without cause.

D. VIABLE SELF-PUBLISHING APPROACHES

If you consider yourself a pure self-publisher, with the goal of more than just minor commercial success, it may not be such a wise decision to take a test ride with your writing future by using an Internet publishing relationship as the launch vehicle. My recommendation for most committed authors is to take the bull by the horns and do it all yourself.

Learn the business. Control as many elements as possible. Save up the funds, and take the risk of the first printing run with a traditional printing organization—or POD printer. Don't participate in the book-trade consignment business. Prove your book can sell, and equitable opportunities will multiply from there.

Avenues now exist for self-publishers to become effective players in the book-trade game and, at the same time, eliminate the consignment risks. New printing and formatting technologies, reasonably priced business-communications systems, and the Internet are forcing changes in how booksellers do business, as well as opening up promotional access to the book trade and media for announcements, press releases, articles, and invitations to review books. A savvy self-publisher can now place well-thought-out, key information directly in front of potential individual buyers, as well as create and deliver high-quality, PDF review-books as attachments to e-mail, or on CD-Rs.

According to an article by Steve O'Keefe in the July 2002 *Publishers Marketing Association Newsletter*, "...there are anywhere from 25,000 to 55,000 self-publishers, depending on whose numbers you use." The road less traveled is now paved with hundreds of recent success stories.

1. YOU DON'T NEED TO BE ON THE SHELF

Although the book trade (distributor/wholesaler/bookseller) business is still a consignment business, drastic changes have taken place in the past five years, and more changes are surfacing even as I write, changes that facilitate more effective sale/delivery interfacing between self-publishers and booksellers. For example, traditional bookstores are now receiving payments in advance from their customers and special-ordering books, just like the online bookstores. This trend is perfect nurturing for the creative self-publisher. When the bookstores have money in hand, they'll find the order source, your self-publishing business—which has registered the book in all the right places, especially *Books in Print*—and they will order directly from your small publishing business, or from your vendor of record, if the business presents a credible image. Asset-based bookstores must respond quickly to the needs of their customers in the face of Internet competition and changing technology.

Another factor fueling the special-order trend is the decrease in stocking levels at bookstores. This is partially due to shrinking order/delivery times from publishers and distributors who, through a variety of business liaisons, are acquiring access to or control of high-tech printing systems such as POD and PQN, making it possible to respond more rapidly to orders.

2. A PRACTICAL PUBLISHING APPROACH

After you register your book with all the appropriate publishing directories and selected Internet bookstores, a viable publishing approach could include investment in the first printing. A recent check of a respected, medium-sized printing organization found the following estimated base cost for printing a trade paperback of 300-pages, #60 paper; four-color, laminated cover: Cost per book was $3.01 for a run of 1,000, $3.64 for 500, or $5.72 for 200, plus shipping. There were no setup fees, and many generic cover templates to choose from. All you had to do was learn to format the book to their specifications, and there were several alternatives for that requirement.

Then, through a personal promotional plan you design to satisfy your lifestyle and professional modus operandi, and keyed to your state of residence, generate direct sales by:

- Securing book reviews and book news articles from the media.
- Driving potential individual purchasers to sales points—your website or fulfillment-services provider as a first priority—and secondarily to bookstores.
- Creating buzz through announcements to organizations having interest in the genre or subject of your book, and introducing creative, short-term giveaway offers to help drive members to purchase the book.
- Offering to speak and/or conduct workshops at appropriate organizations, clubs, and groups.
- Introducing you, your works, and news story tie-ins to radio and TV interview sources.

The keys to success include the quality of your promotional planning, the careful and creative drafting of promotional pieces, and the diligence you put into compiling contact information for recipients.

You can create a viable self-publishing approach with commitment, discipline, and limited financial resources, and in the process you can cut out the costs and risks of dealing with Internet publishers, distributors, and wholesalers.

Once you learn to do it all for yourself, with net profits ranging from 20%-70% of cover price, depending on the type of sale (online bookstore, general bookstore, library, or individual), you can work toward building sales momentum that takes you to the next logical step, that of establishing an integrated printing and fulfillment relationship. This allows you to increase profits through the cost savings of larger print runs and the elimination of delivery costs to you or your fulfillment-services provider. In addition, organizations that provide these services to small publishers are lending another layer of credibility to sales and delivery credibility, not to mention freeing more time for the self-publishing author to dedicate to his trade of writing.

Another option to consider in fashioning a viable self-publishing approach is to measure the cost in dollars and time saved by doing business with a respected, financially stable fulfillment-services provider, to efficiently store your books and process orders 24/7 from bookstores, libraries, and individuals. Remember, as a self-publisher, you will have to fulfill sales. That means you have the books, you process the credit cards and checks, you answer caller inquiries on your toll-free number, and you package and ship the books.

At costs working out to around 20%-35% of cover, depending on the type of sale—book trade, library, or individual—a fulfillment-services provider can provide inventory control, insured storage, 24/7 order taking through multiple payment means, payment processing, detailed monthly reporting, payment remissions, processing of returns (if you allow returnable sales—I don't), and handling and shipping. You don't give up control of your book, and you set the terms of sale to all segments of the market. If you choose, you can still continue to sell specialty books on your website or elsewhere, for example: autographed books, e-books, and multipurpose products derived from your book or other works. In addition, these relationships usually do not have any strings attached, so you are free to change service providers with short notice.

If you decide to employ a fulfillment-services provider, one major adjustment will be to point potential buyers in your promotions to that provider. In many ways, the formal association with a well-known and respected fulfillment organization will greatly enhance your credibility as a publisher and eliminate any reluctance on the part of buyers to make purchases, not to mention free a big chunk of your time so you can write.

3. ALTERNATIVE PUBLISHING APPROACH

An alternative distribution/fulfillment scheme is to contract with a reputable Internet POD publisher, a partner that manufactures books and has distribution relationships with one or both of the largest wholesalers, Ingram Book Group or Baker & Taylor, and with the major online bookstores. These Internet publishers have developed the clout to negotiate a discount of around 40% off cover price to the wholesalers, instead of the 55% new publishers typically pay (at Ingram Book Group). Bookstores worldwide can then special-order your book through the wholesalers and have it delivered within a few days, thanks to POD printing technology. No inventory is required.

If you choose this route, make an informed choice, one that minimizes the risks previously pointed out and that is contractually limited to a maximum of one year. Remember, you are still the one responsible for the development and execution of an effective promotional plan.

The partner relationship offers the frugal author, who doesn't want to invest the time required for a total self-publishing approach, an avenue to bypass involvement with the fulfillment business, freeing time for promotion and a continuing writing career. Yes, the profit potential is less, but if you find yourself on the brink of a blockbuster, you've only committed for a year. Pushing the pencil around a little, I came to the conclusion that you could add about 15% of cover price to your bottom line if you didn't utilize the Internet publishing partner approach. For writers who desire to be authors first, the cost is a bargain for the time it can free up, as long as the risks are acceptable.

After studying the marketplace, I concluded that an equitable Internet publishing relationship should be feasible, corner-stoned around:

- Close to a 50-50 net-profit-sharing arrangement, with net profits defined as cover price less printing expense at the partner's actual cost, less discounts to wholesalers and/or booksellers.

- Authors receiving a monthly check and complete accounting records.
- Sales fulfillment taken care of through the partner's wholesaler and online-bookstore relationships.
- Unlimited sales of books to authors for any purpose at around cost plus 15%-20%.
- Authors having final say over book cover design, interior formatting, and cover price.
- Provision by the partner, in coordination with the author, of a joint book-launch promotional effort. This effort, though certainly not expected to replace the author's well-thought-out promotional plan, is proof of the importance to the partner of its share in net profits.
- Partner possessing long-term access to, or ownership of, state-of-the-art book-production systems.
- A contractual relationship that doesn't tie up author rights, can be terminated with no more than 90 days notice without cause, and doesn't contain terms subject to change by the partner without agreement of the author.

If you've chosen your Internet publishing partner wisely, you will be able to make your end of the relationship even more lucrative by buying books at cost plus 15%-20%. You are then able to implement promotions to individuals and groups that have interest in your subject or genre and to niche markets (like libraries, in the case of this book), and drive profitable sales to your website or your fulfillment-services provider (vendor of record). In addition, you will save considerably on the cost of review copies, and make reasonable profits selling books through your day-to-day business activities.

In examining the profit potential theoretically accruing to authors who use the services of several of the major Internet publishing partners, I found the author's bottom line ranging from 8%-16% of cover price for sales to wholesalers and online bookstores; these sales can represent up to 90% or more of all book sales from an Internet publishing relationship if authors don't aggressively promote sales to fulfillment locations other than wholesalers or bookstores.

E. THE INTERNET AND THE FUTURE OF PUBLISHING

Where is the Internet going? Judging from the changes in websites I've observed during 2002-2003, the organizations with deep pockets are experimenting with how best to utilize this dynamic commercial resource; they seem to be sitting back and learning from the successes and failures of others, and constantly editing their websites and testing techniques and approaches. I believe we've only seen the beginning, and that over the next decade these major organizations will bring a totally new face to this communications and business medium and the way business is conducted in the world marketplace. For example, it wouldn't surprise me as a shopper in the near future, to be able to scroll down theoretical aisles on a retailer's website and shop in three-dimensional virtual reality, examining items for sale by manipulating the view, reading descriptions and specifications, learning about items through audio-video presentations, paying for them, having them delivered, or picking them up at some mechanized super warehouse using an ID, password, and a retinal scan.

Any attempts to characterize the future Internet are probably destined to fall short, but hang on to your hat as the trends begin surfacing; in the midst of inevitable transformation, the opportunities for self-publishers to effectively and directly reach the buying public are bound to increase dramatically.

Some of the writing is on the wall for the publishing industry of the future. More than one of the major bookstore chains has experimented with book manufacturing and the publishing business. For example, Borders, Inc. has tested small, high-tech POD printing machines in selected stores in its system. According to Kristen French, staff reporter for TheStreet.com, Inc., in a February 16, 2002 article published at http://www.thestreet.com/, Barnes and Noble had already published more than 3,000 titles using POD technology, representing around 3% of their $3.62 billion in annual sales. Both Ingram Book Group and Baker & Taylor, the two largest book wholesalers in the world, now own major POD printing businesses, Lightning Source Inc. and Replica Books, respectively. Baker & Taylor has been experimenting with publishing since 1996, according to a March 15, 2002 news article posted at the website of the American Booksellers Association (http://www.bookweb.org/).

Several of the major publishers have made investments in POD Internet publishing businesses, for example, Random House with Xlibris.com and Warner Books with ipublish.com (which failed in 2001). Iuniverse.com, the largest Internet publisher, now has Warburg Pincus and Barnes and Noble as major investors.

What this all means for the publishing industry of the future is totally up for grabs. Perhaps glimpses of the plausible future can be garnered from comments by David Beers, writing in the February 3, 2001 issue of *The Vancouver Sun* about Jason Epstein's new book, *Book Business: Publishing Past, Present, Future*. The Beers article quotes Epstein saying, "'Everything about books is soon to change. Everything: The way we make, find, buy, read, and value them. Goodbye to the mega-conglomerate publishing houses—the Web soon will put you out of business, now that authors can publish and distribute on their own. Goodbye to chains (bookstores) ... the Web will put them out of business now that readers can cyber-shop. With the big boxes gone, boutique bookstores will flourish again as 'shrines' for readers, tangible, intimate, and local. Or, a coin-operated machine will give you a manufactured-on-the-spot paperback edition of any book ever published.'"

CHAPTER II: Resources, Software and Equipment
(Months 1-6)

On the surface, contemplating acquisition of the skills and knowledge to become a capable self-publisher can be overwhelming. The endless number of directions you can go in pursuit of information on the Internet, and the existence of so much irrelevant or unfocused written material, can lead to a great waste of your limited time resources. If you begin from scratch, you are forced to sift through the countless possibilities. Without a knowledge base of the self-publishing industry and a way to keep credible tabs on changes in the industry and book-buying market, you may not effectively interpret the information you find.

In addition, it's easy to believe the computer expertise you need represents too high a mountain to climb, leaving you feeling impotent and frustrated.

I certainly know all these things first hand. But be encouraged. Proficiency with several key software programs is all it takes; adequate help menus within today's software, and the support offered at the websites of software manufactures, will teach you what you need to know, so long as you are patient. As far as understanding the self-publishing field and keeping current, there are shortcuts to competency and remaining up to date.

A. GROUPS AND ASSOCIATIONS (MONTHS 1-3)

Consider affiliating with the following organizations and subscribing to their newsletters or magazines for networking, keeping current on changes in the publishing industry, and maintaining a handle on major events and activities:

- Publishers Marketing Association (PMA), http://www.pma-online.org/, 310-372-2732, $95/year for a publisher membership (1-9 employees). Go to their website to see benefits. Also check out the locations of their regional affiliates. 3,500+ members.

- Small Publishers Association of North America (SPAN), http://www.spannet.org/, 719-395-8374, $60-$95/year for membership. If you belong to PMA, it's $60. 1,300+ members.

- Small Publishers, Authors, and Writers Network (SPAWN), http://www.spawn.org/, 805-643-2403, $45/year for membership. 130+ members.

- Closest chapter of The National Writers Association. Go to http://www.nationalwriters.com/ to find one, or search the internet to find and join the closest major writer's organizations in your state of residence.

- *Publishers Weekly m*agazine, http://www.publishersweekly.com/. Subscription is $199/year in the United States, but you can always go read it in the library. If you join the PMA, you get a hefty discount.

B. REFERENCES AND INTERNET RESOURCE SITES (MONTHS 1-3)

The books, booklets, articles, and Internet-site resources listed here represent the best guidance I have found on writing and self-publishing. They provide an author/writer/self-publisher with a practical and complete resource base.

1. BOOKS AND BOOKLETS

Books: *The Author's Toolkit: A Step-By-Step Guide to Writing a Book* (2000), by Mary Embree; *Stein on Writing* (2000), by Sol Stein; *Getting the Words Right: How to Rewrite, Edit & Revise* (1983), by Theodore A. Rees Cheney; *The American Heritage Dictionary of the English Language* (2000), published by Houghton Mifflin Company; *The Synonym Finder* (1978), by J. I. Rodale; *Write Right! A Desktop Digest of Punctuation, Grammar, and Style* (1995), by Jan Venolia; *The Self-Publishing Manual* (2001), by Dan Poytner; *U-Publish.com* (2002), a book by Dan Poynter and Danny O. Snow; *The Concrete Guide to Self-Publishing* (2001), by Marilyn and Tom Ross; *Book Selling 101* (2000), by Jean Heine; *1001 Ways to Market Your Books* (2001), by John Kremer; *Jump Start Your Book Sales* (1999), by Marilyn and Tom Ross; *Over 75 Good Ideas for Promoting Your Book* (2000), by Patricia L. Fry; *Book Blitz: Getting Your Book in the News* (1994), by Barbara Gaughen and Ernest Weckbaugh; *How to Publish and Promote Online* (2001), by M. J. Rose and Angela Adair-Hoy.

Booklets: *News Releases and Book Publicity, A Book Publishing Consultation With Dan Poynter*, by Dan Poynter; *Book Reviews From Pre-publication Galleys Through a Continuing Review Program, A Book Publishing Consultation With Dan Poynter*, by Dan Poynter; *Book Marketing: A New Approach, A Book Publishing Consultation With Dan Poynter*, by Dan Poynter; *Book Fulfillment*, by Dan Poynter—all periodically revised and available for purchase at Poynter's website, http://www.parapublishing.com/.

2. PMA NEWSLETTER ARCHIVE

The newsletter archive of the PMA contains a wealth of articles covering the gamut of self-publishing. The archive is searchable, and you don't need to be a member to make copies. Go to their website, http://www.pma-online.org/, and scroll to the bottom of the page. Click on Site Map to find newsletter articles you can read, copy, and print.

3. INTERNET SITES

I find everything I need at or through the websites listed below. If you think you need more, try my favorite search engine, http://www.google.com/. Click the directory on the front page, and use those subjects as a base to narrow your searches; it saves time. My next search engine choices are http://www.northernlights.com/ and http://www.infoseek.com/.

- http://www.forwriters.com/: Helpful writer resources.
- http://www.writerswrite.com/: Helpful writer resources.
- Midwest Book Review, http://www.midwestreview.com/: A nonprofit organization that supports writers and readers with a full gamut of lists and information; it offers a free newsletter.
- Publishers Marketing Association (PMA), http://www.pma-online.org/: The premiere organization for small publishers, authors, and self-publishers. Membership includes a newsletter and many useful benefits.
- Small Publishers Association of North America (SPAN), http://www.spannet.org/: An industry organization. Membership includes a newsletter and many useful benefits. It was founded by Marilyn and Tom Ross, co-authors of several of the best books available on self-publishing.
- Small Publishers, Artists, and Writers Network (SPAWN), http://www.spawn.org/: An industry organization. Membership includes a newsletter and many useful benefits.
- Author Dan Poynter's website, http://www.parapublishing.com/: Writings and resources from the guru of self-publishing. He offers a free newsletter and a plethora of self-publishing articles, lists, and helpful information documents. Many are free.
- http://www.about.com/: Lists of everything.
- http://www.bookwire.com/ (R.R. Bowker): A resource site for authors, writers, and the book trade, with a categorized directory of more than 5,000 links.
- The website of authors Dan Poynter and Danny O. Snow, http://www.u-publish.com/: Covers new technology, creative e-marketing, and offers a free newsletter.

4. LEGAL ASSISTANCE

- For useful legal links, plus some of the forms commonly used by self-publishers, see Dan Poynter's website, http://www.parapublishing.com/.
- Ivan Hoffman is an attorney known for his publishing expertise and the salient articles he authors. His website is http://www.ivanhoffman.com/.
- Cornell University supports a website that accommodates legal searches by topic at http://www4.law.cornell.edu/.
- Another free legal resource to find information on topics of interest to publishers is the Publishing Law Center at http://www.publaw.com/.

5. INTERNET SEARCH AID

Google.com, my favorite search engine, offers a free software program that places two Google toolbars at the top of your browser. These toolbars stay at the top, ready for use no matter where you are on the Internet. They enable you to search the Internet or search any website you are visiting. To download the software, go to the Google home page, http://www.google.com/, click on Directory, Google Tools at the bottom of the page, and Google Toolbar.

C. SOFTWARE (MONTHS 1-3)

The writer/author/self-publisher must invest time in becoming familiar with the software discussed below (or equivalents) to execute the tasks and manage the information necessary to effectively carry out the functions of dynamic self-publishing.

If your budget allows, specialized software is available in the market to effectively accomplish self-publishing tasks, especially in the editing, writing, and formatting areas. Several of the Internet writers' resource sites noted in this section have links to appropriate software information.

My purpose in this chapter, regarding both software and equipment, is to summarize what I obtained to perform necessary self-publishing functions, but within a waiter's limited budget. In general, two- to three-year-old software and equipment are available on the Internet for as little as 10%-20% of original cost. To check out what's available, an effective start is to visit http://www.pricegrabber.com to compare prices on practically any item for sale on the Internet. Online auction sites, for example, http://www.ebay.com/ and http://www.ubid.com/, are other major sources where you can get a feel for pricing and availability.

Below is a brief outline of the major uses of software I accumulated.

1. MICROSOFT WORD

To compile promotion lists; create faxes and e-mails to send directly from the program to WinFax PRO or Outlook; create promotional pieces as files to attach to e-mails; convert promotional pieces, books, and book products into PDF files using the automatic link to Adobe Acrobat 4.0 or higher; and provide acceptable book formatting for most printing organizations.

2. MICROSOFT PUBLISHER

To create fax letters, e-mail attachments, newsletters, promotional pieces, business cards, bookmarks, address lists, brochures, flyers, and initial cover designs. You can use templates available in Publisher's catalog for business forms. Publisher can also be used to construct adequate websites that can be uploaded directly from your computer to your chosen Internet host server (the host server must accommodate Front Page extensions).

3. ADOBE PAGEMAKER 6.5

Using this program's layering capabilities, you can design and create book covers, as well as construct an index and table of contents. The program can work with other design complexities in the formatting and laying out of an entire book. It also can automatically link to master documents you place into a PageMaker 6.5 document, so you can edit and make changes to those master documents and have the changes automatically reflected in the PageMaker document. The program allows you to import files from many common software programs on the way to creating PDF files.

4. ADOBE ACROBAT 4.0+

This program is also used to create PDF files from files created in many common software programs. A limitation is that you can only make minor editing changes to the documents you create. This program allows you to add security elements to PDF files—for example, assigning a password to open the file, disabling editing, and disabling copying and printing—that help inhibit abuse of the files you place on your website for downloading or files you send out as e-mail attachments.

This program works seamlessly in Microsoft Word; the Acrobat convert button is automatically inserted on the toolbar in Word 97 and up during setup, so any graphics or text you can copy and paste into a Word document can be perfectly brought into Adobe to create a PDF file. I use this program to create the larger documents (for example, my media kit and the excerpt of Chapter I of my upcoming novel) I place on my website for easy downloads. I even used it to create the PDF e-book of this book for media review copies, complimentary copies offered in promotions, and for sale at my business website.

5. ADOBE READER

In order to open and read PDF files you must have Adobe Reader software on your computer. This software is a free download at http://www.adobe.com/.

6. WINFAX PRO 10.0

I use this program to manage broadcast faxing. It facilitates importing and storing promotion lists you create that contain recipient names and fax numbers. WinFax can send faxes automatically, on a schedule you set up, through a telephone line hooked up to your PC.

7. MICROSOFT OUTLOOK

This important, multifunctional business-affairs software stores, manages, and manipulates business and personal contact information; facilitates the scheduling of events and appointments; offers administrative-support and time-management functions; provides a robust platform for creating and sending e-mail messages; and allows you to receive e-mail messages—from all your accounts on the Internet—that are filtered, sorted, and stored in designated sub-inboxes according to rules you create in the program. Through its import/export wizard, it facilitates importing contact lists from many common software programs, for sending broadcast e-mails.

8. MICROSOFT FRONTPAGE

This program is optional. It's included in several of the Microsoft Office packages and is used for creating and managing a more sophisticated business website than can be created and maintained in Microsoft Publisher. As this book went to press, I am still satisfied using Publisher for my business website.

NOTE: I have heard good reports about the ease of use and sophistication of Dreamweaver software for the average, do-it-yourself webmaster. As this book was being written, more and more website-creation software was coming to the market at affordable prices.

9. MICROSOFT ACCESS

This program provides a high level of database management for effectively storing and manipulating contact information. It is especially useful in facilitating e-mail promotions. It easily works with large and complex databases; for example, the CD of the *American Library Directory* ($499), comprehensive media lists (around $250), or opt-in e-mail lists ($10-$20/1,000), should you decide to purchase them.

10. QUICKBOOKS

This is a complete accounting-software program. It allows you to easily manage all your banking affairs, billing, invoicing, processing of payments, issuing of sales receipts, maintaining of accounts for income and expenses, preparation of tax-forms, and production of financial statements. I elected to purchase an upgrade from a six-year-old, 4.0 version directly from the manufacturer for $149.

The program includes the capability of processing charge-card payments received by phone, e-mail, fax, postal-mail, or directly from your website payment forms. It makes automatic deposits to your bank account online from these transactions. Through an account you set up with a QuickBooks merchant-account partner, cleared charge-card payments are credited to your business account in four to five business days. There aren't any equipment rental, Internet access, or setup fees, and confirmation of payment clearance is sent to you by e-mail. All you need is a current version of QuickBooks and your own Internet connection.

Resources, Software and Equipment 35

In addition, you can fax or e-mail paid invoices, invoices to be paid, or any other form from QuickBooks directly to your customers by using the program's interactive capabilities with WinFax PRO 10 and Outlook.

11. MICROSOFT EXCEL

Accounting-wise, an alternative I found useful prior to receiving significant, recurring income from my fledgling business, was to create simple expense worksheets in Excel. Using the standard worksheet default page, I customized the column layout to list expenses (using the Schedule C, IRS nomenclature to name expense categories) by day and month, inserting columns at the end of each month and cumulatively at the end of the year for totals. This gave me an adequate, credible record. I did this for four consecutive tax years, using copies of the worksheets as attachments to Schedule Cs when I filed my individual 1040 Forms.

As soon as I began to receive significant, recurring income, I set up the business in QuickBooks, using its easy tutorial in the Help menu, and converted all the transactions from the Excel expense worksheet since the beginning of that current year. It took me two days.

NOTE: You can use the credit-card-processing functions and invoice faxing and e-mailing functions of QuickBooks without using the software as a total accounting program.

12. IMAGE-MANAGEMENT SOFTWARE

In my case, I found the ArcSoft PhotoStudio 2000 software that came with purchase of a $100 Canon scanner to be sufficient. It works with the scanner, or independently, to clean up, crop, and resize picture images for use in different promotional pieces or in books.

For example, in creating a book cover, I take 35-mm pictures with a basic camera and have standard 8 X 10-inch glossies made from the pictures I want to save for possible use. This size allows me to proportionately size down to the actual dimensions of the front and back covers for hardback or trade-paperback books without affecting resolution quality, as well as create smaller images of the same quality for many other purposes.

Then I can place a picture as a background layer when I create a book cover in Adobe 6.5 PageMaker—or insert it in Publisher—and layer text over it.

With most image-management software, you can select parts of any picture, resize them, and make new images for a variety of paste-in uses in creating documents, websites, and promotional pieces. You can also insert images as e-mail attachments through Outlook or have the images display directly in an e-mail message by copying and pasting. Images can also be imported directly into faxes in WinFax PRO.

A delightful surprise in the ArcSoft PhotoStudio 2000 software was the ability to create, using a large variety of design tools and importing capabilities, my own images from scratch. For example, I created my own TIF and JPG images of logos—at various resolutions depending on what they were to be used for—by using text, text effects, color, and background options available in the program. The program even lets you work in different layers if you need the complexity. In addition, it's Windows-compatible for copying and pasting directly from the program; and you can access and work with most any image file on your computer created in other programs or downloaded.

13. ENCYCLOPEDIA BRITANNICA CD ROM

I suggest buying the encyclopedia CD-ROM for about $49 (recently $69 minus a $20 rebate) at http://www.britannica.com/. This is a fantastic research resource at an unbelievable price. It even comes in an optional DVD/CD-ROM. The program on CD has a powerful, built-in search capability.

14. BULK E-MAIL SOFTWARE

This is an optional move for the guerrilla self-publisher. Searching the Internet will give you websites to investigate that offer this kind of software. A typical attribute of this software is to facilitate using your desktop as a mini-server, bypassing your Internet-service provider (ISP) and allowing you to send bulk e-mail out without the size and number restrictions typically set by an ISP and, concurrently, eliminating the embedded stamp of the ISP on the outgoing e-mails.

Some other typically present features of this type of software are:

Resources, Software and Equipment

- Automatic gathering (extraction) of e-mail addresses present on websites throughout the Internet—defined loosely by keywords or specific groups.
- Bulk posting to newsgroups.
- Access to current lists of harvested e-mail addresses located on a website maintained by the software business and categorized by interest group.
- Limited-time demo downloads
- Free technical assistance.

The costs vary considerably, with most falling in the range of $80-$800. In addition, there are a variety of websites that provide services directly to handle bulk e-mail needs on a monthly fee basis, starting at around $200/month and moving up from there, depending on your sending frequency, number of messages, and list compatibility.

15. LEARNING TO USE SOFTWARE

Take heart. Learning to use software doesn't have to be a daunting undertaking. You'll receive plenty of positive feedback and confidence building along the way when you successfully tackle challenges and learn to satisfy your needs using the software programs. Even if you're a computer novice, you have many months to learn, practice, and perfect your skills. Remember, there're guides for idiots—and if there's a club, I claim default membership—universally available for most software at bookstores and software manufacturers.

In my case, I found the Help feature on the toolbar of programs, and the free support of manufacturers at their websites, to be adequate teaching resources, except for some quirks in Outlook and Publisher that I just plain had to learn by trial and error.

For example, the Microsoft website http://www.microsoft.com/ has a slew of staff-written articles posted that will help you understand how to work through or around most quirks in their software. In its Knowledge Base articles, Microsoft also posts comments from the practical experiences of users on issues and problems confronted and resolved. I found that the websites of most major manufactures provide similar services.

D. EQUIPMENT (MONTHS 1-3)

The equipment needed to effectively self-publish while conserving limited financial resources is suggested below:

- Scanner: These typically cost under $100 at office-supply or computer superstores. Purchasing a low-cost item online is usually not beneficial due to the cost of shipping, but going to appropriate sites can give you pricing perspectives.

- CPU: 700+ MHz with 128+ MB of RAM and 20+ GB of disk space is really all you have to have—three-year-old technology with most of the necessary bells and whistles. Mid-2003 checks at office-supply and computer superstores found major brands under $600 with Pentium-based processors of 2.4 GHz; 256 MB of RAM; 120 GB of disk space; DVD-CD player; CD writer; networking, digital photo, and wireless capabilities; and full upgradeability.

- Monitor: Again, go to appropriate Internet sites to check on prices. Recently, major-brand, 17-inch monitors being phased out at superstores were less than $100, and 17-inch LED flat screens were coming down to the $250-$300 range.

- Color printer: Good inkjet printers (claiming photo quality) were recently priced less than $100 new from office-supply and computer superstores. Picture-quality laser printers were less than $150. These printers make it possible for you to print out pictures of acceptable quality, brochures, flyers, CD-R labels, business cards, post cards, bookmarks, and any other small-scale, hard-copy promotional materials. You can even create masters to take to a professional printer.

- Fax and copier combination unit: Black-and-white units from major manufacturers were recently running $65-$100. You can keep the fax on 24 hours/day on a dedicated telephone line. Telephone-service providers usually have a separate telephone number with a special ring that you can purchase as an option for around $3/month. You use that number as your business fax number. You will also need this combination unit to fax hard copy from outside your computer, and to make copies on a daily basis.

Resources, Software and Equipment

- Laptop computer: I consider the laptop as an emergency backup for my desktop. The laptop is the primary tool for a writer on the road. It should allow you to accomplish most creative-writing and self-publishing tasks. For the frugal author/self-publisher, the laptop has to be able to do the basics, no more. For perspective, you need a minimum of 266 MHz and 64 MB of RAM to adequately run all the software listed in this book, as well as to operate effectively on the Internet through an internal 56k modem. The cost at auction sites could be as low as $200-$300. If you can afford it, a newer laptop with digital camera input and wireless capabilities may be important, and might run up to around $1,100, complete with all the bells and whistles. As far as batteries are concerned, they are very expensive (replacements run around $140), and battery life is commonly limited (two to four hours per charge). It's usually pretty easy to find an electrical outlet most anywhere you go anyway, and airplanes are beginning to offer 100% facilitation complete with Internet connection, so I don't care if the laptop runs on batteries or not.

- CD writer: A CD writer is a necessity for producing any CD-Rs you decide to create for the media, special promotions, or for product delivery. For instance, you may package PDF files of writing products, a media kit, a review-book, audio and video interviews, etc.

  CD-RWs are ideal for holding backup files from your desktop hard drive. For example, I can get everything I've ever created, plus an exported copy of the Personal Folder (PST file) of all the contents in my customized Outlook folders, and a current copy of the Windows My Favorites folder, in the space available on one CD-RW (around 700 MB of total capacity per CD).

  I purchased an Iomega external CD writer drive for about $150 new so that by placing my files on a CD-RW, I could take it—and everything I needed from my desktop—with me to use with my low-tech, laptop (with only 2.2 GB of disk space) when I'm on the road or using the laptop as a backup to the desktop.

NOTE: Typically, for software, computers, accessories, and equipment of all kinds, the online auctions and equipment wholesalers will have most of what you need (for example: monitors, laptops, and desktops) new, used, or rebuilt, and usually warranted, often in blocks of hundreds and thousands. The best values seem to be items one- to three- years old. In the computer industry, March is the month for new product releases, so the prices on everything go down in April each year.

CHAPTER III: Book Development (Months 1-24)

This chapter contains an overview of my writing and editing procedures, in case some of these concepts may be of interest to writers and authors. It also reveals just how much time and effort needs to go into a book for it to be the best you can produce.

A. BOOK FIRST DRAFT (MONTHS 1-6)

There are as many ways to get the first draft of a book on paper as there are rise-and-shine routines. Every writer is different. I share here a brief description of my routine, developing and writing fiction books, with the hope of being able to add some useful ideas to your creative-writing process.

1. GENERAL STORY FOLDER

First, I create a first rough draft of the synopsis, and then a three-to-five-page description of the general story. I keep these individual files in a Story file folder in My Documents on my computer. I will constantly go back to this folder to revise individual files. I recommend not deleting any of the ideas and concepts you end up revising; just move them to a discarded ideas and concepts file. You never know what will become material for other books.

I organize the general Story folder into files, including the following:
- Possible beginnings.
- Major conflicts.
- Possible endings.
- Major twists.
- Secondary conflicts and twists.
- A log of bright ideas and miscellaneous thoughts about the plot and characters.
- A list of potential characters and descriptions—everything from personality quirks to upbringing and experiences, including family, friends, psychological foibles, phobias, habits, physical and behavioral characteristics, etc.
- Discarded ideas and concepts

2. SCENIZING

Next, I write scene after scene without much forethought as to exactly how or where they will appear in the story. This scenizing (new verb from a noun—I like this technique) methodology marks the beginning of the writing and constructing of chapters. It's a useful tool for developing breadth and depth to the storyline and characters.

3. WRITING VOICE

My primary writing voice is the first-person present point of view. I also use short mental flashbacks, spontaneous internal dialog, and mental comments to provide information and build context for readers. When I narrate (and I try to find ways not to do this), I use the first-person present when I can and the omniscient point of view when I can't. For me, the limitations of the first person are outweighed by the opportunity for direct stimulation of readers through experiencing internal mind-talk, action, sensory perception, and dialog spontaneously as it occurs. I want readers to think they're there in the story, involved and engaged.

4. SCULPTING

Then I organize the scenes into chapters, smooth them out—only a little—and start inserting basic story-writing elements (and notes on alternatives) that make will make them complete. This is a sculpting process. The process is similar to structuring a short story, making sure the story-writing elements of danger, fear, conflict, tension, victory, defeat, action, suspense, clues, false trails, and character development are all present. I want each chapter to be like a little book, but with the end either left crying out for closure or shrouded in mystery.

There's a point where I feel like the story is just about all out. That's the signal that the first draft is complete. There will be a lot of editing from here, and the book will most likely be chopped and revised, even drastically, but I know at this point I have a potentially good book built around a worthy story that employs basic story-writing elements.

B. AUTHOR EDITING (MONTHS 7-18)

My first, second, and final edits take about twelve months: six months to complete the first and second edits and another six for the final edit, threading the work around necessary self-publishing tasks. I allot an additional six months for outside editing and revisions during months 19 to 24.

1. FIRST EDIT (MONTHS 7-12)

In the first edit, my objectives are to: cut and trim; sharpen and focus; smooth out and begin to give rhythm and pace to the structure and positioning of chapters; devise subtle linkages between chapters; ensure realism in the dialog; create credibility and consistency in actions, events, and objects; make sure characters change and grow; and create a consistent writing voice.

Many scenes will be drastically altered, or even cut and saved for another day. Creative ideas will pop up and become additions to scenes or new scenes. This phase includes the incorporation and development of ideas and concepts I've been jotting down in the files of the general Story folder. The plot thickens, so to speak, as I begin to create a compelling and provocative reading experience.

One of the techniques I use heavily is to leap from one scene or chapter to the next, always leaving the end of each chapter immersed in mystery or crying out for closure. In the beginning of the book, the scenes appear unrelated. As I jump back and forth, I create linkages that slowly bring out relatedness.

I prod and drive readers; I want them to become progressively hooked into building their unique perceptions of the story. I want them wrongly guessing what's going to happen next. To help me accomplish these reactions, I insert incomplete picture flashbacks, mental projections, and scenes that foreshadow, and I weave several mini-stories together. But I try not to overwhelm the reader with complexities that lead to confusion.

In bringing the story along, I construct trails of information that provoke the reader to make logical guesses of where the story is going and what the explanations are for the mysteries. I go to great lengths to make sure the correct guesses are well-grounded and the incorrect ones are justified.

Word effectiveness and word economies are not paramount concerns in the first edit. I need to remain loose, without grammatical or editorial boundaries or rules, to allow the maximum of creativity to flow out in developing the story. Honing style, selecting words, and crafting clauses and paragraphs comes in the second edit.

2. SECOND EDIT (MONTHS 7-12)

The second edit concentrates on showing, not telling, using economy of words, developing consistency in voice, and ensuring authenticity in actions and dialog.

I polish descriptions; make actions crisp and vivid; add vitality and legitimacy to the thoughts, feelings, and sensory perceptions of the characters; ensure dialog is natural and spontaneous; tighten up the realism in foreshadowing; and bolster and refine the linkages between chapters. At this stage, I'm still open to adding, subtracting, or reorganizing scenes to make the book better.

I want my end product to be the most realistic, fast-moving, unpredictable, in-the-moment, riveting reading experience possible, and I don't care about literary correctness.

Book Development

3. FINAL EDIT (MONTHS 13-18)

At this point, I lay the book down for a month to six weeks and work solidly on scheduled tasks in the self-publishing plan. Then, allowing six months, I come back with a vengeance to perform the final edit.

First, I read a printout of the book from cover to cover, only making notes in the margins on general plot, character development, and possible inconsistencies.

Next, I go back to the beginning and execute what I call my story metamorphosis, a chapter-by-chapter maximizing of story development, taking the plot to more intricate and realistic levels of development and reaching new heights of word economy, smoothness, and effectiveness, until I perceive the whole book as slick, credible, and flowing like a raging river. I don't let anything interrupt the final edit, outside of tasks required by my self-publishing plan.

Keep in mind that at the end of the final edit, if you look anywhere in the manuscript, you will still want to change this or that. The completion of the final edit is just that, the place to stop. Perfection is an unrealistic goal. You already have a good book. Rely on the next step, fresh perspective from the services of an outside editor, to provide developmental and writing-style suggestions and corrections in grammar that will help you polish the book into excellence.

C. OUTSIDE EDITING (MONTHS 13-24)

Finding and developing a professional relationship with an accomplished editor is almost as important as writing the book. So many trees remain hidden in the forest that most writers are bound to overlook important elements in performing their edits. Many authors and writers admit outright to not being accomplished editors.

The search and selection process for a magical editorial relationship should start when you begin the final edit (month 13), giving you six months to establish this vital relationship. The actual outside editing, and the author revisions from that edit, will likely take about another six months (months 19-24).

In general, finding an appropriate editing relationship for a nonfiction book will be considerably easier than finding one for a fiction book. Usually, writing a nonfiction book makes you the expert, and development, style, and writing-voice qualities are not important editing issues. For a fiction book, successful editing and writing experience in your genre will be a key criterion in editor selection, and you should budget for the cost. This expense will probably be the largest expense in your self-publishing plan.

1. SOURCES

- Use Internet search engines to compile lists of organizations of senior citizens, writing organizations, editing organizations, local newspapers and magazines, and college and university English departments in your state of residence.

- Go to http://www.yahoo.com/, and http://www.aol.com/ to search the clubs and groups formed around editing and writing. Join those that are appropriate and put out your queries. There are hundreds of these clubs and groups, some with thousands of members.

- Do an Internet search for editing or editing services. Many Internet websites, for example, http:/www.nupedia.com/ and http://www.content-exchange.com/, offer peer-review and editing services for a fee (usually around $5/page). Also check out the editor and writer referral services at the American Society of Journalists and Authors, http://www.asja.org/ and the Editorial Freelancers Association, http://www.the-efa.org/. In addition, look into services offered at http://www.scribendi.com/, http://www.editavenue.com/, and http://www.authorshowcase.com/. Fees charged by editors vary considerably; I've seen from $0.015-$0.04/word, depth of experience being the major factor.

- If you are a PMA member, use the annual PMA *Resource Directory;* or look in the PMA newsletters for advertisements in the back, under Classified Mart. Past newsletters are archived and accessible to nonmembers at the PMA's website, http://www.pma-online.org/.

- Go to http://www.publishersweekly.com/ and look through the ads, buy the magazine at a bookstore, or view and copy from it at the library.

2. CONTACTING

Send e-mails that describe your needs, and post queries at clubs, groups, and organizations on the Internet. Communications should be structured according to their destination, for example:

- Post editing help-wanted ads in the newsletters and on the websites of potentially synergistic organizations. This can be free.

- Send requests to English-department heads of colleges and universities to post the editing project to faculty and graduate students. Offer potential editors literary credit, experience, and some pay. I've heard that around $100/10,000 words is an equitable, straight-pay arrangement.

- At the clubs and groups you join, post messages at the websites and send messages to the master e-mail addresses (usually provided), so individuals in the clubs or groups receive your query directly.

- Submit invitations soliciting interest and/or referrals to editors of newspapers and magazines in your state of residence.

- Senior citizens may be one of the best sources. You will be surprised at the number of candidates in your local area, especially if you live close to popular retirement regions. Retired editors are often not as submerged in their own activities, or as stressed out with the day-to-day routine of their lives, so they may have time for an upstart, enthusiastic, confident author. Be advised, editors away from the action never lose their juices. Even highly experienced seniors may be able to give you a break on cost. I recommend posting queries on bulletin boards of housing developments in your local area, and contacting seniors' organizations in your state of residence for query-posting assistance.

Be brief, polite, and professional in all your e-mails and postings. Mention that sample chapters can be attached to e-mail on request, and/or send them to a special page on your website for downloads of the synopsis and sample chapters you have edited. Use the hooks and taglines you've developed that set your book apart from the herd. Offer your website for background information and to solidify credibility. If you don't have a website, you will by the time you get through this book. Chapter VII has been dedicated to discussing the rationale and creation mechanics for this critically important ingredient of successful self-publishing.

3. SCREENING

In screening identified candidates, take the time to get to know them—initially you are looking for personal rapport, reliability, experience, degree of excitement with sample chapters of your book, interest in your book's genre or subject, and a mutually agreeable time frame for the potential edit. Editors should communicate a potent belief in being able to help you accomplish the specific publishing goals you've set to define success. How much digestion of the background information you've provided at your website, and the degree of story understanding and excitement expressed by interested editors, will go a long way in convincing you of an editor's genuineness.

Keep a high priority on finding your editing relationship as close to your residence as possible; face-to-face contact could be important throughout the relationship.

After the screening process, your final choice of an editor relationship will hinge on evaluation of the editor's ability to enhance your writing style and story development. This is the time to request a sample of his or her editing. With complete command of the story you have provided, the final proof is in the pudding.

So, if you have not completed the final author edit of your book, you will want to give the editors you invite to submit sample edits a chapter-by-chapter description—just the salient story and plot elements to fill out their story understanding. If you've completed the final author edit of the book, make a PDF copy, place it along with a cover letter on CD-Rs, and send them to your candidates by postal-mail. Editors should be able to fully demonstrate their developmental and story-enhancement skills through the sample edit process, and you should be able to narrow your search.

4. FINAL SELECTION

The final stage in the selection process should include requesting and thoroughly checking out business and personal references. Prior to requesting these references, negotiate the terms of the relationship. Then, attach a copy of your proposed editorial agreement along with the request.

Search the Internet to research the elements that should be covered in a proper contract. Use the legal resources cited in this book as starters. You should be able to find sample contracts to work from, and then choose a qualified publishing attorney to draft the final document after you come to terms with an editor. The key issue is signing over all ownership rights to any changes and suggestions that you might derive from the editing work. There may be other issues that need to be formalized, depending on the situation you negotiate; for example, possible sharing in profits from the book, the wording and placement of the acknowledgment in the book or on the cover, and remuneration.

One thing is for sure; investment in a close editorial relationship will be worthwhile. You will produce a better book, and learn a great deal more about effective editing through the experience—knowledge that will immensely enhance the quality of your future writing and editing.

CHAPTER IV: Promotional-List Compilation and Use (Months 1-24)

During the same 24 months when you are drafting, editing, revising, and polishing your book, many organizational tasks must also be accomplished, including acquiring access to promotional contacts. If you have the financial resources, you can save time by paying outside providers for access to the promotional lists you will need.

If you're strapped, the compilation of the contact lists needed to succeed in self-publishing is time-consuming and continuous during this period. Adding to these lists will remain an ongoing activity. Your later promotional activities will rely heavily on sending review invitations, announcements, blurbs, and media releases to important segments of the publishing industry and directly to potential buyers in the marketplace.

A. GENERAL MECHANICS

Ideally, the contact data needed for these lists should include: organization or company name, address, telephone number, fax number, e-mail address, website, and the full name and title of the contact person.

NOTE: Names, titles, and functions within organizations change too often for it to be worth pegging contacts from directory lists copied in the library; contact information is already almost two years old when a current directory comes out. If you send promotional communications to these individuals, a large number will not be delivered because the individuals have left their positions. E-mails will be returned with notes, and faxes will be discarded.

I recommend that authors put the effort into contacting a specific person when communicating/promoting by fax and e-mail. For many contact lists, this will mean a lot of website surfing and telephone calls.

B. EXAMPLE OF LIST CREATION USING MICROSOFT ACCESS

I recommend using Microsoft Access for compiling, managing, and manipulating contact lists. These lists can be sorted and/or filtered into sub-lists (tables) for importing directly into fax and e-mail software programs like WinFax PRO and Outlook respectively.

In constructing contact lists, you create columns for your information. Among these, I suggest defining "importance-indicator" data-lines (columns). For example, for news-media lists, I add the data-lines Review, Size, and Daily or Weekly. You will come up with other custom data-line needs; just remember to think out how you will be using the list, and define the lines from the beginning. Better too much information than too little.

Continuing with the example, I enter G on the Review data-line if I want the contact to receive an automatic galley-book, R in the Review data-line to receive an automatic review-book, G and R for both considerations, a number representing the definition of circulation size (range) on the Size data-line, and D or W for daily or weekly on that data-line.

As specific examples, all the super newspapers, like *USA Today, The New York Times,* and several others, and important reviewers and syndicators, get a G and an R. Additionally, I define newspapers with a 1 if daily circulation is over 100,000, whether it's a daily or weekly, and

2 and 3 for lesser circulations. Some of the biggest newspapers also get both Gs and Rs. You can set your own criteria. I enter Gs for major magazines that have specific interest in my subject matter or genre, if they review books no matter what their size. I give Rs to those with interest in reviewing books in general, as long as circulation is over 100,000.

By sorting and filtering your lists, you can develop test groups for different e-mail and fax promotions. For example, you could create a sub-list (table) within your list of newspaper by sorting out those with Florida in the State data-line and R in the Review data-line, and then save it (as a table) with an explanatory name as part of the larger, inclusive Access list document.

C. IMPORTING LISTS FOR BROADCASTING

Importing a text file you've created, or a list compiled in another compatible file format like Access or Excel, into Outlook or WinFax PRO, is accomplished by using the import wizards located in the File menu of these programs. By working with these programs in advance, you will know where to store lists when they are imported and how to select them for broadcast e-mails and faxes. The wizards are relatively straightforward.

In a general case, importing into Outlook for example, go to File and select Import Export. At the end of the process before you click Finish at the last screen, map the fields you want to import from your file to the corresponding fields available in Outlook. You do this because the fields will probably be different in the data file being imported unless you've created the file and designated the names of the header fields to correspond to the Outlook names.

Contact lists created as Access documents are directly importable (Access is a file-type selection option in the import/export wizard) into an Outlook contacts folder you create to store the list. The titles of the Access columns need to correspond to Outlook names defined in Outlook contact folders (Right click on any column heading at the top of the opened contacts folder on the right-hand screen; then click on Field Chooser and select and move to the column heading the column names you want to show for the list you are importing.). Or, you must use the same mapping process described with the Outlook import/export wizard. Outlook contact folders are automatically available (selectable) in WinFax PRO.

Notepad and WordPad are handy software programs for creating text lists that are directly importable into Outlook and WinFax PRO. You can find them in Windows by going to Start, Programs, Accessories and choosing either one. I place shortcuts to the programs on my PC desktop. For example, when working on the Internet compiling a new list, you would open the program and minimize it, so it goes to the bottom of the screen. You can copy and paste or type the contact information from a website by restoring the program from the bottom of the screen, and then minimizing it when you're finished pasting or entering.

You format the list document by creating a line of Outlook-compatible headers—contact-information names, like "E-mail Address"—on the top line. Separate each header with a comma or tab and use the carriage return at the end of the line. Organize your inputs into the document by entering each under the header line in sequence, using commas or tabs to separate the items as defined by the header line. No spaces are utilized, and at the end of an entry, you use a carriage return to start another entry. Save the list as a text document to an appropriate folder in your My Documents folder. A generic example of a header line and an entry line using commas is as follows:

Company Name,Full Name,E-mail Address,Fax (carriage return)

ABC Company,John Brown,,jbrown@abccompany.com,941-339-9820 (carriage return).

D. PURGING THE LISTS

Purging lists as you complete them, to identify incorrect fax numbers and e-mail addresses, allows you to gain experience with broadcasting as well as putting out your first promotion as a self-publisher. Make it short and sweet, leaving positive name recognition. Then you have to make a decision as to whether visiting websites and calling the businesses to track down the correct fax numbers and/or e-mail addresses is worthwhile.

E. LIST DESCRIPTIONS

I manually compiled the lists described below over a two-and-a-half-year period. I've indicated the number of contacts for each in parenthesis, and offered sources.

Several of the lists became ongoing projects, for example, locating individual potential book buyers using Internet clubs and groups. In the cases of media and libraries, in the beginning I compiled lists of just the majors, realizing I would have to budget for the later purchase of databases for these important sectors. Most of the lists you'll want to compile can be found in reference books at a good library.

In compiling the majority of your lists, I recommend you omit entering the full name of your selected contacts, in favor of later website or telephone contact to identify the appropriate current person and confirm the e-mail address.

The contacts in nearly all of the lists I recommend compiling will receive a galley-book review invitation, a review-book invitation, and other communications as appropriate.

1. LIBRARIES

Sources: Buy the CD (about $495), or copy the information at the library from the *American Library Directory*, published now by Information Today, Inc. (as of the Fall 2001. It used to be R.R. Bowker). The customer-service number is 800-300-9869 or 609-654-6266, and the directory comes out annually in June. The disk was not available online when I last checked at their website, http://www.infotoday.com/. This directory includes profiles of more than 30,000 public, academic, special, and government libraries and library-related organizations in the United States, Canada, and Mexico.

An alternate source is the University of California at Berkley's site, http://www.sunsite.berkeley.edu/libweb/public_main.html. It has hyperlinked lists of U.S. public libraries on the Web, organized by type and geographic location.

I started out at the public library copying contact information for the major public library systems from the *American Library Directory* (84). I didn't fill in the full name of the appropriate contact, but I did enter "Selection Librarian" for the Title. I plan on developing a larger—

perhaps state by state—list further into the promotion-planning process as sales from pointed promotions justify, or I may buy the CD later. Libraries are of particular interest to me for potential sales of this book, as I see the book as an excellent reference.

In addition, I decided to compile lists, from a locally produced directory of libraries in Florida (my state of residence) for the major library systems and bigger branches (86), and libraries at centers of higher education (161).

In the case of my upcoming fiction book, I served with the U.S. Marine Corps and plan to build a promotional tie-in with that affiliation and the hero's military background. So, I decided to compile a list of all the U.S. government and military-base libraries (275), also copied from the *American Library Directory*.

If your subject matter and/or genre are appropriate, a list of high schools (to get to the librarians) can be copied from Patterson's *American Education 2002*, including most fax numbers. If you wanted to conduct tests, ASCII tab-delimited CDs can be purchased from Patterson's for about $60/1,000 names (call 800-357-6183 for information). I took the time and compiled my list of Florida high schools (423) by copying directly from the Patterson publication, and adding a list I came across of county education media centers (43) from the State of Florida website.

The first time I will utilize these lists will be seeking book reviews from libraries through a galley-book review promotion. I hope the testimonials I can add to the final book will enhance salability to the general library market.

The library market deserves serious promotional attention, because sales to libraries don't come back, and libraries are conditioned to paying full retail price or accepting small discounts for volume when dealing directly with publishers. For context, Ingram Book Group and Baker & Taylor typically offer libraries a discount of 20% across the board.

2. BOOKSTORES

Source: The *American Book Trade Directory*, published by Information Today, Inc. Go to the library and compile an in-state list, with store names, owner/manager names, e-mail addresses (when given) and fax

Promotional-List Compilation and Use 57

numbers (306 in Florida). I plan on doing some promotional testing with these bookstores after the book has been out in the market for a while.

3. MAJOR AUTHORS

Source: Internet search engines. Use their names or keywords, for example: fiction authors, best-selling authors, author directories. My target here is e-mail addresses for 100 well-known authors in my subject or genre. I also look for any other contact information, like addresses, telephone numbers, and fax numbers.

Often you will have to graze the sites to find the elusive e-mail addresses, and many times you will strike out totally. But persevere; you will use this list to beg for galley-book reviews (cursory peer reads) with the hope of capturing useful testimonials for the final book.

4. FILM PRODUCERS AND FILM AGENTS

Source: *Writer's Guide to Hollywood Producers, Directors, and Screenwriter's Agents*. At the library, copy the descriptive pages of listings that strike you as possibilities, according to your subject. Make two lists, one for film producers (153) and one for film agents (44). If the library doesn't have the book, ask it to use the inter-library loan service. Compiling this list is appropriate for writers structuring books that will be of interest to the film/TV market.

5. NATIONAL MAGAZINES FEATURING BOOKS

Source: *Literary Market Place*, now published by Information Today, Inc. Copy the listing information for those who review books in your subject or genre (152). When you send galley-book review invitations and review-book invitations to these magazines, you'll tailor them to win reviews of the book, generate possible articles, and whet appetites for purchasing first-serial, second-serial, condensation, and/or excerpt rights to your book. My list included nine Gs and 21 Rs (entries on importance-indicator data-lines, discussed in the "General Mechanics" section, above).

6. NATIONAL, DAILY, AND WEEKLY NEWSPAPERS

A critically important ongoing promotional effort after your book is available for review will focus on obtaining free publicity through reviews and articles published in these important publications.

Sources: I began this task by copying the contact information at the library from the "Newspapers Featuring Books" and "Newspapers with Weekly Magazines" sections of the *Literary Market Place* (370). This publication gives you most of the majors. Then I went to a current copy of *Bacon's Newspaper Directory*, published by Bacon's, a part of the Swedish company, Observe AB, and added newspapers with circulations of over 100,000 (137) that were not included in the *Literary Market Place*. Next, I checked with Dan Poytner's list of "must" reviewers to make sure I didn't miss a key newspaper or review source. When I finished, the list had 37 Gs and 173 Rs.

An alternative source on the Internet is http://www.newspapers.com/. Here you'll find an extensive listing of different types of newspapers, selectable by state and all hyperlinked.

Media database CDs are available from: Bradley Communications Corp., http://www.rtir.com/, 800-989-1400; Bacon's Media Directories, http://www.bacons.com/, 800-972-9253; Media Made Easy at http://www.workshopinc.com/, 704-528-8260; Media Directories at http://www.oxbridge.com/; and *All in One Directory* at http://www.gebbieinc.com/, 845-255-7560.

Each of these lists on CD has pluses and minuses. I found Bacon's and Oxbridge's to be too expensive ($800+), and Gebbie to be too limited (lacking editor names and a program for creating and manipulating target lists). I settled on Bradley's *Publicity Blitz Media Directory* ($295). It has newspapers, magazines, syndicates, and radio/TV/cable talk shows. Although only about one-third of the entries have e-mail addresses, almost all have websites, fax numbers, editorial and producer/host contacts, and all the necessary organization information. There are around 20,000 entries, formatted so data specific to your use can be easily identified, sorted, and saved in sub-lists as tab-delimited and/or comma-delimited text files or brought into Access for management and creation of sub-files to import into broadcast fax and e-mail software programs. Bradley recommends Access 2000 or its equivalent to manage the database. The new CD comes out each year in July with a 30-day, money-back guarantee, giving you time to experiment. Free technical assistance by phone is included.

Promotional-List Compilation and Use

NOTE: *If you're on a shoestring, don't commit to the expenditure until you feel your book has gained sufficient sales momentum. This decision, like the one for the library CD, can be effectively made later on as part of the continuing creative promotional process outlined in the last chapter.*

Other alternative approaches include:

- Joining a respected media-information service provider on the Internet, for example, YearBook of Experts, http://www.yearbook.com/. This business is owned by Broadcast Interview Source, Inc of Washington D.C. Here, for an annual registration fee of $795, you can list yourself (a profile of your business and a description of what you do) for perusal by the media. You are allowed to submit news releases weekly, which are sent to 12,000+ journalists who have opted-in to use the service. For the investment, the prestige associated with this mature website business, the advantage of media editors having opted-in to receive promotions, access to instantly changing your account profile, and the ability to literally manage all your media-contact promotions online from any computer with Internet access, I consider this an excellent value. In addition, Yearbook.com has other quality services it offers as part of the membership package.

- At http://www.parrotmedia.com/, for $49/month you can have unlimited access to their media databases online. They're kept current and maintained by Parrot Media Network. This may be an equitable way to go for the frugal self-publisher, considering you could turn the service on or off according to your promotional schedule and budget, and you're assured of current information.

7. MAJOR PUBLISHERS

Source: *Literary Market Place*. Copy contact information for publishers that have an interest in your book's subject matter and/or genre (28). These biggies should all be tagged with Gs and Rs. As a self-publisher, you'll want to keep the major players in the industry aware of you and your work; it makes sense to do what you can to keep all the avenues open. Finding e-mail addresses for appropriate contacts is difficult. The first step is to review their websites. Worst-case scenario is you will have to call and beg.

8. LITERARY AGENTS

Source: *Literary Market Place*. Copy contact information for those that have interest in your book's subject matter and/or genre (182). They'll receive galley-book review invitations as another means of networking and keeping the doors open to the traditional publishing industry.

9. TRADITIONAL BOOK REVIEWERS AND SYNDICATORS

Source: *Literary Market Place*. Copy contact information for those interested in books (163). This list received 21 Gs and 101 Rs.

10. INTERNET BOOK REVIEWERS

Sources: Hundreds and hundreds of websites have something to do with reviewing books. I suggest developing several lists, for example: e-zine and newsletter reviewers, book-review interested organizations, miscellaneous and independent reviewers, etc. You will be continuously revising these lists as the Internet expands and matures. Choosing a limited number of credible resource sites for obtaining lists of reviewers will help you stay effective, relying on them to remain current and do the initial screening and categorizing.

I recommend the resources below, and suggest you surf their lists of hyperlinked sites for key contact information (organization name, contact person and title, telephone number, and e-mail address). In the process of visiting these sites, you'll discover other lists of links. Don't get sidetracked. Complete the lists presented by your selected resource sites first, but you may want to take notes on the existence of lists on other sites and put them aside for future investigation and cross-referencing.

To start the journey, I would first go to the Book Reviewers and Other Reviewers, a list maintained by Midwest Book Review, http://www.midwestbookreview.com/. A significant covey of individual, professional reviewers can be found at http://www.amazon.com/. You can track down e-mail addresses for Amazon's reviewers by going to the pages at Amazon that contain profile information on the top 100—just search for reviewers on the Amazon site; I found 73 reviewer profiles that included e-mail addresses.

A good e-zine list is still present at http://www.meer.net/~johnl/e-zine-list; it was current up through March of 2000, listing thousands of e-zines, searchable by keyword. For example, reviews brought 308 entries, all hyperlinked.

By the time I finished the final edit of this book, the total number of reviewer contacts in all my sub-lists was over 700.

11. CATALOGS

Sources: *National Directory of Catalogs*, published by Oxbridge Communications Inc., "Books and Book Trade" section; and *The Catalog of Catalogs*, by Edward L. Paulder, published by Woodbine House. At the library, copy information on those catalogs appropriate to your subject and/or genre (127).

Many organizations offer books through periodic publication of catalogs to their members. One or more catalog deals could materialize during the galley-book review process to help defray the cost of the first printing. What at first appears to be a break-even agreement, or below cost, may produce a decrease in unit-printing cost if it enables a larger first printing run that converts into increased overall profit from selling it out. Early contact with these players is important; they want access to book products before the rest of the market.

I pegged the 19 biggest of these catalog organizations with a G for automatic receipt of a galley-book review presentation; these potentially important organizations should be contacted by telephone to introduce the coming of the presentation. Of course, all the organizations you've identified should receive galley-book review invitations.

12. BOOK CLUBS

Sources: Copy appropriate contact information from *Literary Market Place* and check out http://www.midwestbookreview.com/ for their book club listings.

Dan Poynter's book, *The Self-Publishing Manual* (2001), indicates that a contract with a major book club may typically bring in a 7%-10% royalty from their club offering-price (usually 20% off cover), plus a negotiated amount up front for publication. Again with consideration to the economies of scale from a larger first printing due to an order from a book club, and the promotional value of the club's endorsement, a deal with one or more book clubs can be extremely valuable. If you can just cover printing cost and shipping in the up-front arrangement, you've made a great bargain.

The list (37) receives galley-book review invitations. The major book clubs on the list got Gs (17), and will be telephoned directly to introduce the coming of the galley-book review presentations. Like the catalog organizations, these powerful movers of books want to see potential products well before the general review market.

13. MAJOR PAPERBACK PUBLISHERS

Source: *Literary Market Place*. I want to keep this market segment constantly appraised. These publishers may be interested in the paperback rights one to three years after a book's publication date, assuming you have been successful in generating sales that attracted attention and the book fits their subject and/or genre interests.

14. MAJOR DISTRIBUTORS

Source: *Literary Market Place*. My list turned up 34. The super major distributors (pegged with G and R data-line entries) should automatically receive the galley-book review presentation, and later the review-book presentation. These key players should be kept informed about you and your works. You want to be on record as having touched all the bases, even though the distributors may not be a part of your immediate plan. As self-publishers, because we can't know what the future holds for the industry (consolidations, re-purposing, spin-offs, etc.), it's a good idea to keep our options open.

15. MAJOR WHOLESALERS

Source: *Literary Market Place*. Out of my list of 37, four of the super majors received Gs and Rs. As with the major distributors, covering this segment of the publishing industry with your promotional efforts helps to create awareness, buzz, and credibility.

16. FOREIGN RIGHTS PUBLISHERS

Sources: *Literary Market Place* and the *American Book Trade Directory* have sections for foreign publishers with offices and/or representatives in the United States. Screen these organizations for interest in your book's subject and/or genre (51). This list is most certainly not complete, and there are other methods you will add later to your promotional efforts for communicating with this market.

17. ALTERNATIVE NEWSPAPERS

Source: Association of Alternative Newsweeklies, http://www.aan.org/, 202-822-1955. These are the in-generation tabloids. For about $25, you can purchase the current directory to access contact information for North America's metro weeklies (119).

18. NATIONAL CHAIN BOOKSTORES

Source: *Literary Market Place*, "Major Chain and Franchise Headquarters" section. This list (93) contains the club and super retailer chain stores like Sam's and WalMart, as well as national bookstore chains, and drugstore, supermarket, department store, airport, and college-bookstore chains. Again, the purpose of promoting to these outlets is to create recognition for you and your works by keeping the doors open.

19. NATIONAL INDEPENDENT BOOKSTORES

Source: Using the American Booksellers Association (ABA) member directory online at http://www.bookweb.org/, you can sort out bookstores by specialty or geographic location, and print out lists. About 70% have fax numbers and 50% have e-mail addresses. I compiled two lists of specialty bookstores for test promotions involving the release of my fiction book next year: Metaphysical (75) and Science Fiction (78).

For developing more detailed lists, a current *American Booksellers Directory*, published by the ABA, can usually be found at major libraries.

After this book is available in the market, I will be experimenting with promotions to my list (350) of Florida bookstores (including the branches of the national chains) that are tied to offering self-publishing workshop/signings.

20. PRINT NEWSLETTERS THAT REVIEW BOOKS

Source: *Newsletters in Print*, published by the Gale Research Company, and found in most libraries. Copy those appropriate to your subject matter and genre (18).

21. INTERNET LISTSERVS AND GROUPS

The ideal is to be able to directly contact individuals who are interested in the subject matter or genre of your book. An effective means to help accomplish this seemingly impossible feat is to search the Internet and join appropriate listservs, groups, and clubs. By joining, you can compile lists:

- Of their master e-mail addresses; these are the addresses used by members to send messages to all the members.
- Of individual members who send messages to members.

In addition, I suggest adding the home pages of all the groups, clubs and subject lists you join to a Groups and Clubs folder in your My Favorites directory. My Favorites is an organizational capability in Windows Explorer, opened through a tab at the top of the browser page, or the equivalent in another browser, like bookmarks in Netscape or AOL. Using this helpful feature allows you to have all of these connections in one place.

LISTSERVS

Source: According to information on the website identified below, listservs are lists managed by software that began service in 1986. With the advent of the Internet, the business of online list management has grown to more than 213,000 lists.

Explanatory information and index/search capabilities for listservs can be found at http://www.lsoft.com/. Go to this home page and click on Catalist in the left-hand column. This takes you to a searchable list of listservs by subject. It also includes a list of the largest lists.

More than 56,000 of these lists are public, meaning almost anyone can join. Some lists are set up so you can e-mail the management software, sending your message to everyone on the list. Others are just one-way, depending on the purpose of the list; for example, members can only receive product updates, news in an industry segment, digests of commentaries, tech-talk, etc., from the list manager. The ones of interest will be those that allow messages from members to go to every member of the list.

I found it effective to join selected lists, using the same business e-mail address each time; and then unsubscribe from the ones—I discovered from their membership-confirmation e-mails—that didn't allow messages to be sent directly to the whole list (you have to join to find out).

To date, I've joined about 100 listservs that have to do with writing and self-publishing, giving me direct access to nearly one million potential buyers of this book.

GROUPS AND CLUBS

Sources: The major Internet directories, such as Yahoo! (Groups), AOL (Communities), Excite (Boards), MSN (People and Chat), Topica (Newsletters and Discussions), and Lycos (Communities), facilitate free creation of clubs, groups, and subjects (I'll call them all groups from now on). There are groups based on practically any topic you can think of. The idea is to join those that have something in common with your book. Finding these groups and joining them is a worthwhile ongoing activity.

Considering Yahoo! Groups as an example, the groups range in size from one to thousands of members. Find the ones involved with your book's subject or genre by browsing through the categories and checking out the sub-lists of groups displayed. I suggest joining those screened for the following attributes:

- Have over 100 members.

- Allow members to post messages to the group.

- Don't have moderators screening the messages that go to the membership; this presents a stumbling block you don't want to invest the time dealing with—unless the group is so important you decide it's worth your time to treat it separately.

- Presence of sufficient message volume between members. This is easily discernible from the graph on every group home page, which displays these numbers by month.

As part of joining a group, typically you can elect to receive individual e-mail messages from group members. The reasons to activate this feature of your membership could be to keep current with the topics of interest to the group, tap into good advice from members, and/or process the messages into a list of potential individual buyers.

Upon joining a Yahoo! Group, you receive an e-mail that explains the group and lists the master e-mail address to use when sending messages to all the group members. An additional characteristic of e-mailing to the members of a Yahoo! Group is that the messages sent are also posted at the group home page.

As a member of Yahoo!, you can select a module called My Groups to be a part of your My Yahoo! page. All the groups you've joined are neatly listed with key information, and hyperlinked to each group home page. This is a great management tool.

ORGANIZING MEMBERSHIPS FOR SENDING E-MAILS

Using Outlook as the example, an effective way to organize memberships, is to create categories in Outlook's Master Categories list, accessible from any contact folders you've created in the program. When adding a new contact to a Contacts sub-folder, enter the name of the group or listserv and the master e-mail address, and click on categories to select from those you've defined.

For example, I created the categories, Listserv Writers, Listserv Fiction Readers, Listserv General Markets, Group Fiction Readers, and Group Writers, and entered the new contact information for each of my memberships into the Business Contacts folder (I created this folder as a sub-folder of the Contacts folder). When I click on the Business Contacts folder, the screen shows all my contacts organized by category (a view selection in the toolbar at the top of the Outlook page).

To take this example further, when you want to send e-mail to the master e-mail addresses in a category, open the Business Contacts folder and right-click the category name that holds the contact information. Then, right-click the category and select Move to Folder. Select the temporary Contacts sub-folder you created for these kinds of manipulations.

When you're finished creating and sending the broadcast e-mail, you move the category list in the temporary sub-folder back to the Business Contacts folder.

Now, create a tailored message you want to go to the contacts (master e-mail addresses) in the temporary sub-folder. Select BCC in the e-mail header, and select the temporary sub-folder from the screen.

Promotional-List Compilation and Use

Then, select all the contacts by scrolling down the screen and holding the shift key. Click the Add button and OK, and all the master e-mail addresses will show up on the BCC line.

The last step is to send the e-mail through the e-mail account (also selectable in Outlook) you used when you joined the listservs and groups. The e-mail goes to all the master e-mail addresses, and subsequently to all list members.

It is important to draft these communications creatively, and at the same time respect current non-spamming practices. I have more to say about this subject in the last chapter of the book.

22. POTENTIAL INDIVIDUAL BUYERS

Sources: I compile this list on an ongoing basis from e-mail messages automatically received from members of the groups and listservs I've joined. Receiving e-mail messages from members at a specified e-mail address is usually an option you elect during the process of joining a group. With listservs it's automatic.

In addition, I recommend setting aside a daily block of time to search the Internet for organizations related to the subject or genre of your book in order to collect and add the contact information of staff, officers, and members to the list. This effort is also part of compiling the Book-Related Organizations list discussed below.

ADDING GROUP AND LISTSERV MEMBERS

I use Outlook to manage all incoming e-mail messages from group and listserv members. Using the Organize tab in the standard toolbar at the top of the page in Outlook, I set rules for directing these messages to Inbox sub-folders I create, for example, Listserv Fiction Readers, Group Fiction Readers, Writers, etc. The objective is to extract names and e-mail addresses from these messages, and add them to the Potential Individual Buyers list.

Group Messages: To accomplish the objective, periodically process e-mail messages in the inbox sub-folders you've created to Access or Excel files by exporting the contents of the sub-folders, using the import/export wizard in Outlook under File, and selecting Access or Comma-Delineated Windows format (this format selection automatically creates an Excel file) during the process. I recommend storing lists in folders created in your My Documents directory.

Next, you edit the Access or Excel files by deleting all the columns except for those that contain the individual names and e-mail addresses of sending members. Then, rename the columns to the same ones you've set up in the Potential Individual Buyers list (also an Access file), and copy and paste the contact information into that list. Once you've done that, the Access or Excel file can be deleted.

Listserv messages: Exporting the messages to Access or Excel doesn't separate the information into separate columns (don't ask me why). Compile the information by opening the messages individually, taking down the sender name and e-mail address, and entering the information into the Potential Individual Buyers list.

In all cases, when you're finished processing messages from an Inbox sub-folder of Outlook, delete the contents, freeing space for fresh messages.

USING THE LIST IN BROADCAST E-MAIL

When you want to use the Potential Individual Buyers list for a broadcast e-mail message from Outlook, import the list into a sub-folder you've created in Contacts, for example, a folder called Temp Holding.

Then, create the broadcast e-mail message, and click on BCC in the message header to choose the contacts in the Temp Holding folder. Scroll and select (holding down the shift key) all the contacts in the folder, click the Add button, and then OK. All the contacts will appear in the BCC header line, and you're ready to send the e-mail.

After you finish, delete the contents of the Temp Holding sub-folder. This leaves the folder empty and ready for importing another list. Your master Potential Individual Buyers list remains intact in whatever file you have it stored in My Documents.

23. BOOK-RELATED ORGANIZATIONS

Sources: *The Encyclopedia of Associations,* published by the Gale Research Group, 800-877-4253, http://www.gale.com/. For example, if your book's subject is gardening, you could develop a list of associations, clubs, and organizations by searching through the index for keywords like horticulture, plants, botany, gardening, etc. You should be able to identify the major national, regional, state, and local associations and organizations that have anything to do with your subject or genre. Most of the time, the *Encyclopedia* lists websites, fax numbers, and e-mail addresses for the business, and contact information for key staff/officers. Going through this reference book will give you additional keyword ideas to use in Internet searches.

Search the Internet for websites of genre- and subject-related newsletters, e-zines, newsgroups, organizations, clubs, and groups not associated with a directory (like Yahoo!); for example, for a book about business you might additionally seek out business-news and business-magazine editors and publishers; heads of university business schools; well-known business analysts; and senior executives of investment-banking firms, mutual funds, and bank investment departments. Keep an open mind to discovering unique tie-ins; this will be an ongoing project.

Some of the key elements of information you would be looking for:

- Potential for working with the organization in special offerings of your book for sale to members.
- Access for posting announcements on the website.
- Acceptance of announcements for inclusion in newsletters.
- Experts and movers and shakers in your subject and genre to invite to review your galley-book when the time comes.
- Names and e-mail addresses to add to your Potential Individual Buyers list.

ORGANIZING KEY ELEMENTS OF INFORMATION

To help organize the Book-Related Organizations list, I suggest creating an importance-indicator data-line in the list-creation software you are using, such as Publisher, or a new column in Access, that lets you identify your business interests in the organization and its website, for example, a line called Business Actions. You could then enter a P for a direct-posting site, G to send a galley-book review invitation, N for submitting announcements to their newsletter, O for those to send special-offer invitations for their members, R to send review-book invitation, M for movers and shakers (key people in an appropriate industry, subject, or genre)

If more than one contact person and/or e-mail address is associated with these interests, make the list reflect this by making several separate list entries; for example, John Jones, ABC Corp, e-mail address, and N entered on the Business Actions line so you know he's the one to sent announcements for inclusion in the organization newsletter. The list can then be easily sorted to create sub-lists for special purposes.

ADDING TO THE POTENTIAL INDIVIDUAL BUYERS LIST

For the book-related organizations you track down, acquire names and e-mail addresses of members, officers, staff, members of boards of directors, as well as any chapter contacts and their officers, staff, board members, and members. As mentioned above, these contacts should also be added to the Potential Individual Buyers list.

SOME COMPILING SUGGESTIONS

For those organizations that allow posting of messages and/or news, add the URLs of those website pages to a My Favorites folder for use in later promotions.

When you're on the Internet searching websites, keep the Book-Related Organizations list, and the Potential Individual Buyers list files open and minimized, so you can pull them up to copy and paste where effective.

An idea that may work for you, if you can budget for it, is to create properly formatted Notepad files with three comma-separated values as headers at the top (Name, Company, E-mail). Copy the formatted file to several 3.5 floppies, and use one or more neighborhood teenagers to perform the no-brainer data-entry work at websites you assign to them, or folders you create of copied listserv messages that each have to be opened to get the information. Since almost every computer has Notepad, they do the work for you at their homes, using their computers and Internet access. You can copy and paste the contacts into your Potential Individual Buyers list.

24. BOOK PRESENTATION AND AUTHOR POSTING SITES

Sources: Depending on your purposes as a self-publisher, you will choose to post your book presentation at various sites appropriate and synergistic with your subject matter and/or genre to obtain exposure. There are hundreds of sites to confuse your attention. In general, I elected to concentrate on defining the major players, and developing relationships with these organizations.

For example, if your book is in the fantasy or sci-fi genre, and you want maximum exposure to the reading and publishing market at a minimum of cost, it would make sense to consider having the book presentation available at:

- Website bookstores or member pages associated with one or more major, fantasy/sci-fi, author organizations like SFF Net at http://www.sff.net/, the premiere sci-fi/fantasy/horror organization for authors and publishers ($99/year for basic membership).

- One or more specialty sites set up for media editors, publishers, agents, and film executives looking for stories and talent, for example: Authorlink at http://www.authorlink.com/ ($129/year), AuthorShowcase at http://www.authorshowcase.com/ ($70/year), and JLBooks at http://www.jlbooks.com/ ($30 for two years).

- Major online bookstores such as Amazon (http://www.amazon.com/) and Barnes and Noble (http://www.barnesandnoble.com/) for exposure to the general book-buying market. Although these relationships are free of setup costs, net profits, with the steep discounts required, may keep many self-publishers away from this avenue until sales justify larger print runs with inherent volume economics.

- http://www.allreaders.com, a website for readers. Using its powerful searching capabilities, readers can be quite specific about what books are of interest. Writers may promote their books by completing a voluminous review form online. The service to writers is free, and the website recently claimed its visitor volume was about 15% of Barnes and Noble's, http://www.barnesandnoble.com/. That's big, approaching two million visitors a day.

In addition, authors, writers, and self-publishers can post appropriate information about themselves, their works, or events at many important websites that maintain directories of information for their visitors or members. Track these down by diligently searching the Internet. Examples of entrenched and respected sites that offer free registration are http://www.google.com and http://www.authorzone.com/.

In most cases, submissions and registrations are facilitated directly at the websites. So, creating a folder in My Favorites to store the URLs of appropriate pages will enable you to quickly go to each one when the time comes to submit.

25. OPT-IN E-MAIL LISTS

Sources: Use a search engine to find the latest service providers of opt-in e-mail lists. Typically, these providers will e-mail promotional pieces to the number of contacts you buy, by geographic location and opted-in interest. Many of these lists have been gathered by harvesting software that grazes the Internet, tracks surfers through the sign-up process for various benefits at websites, and captures their e-mail addresses. The addresses are usually sorted into interest groups and sometimes by geographic location of the owners.

The cost is typically around $0.15/name, but the providers keep control of the list(s); you pay every time you send to the list(s). If you have interest, it may be wise to concentrate on the services offered by providers whose credibility you can check out, for example, http://www.postmasterdirect.com/.

I haven't utilized opt-in e-mail sources yet. I'll wait until the providers get to the point of offering list packages, formatted for ease of manipulation by database-management software, delivered on CD-R discs, and at reasonable prices.

26. BULK E-MAIL LISTS

Sources: Search on the Internet. I receive offers daily by e-mail for tab- or comma-delineated lists on CD with e-mail addresses, often with e-mail management software. The offers I've seen range from $59-$399 for 1-174 million addresses plus accompanying software, and

Promotional-List Compilation and Use

purchases can be made by charge-card at websites. Using these lists effectively requires knowledge of e-mail spam rules, common e-mail courtesies evolving on the Internet, and adroit as well as creative message-drafting skills.

NOTE: Look at the bottoms of e-mail advertisements you receive daily from reputable sales organizations to help you derive up-to-date terminology for disclaimers used with e-mail broadcasting.

So far, the lists available for sale are not interest-oriented, just valid e-mail addresses (but by the millions). It would seem to be the cheapest way to expose a large segment of the total market to a book's availability. A test of a block of 1,000 might be a way to experiment. Draft a short, creative, nonintrusive announcement; for example, the Subject field, the key to getting a recipient to open the e-mail, might say something simple like, "Only readers interested in ABC."

I haven't done it yet, but it's tempting to think that at a nominal cost you have the opportunity to get creative sales hooks directly into millions of people all over the world with the push of a few buttons.

27. RADIO AND TV PROGRAMS FEATURING BOOKS

Sources: *Literary Market Place* or the *Gale Directory of Publications and Broadcast Media*. Stations are listed by state with good contact information; these reference books are commonly available at public libraries.

Alternatively, the information is available on CD from Bradley Communications ($295), http://www.rtir.com/; Bacon's Media Directories ($295), http://www.bacons.com/; and Gebbie Press ($295), http://www.gebbieinc.com/.

Another option is to purchase a subscription at the Parrot Media Network for $49/month, http://www.parrotmedia.com/, and receive online access to media databases kept current daily. Parrot offers a free short trial of the service. This resource might be an equitable answer for the frugal among us, if you can plan to use it intensely during scheduled periods.

28. NICHE LISTS

The objective is to identify the most important niche markets for selling your book, and then search for list sources.

For example, my upcoming fiction book is concerned with subtle metaphysics, science fiction, and some military-fringe actions; the heroes have military backgrounds, and the author is ex-U.S. Marine Corps. So, I found a breakdown of bookstores by specialties in the *Bookstore Directory* at the American Bookstore Association website, http://www.bookweg.org, and compiled a list of those with a metaphysical specialty (75) and those with a science-fiction specialty (78). I'll test a creative sales approach to those stores as part of my promotional plan.

I also decided that military-base libraries would make a good niche candidate. I had already compiled a list of military bases (273) from the *American Library Directory;* so, when the time comes, well after I use the list to invite the Commanding Officers to review the galley-book, I will send unique sales offers to base libraries, using the central base fax numbers. I will be sure to mention the Commanding Officer by name and the date he was invited to review the book.

NOTE: When I send my creative fax invitation to the Commanding Officers of the military bases to review the galley-book, I'll be directing them to my website to establish credibility, spark curiosity about the book, and encourage them to fill out the Request for Review form. In addition, I'll request that the book be made available in the base library. So, I'll be laying the foundation for sales directly to the libraries. We'll see; it's worth a shot.

In another example, if your book was about rocks, you might consider compiling a list of museums with rock collections, national and state parks, gift stores that sell rocks, and other appropriate novelty stores.

The Internet is the best place to look for lists of retail locations with a tie-in to your book, but remember, in the case of stores, you would be entering the world of consignment. Sales made by these establishments are impulse sales, and books would have to be in stock.

29. SUPER MAJOR REVIEWERS

Much of the information below is derived from *Document 112, Poynter's Secret List of Book Promotion Contacts.* A current edition is available at nominal cost from Dan Poynter at his website, http://www.parapublishing.com/.

- *ALA Booklist,* Up Front: Advance Reviews: Contact Bonnie Smothers (adult fiction), Salley Estes (young adult), and/or Chris Anderson (submission guidelines), 50 East Huron Street, Chicago, IL 60611. Telephone: 800-545-2433. Fax: 312-337-6787. Go to http://www.ala.org/ for additional contact persons.

- *Kirkus Reviews:* Contact Anne Larsen (fiction) at Library Advance Information Service and/or Mary Daley (review submission guidelines), VNU eMedia, 770 Broadway, New York, NY 10003-9595. Telephone: 646-654-4602. Fax: 646-654-4602. (No poetry or children's books). E-mailing kirkusrevs@aol.com/ or info@kirkusreviews.com/ might be effective. Kirkus usually gets two copies of a galley-book. Go to http://www.kirkusreviews.com/ for submission guidelines and other contact information.

- *Library Journal:* Contact Heather McCormack for submission guidelines and procedures, 245 West 17th Street, New York, NY 10011. Telephone: 212-463-6818. Fax: 212-463-6631. For more contacts go to the website, http://www.library journal.reviewsnews.com/.

- *Publishers Weekly,* Forecasts: Contact Laura Siporen for a copy of Forecasts submission guidelines, 249 West 17th Street, New York, NY 10011. Telephone: 212-463-6781. Fax: 212-463-6631. Contact selfpub@reedbusiness.com to inquire about a submission. Go to http://www.publishersweekly.com/ for guidelines and other contact information.

- Quality Books, Inc: This is the largest distributor to libraries, 1003 West Pines Road, Oregon, IL 61061. Telephone: 815-732-4450. Fax: 815-732-4499 (get a new-book submission form). Go to http://www.quality-books.com/ for publisher and contact information.

- *School Library Journal:* Contact Trevelyn Jones, Book Review Editor, 245 West 17th Street, New York, NY, 10011-5301. Telephone: 212-463-6759. Fax: 212-463-6734. E-mail: tjones@chners.com. They usually get two copies. Go to http://www.slj.reviewsnews.com/ for submission and contact information.

- *The Los Angeles Times Magazine:* Times Mirror Square, Los Angeles, CA 90053. Telephone: 213-237-5000. http://www.latimes.com/. Contact Steve Wasserman, Book Review Editor, by e-mail: steve.wasserman@latimes.com or Fax: 213-237-4712.

- *The New York Times Book Review:* 229, West 43rd Street, New York, NY, 10036. Telephone: 212-556-1234. Fax: 212-333-5374. Contact Robert B. Silvers or Barbara Epstein, Editors, editors@nybook.com/.

CHAPTER V: Communications Systems (Months 25-27)

The communications systems that support your business are critical to making self-publishing a success. I recommend investigation of the following subjects in developing effective and economical communications systems: the logo and business header, business cards, charge-card services provider, telephone-services provider, long-distance telephone-services provider, toll-free telephone-number provider, fax-number services provider, e-mail services providers, and Internet-service providers.

Website-services providers (hosting services) are discussed in Chapter VII, which covers the process of developing a business website.

A. LOGO, BUSINESS HEADER AND SIGNATURE

Choose a low-key symbol or icon to set to the left of your business header in all communications as a logo. Keep it simple. Most companies create a GIF, JPG, or TIF color image at 75 dpi (dots-per-inch resolution) for logos on their websites. This is easily accomplished in most basic image-manipulation programs. Usually the program that comes with your scanner is adequate. Go to various websites and check out examples.

The information in the business header should be kept short and professional. I recommend: P.O. box mailing address (only); general-purpose, 24 hours/day fax number; voice-mail (only) telephone number; toll-free, 24 hours/day, customer-service number; e-mail address; and your website URL.

Attribution-signatures are for use at the bottom of communications; for example: business e-mails, articles you've written, news announcements, any promotional piece you design and utilize. To create e-mail signatures in Outlook, go to Tools>Options>Mail Format> Signature Picker.

If you use Word as your e-mail editor (a selection in Outlook: Options>Mail Format), go to Tools>Options>General Tab>E-mail Options to create your signature(s). I ended up creating different attribution-signatures for different uses, including a business header as a signature. The signatures you create are then available for selection at Insert>AutoText in Outlook and in Word.

B. BUSINESS CARDS

Business cards offer you an important promotional opportunity for getting the key elements of your message across. I use them as my primary sales piece. I leave 10 or more anywhere people might see them and pick one up: doctor's offices, bookstores, libraries, meeting rooms, gyms, office-supply stores, restaurants and bars, etc. I recommend a two-sided card, which you can easily design in Publisher. The front of the card could include:

- Your full name and profession, for example: Author, Publisher, Speaker.
- Business e-mail address—not the one you give to your friends and family. I use author@gracepublishing.org.
- Business website URL.
- Business name; mailing address (P.O. box); voice-mail (only) telephone number; 24 hour/day fax number; 24 hour/day, toll-free, customer-service telephone number.

  The back of the card could display your major business activities and products for sale. You could go to a double card that folds and include a miniature picture of your book cover in black-and-white or color, and have more room for describing your services and products. In either case, I suggest using laminated card stock or the new waterproof stock.

NOTE: I have elected to keep the style of most of my promotional pieces, including business cards and bookmarks, associated with the theme/style (fonts, colors, borders, logo, etc.) of my website.

C. CHARGE-CARD SERVICES PROVIDER

Discussions with many self-publishers indicate that more than half of your customers will want this method of executing a purchase. Many reputable merchant-services providers are available for consideration in providing this important processing vehicle. Check the advertisements in current editions of the PMA and SPAN newsletters; ask for recommendations from these organizations. If you are a member, they will respond. Check with your bank, or do a search on the Internet. I have outlined my investigations below and reveal where they led me for the best deal.

My bank offered a merchant account for: a $95 setup charge; a $30/month minimum transaction fee; an average transaction fee of about 3.8%, using a modem they provide and a telephone line from my location; and a charge of $0.30/transaction. The bank is one of the largest in the United States, so it's probably representative of the industry.

Following up extensively with several of the suppliers offering merchant accounts over the Internet, for the most part I found them to be independent representatives touting banks' merchant-account processors. Typical costs were: a $295 application fee; $200 for the initial downloaded software; $49.95/month for 36 months, with a 12% buyout at the end of the term, to purchase the equipment (a modem that hooks the computer to the telephone line); a $10/month, secure-gateway fee for transactions over the Internet; $0.30/ transaction with a minimum of $15/month; and 2.5%-3.5% of the sales, depending on which charge-card is used. A recent search of charge-card processing on Google turned up 512,000 responses.

I chose to utilize the services of an Internet full-services provider, http://www.paypal.com/, to process charge-card orders directly from my website. At the time of this writing, PayPal didn't charge a setup fee; transaction charges were 2.2% plus $0.30/transaction, and they charged 0.06% of the total amount of your transactions when you swept the money from your money-market account with them to your bank account.

This service provides my customers with a secure means for utilizing charge-cards at my website, and it cost me nothing to organize and nominal charges to utilize. A drawback is that a buyer has to fill out a PayPal form.

PayPal offers secure access to your PayPal account and a record of all transaction details online, 24/7. The only disadvantage I see is not being able to process charge-card transactions received over the telephone or by e-mail, fax, or postal-mail directly through PayPal. Transactions must be processed directly by PayPal with the payee (your purchaser) through PayPal's website and its secure processing software.

However, the PayPal service offers all its registered accounts the service of receiving money. PayPal will send an e-mail request for payment to customers who want to purchase your merchandise. If your business has not established a merchant account for processing charge-card purchases, this is an optional way to satisfy charge-card purchases that come in on your toll-free number and by fax, e-mail, or postal-mail. You instigate the service by filling in a Request Money form online at your PayPal account location with information describing the purchase and purchaser, including the purchaser's e-mail address. PayPal does the rest. They send e-mail instructions to the purchaser requesting payment to your business via their secure charge-card processing system. The purchaser fills out the PayPal form, submits it, and PayPal pays your business account and adds the purchase information to your account records.

There are other experienced processing services you can find by searching the Internet, such as http://www.verza.com/ and Yahoo! PayDirect, http://www.paydirect.yahoo.com/.

I decided I still needed an economical way to process charge-card purchases received through my toll-free customer-service number, e-mail, fax, and postal-mail. The answer was contained in my QuickBooks 2001 software. Intuit, the company that produces

QuickBooks, had linked up with Chase Bank and Wells Fargo Bank to process charge-card transactions entered in QuickBooks. The beauty here was that the setup fee was nominal and there were no equipment-rental or software-use charges.

In a nutshell, the process is to put customer, product, shipping, payment, and any other information you set up into a QuickBooks Sales Receipt form. Entering this information into the QuickBooks form (when you save it, the information is stored in the proper accounts within the accounting system you've set up for your business), allows you to send charge-card payment information to Chase Bank or Wells Fargo Bank for approval and automatic processing into your bank account (in three to five days). The service communicates approvals while you're in the QuickBooks program.

Then, with an approval, you can fill in a QuickBooks Invoice form, showing the same purchase information as you entered on the Sales Receipt form, but showing that it is a paid invoice with a zero balance. When you're done with the invoice, you have the option (when you save it) of sending a copy to the purchasing customer by e-mail or fax. I use this capability to confirm receipt and clearance of payments to the purchaser. I also include an estimated delivery date on the paid invoice to reconfirm delivery expectations. In the invoice-saving process, you can elect to hold the invoice in a batch and send it by e-mail with others when you're processing over the Internet. In the case where you don't have an e-mail address for a purchaser, you can print out the invoice and use your fax machine (or your fax software) to get the confirmation to the customer. If all else fails, use postal-mail.

You can sign up for the QuickBooks online fax service, and batch and send the invoices much as you would do with e-mail. I found the fax service much too expensive compared to the telephone charges offered by my long-distance services provider, using my own fax software (WinFax PRO 10.0).

The costs for getting aboard this QuickBooks charge-card processing program, using Chase Bank as the merchant services provider were: $10 setup, an Internet-service fee of $5.95/month, $0.20/transaction, $4.95/month statement charge, and 2.35% of the amount of transactions for Visa and MasterCard. I recommend only using these two because Discover and American Express are separate deals with higher rates. Everyone has a Visa or MasterCard.

The application for this QuickBooks service is painless at http://www.quickbooks.com/. Chase Bank approved me although I had no self-publishing track record, no credit showing on my credit report, and had only had a bank account for six months. I hooked them with copies of my workshop brochures, book-release announcements, book chapters, a short biography, and a business description sent as a PDF e-mail attachment. The approval was an unexpected pleasant shock.

D. TELEPHONE-SERVICES PROVIDER

A telephone-services provider should be chosen on the basis of reliability, flexibility, services, and price. I elected to consider only the local service providers that were national and international, the ones that are likely to be around forever, for example: AT&T, the Bell Companies, and Sprint. The services I found valuable and affordable were:

- Number with a distinctive ring: It's a separate number that comes in on the same telephone line as your personal number. I use it as my primary fax number. The cost is around $3.25/month with Sprint. When it rings, my fax machine recognizes the distinctive ring and automatically takes the call, and I don't pick up the phone.

- Caller ID: This service shows the number, and sometimes the name, on my cordless phone receiver coming in on my (one) personal/business line. By checking out the caller ID window, I can decide to answer or let it go to voice-mail; this makes it possible to screen out most undesirable calls. Any serious callers will leave messages I can check periodically at my leisure. The cost is bundled up with my other Sprint services, but is nominal by itself.

- Voice-mail: Sprint gives me a separate telephone number to use that goes directly into the voice-mail service. The cost is $7.95/month. I use that number to call into voice-mail for messages, and I use it as my main business number, so it doesn't ring at my residence. I also have my toll-free number set up with my long-distance services provider (see the next section) so that it terminates at the voice-mail number.

Voice-mail messages can be constructed to let callers leave messages for specific individuals involved with the business, to provide direct product-purchase information, and to direct requests for certain specific information to the website.

Don't get call waiting. An interruption by a beep in the middle of a business call is irritating to the person on the other end, and it indicates you're on your home phone.

E. LONG-DISTANCE TELEPHONE-SERVICES PROVIDER

Examine all the providers that service your geographical location. You can't rely on the telephone book to provide this information. I did a search on the Internet of long-distance services and found a list that compared providers and defined the geographical areas covered, costs, and services provided. I settled on http://www.americom.com/, a sales organization that represented the capabilities I needed. It provided long-distance service with:

- No monthly fees or hidden taxes.
- Six-second, incremental billing.
- Rates of $0.054/minute anytime, anywhere in the United States outside your state of residence.
- A calling card with unrestricted use in the United States at a flat $0.10/minute rate anytime, from anywhere in the United States.
- In-state long-distance fees at a set rate—it was $0.088/minute for Florida—again with six-second, incremental billing. I elected to use their in-state service to avoid using Sprint, which charged various taxes that made its package deals for minutes more expensive.
- A free, toll-free number for customers to call you; the rate was $0.054/minute anytime, anywhere in the United States.

A recent Internet check of long-distance providers reflected a narrowing of competition, with several substantial providers (for example, http://www.idstelcom.com/) offering around $0.05/minute anytime, anywhere in the United States outside your state of residence, with six-second interval billing.

F. TOLL-FREE, IN-BOUND TELEPHONE NUMBER

It's absolutely necessary to have a toll-free customer-service number, accessible 24/7, if for no other purpose than to demonstrate credibility. Utilize the toll-free number on all your promotional materials, including business cards. Owning a toll-free number serves an important control function. Typically, you can set the termination number that calls go to when it's used, allowing you the flexibility to change how you handle customer-service calls. At my account location on Americom.com's website, I can choose to change the termination number for my toll-free number anytime I want.

Since you will bear the user-costs of the toll-free number, it is important to use a long-distance telephone-services provider that has the same low charges (and incremental six-second billing) for use of the toll-free number as it offers for long-distance use of your regular telephone number.

As a self-publisher, you have several options for selecting a termination number for your toll-free number, depending on the complexity of your business and your budget:

- You can have the number terminate at your voice-mail, directing callers to leave a message, go to a website (yours, an online bookstore's, or your fulfillment-services provider) to make purchases or get information, or direct them through charge-card purchases. The larger telephone companies usually provide a multiple mailbox service to help you facilitate and process different types of callers. At Sprint, two extra boxes cost $6.95/month.

- If you can afford a more sophisticated approach, have your toll-free number terminate at a professional answering service instead of your voice-mail. The monthly cost will vary depending on the specific services you choose. The ones in my area average around $35 for setup, $89/month, and

$0.58/minute over 150 minutes of usage per month. The answering service can take messages, answer basic questions, take charge-card orders for your books and other products, and e-mail or fax information to you daily. You don't have to interact with the service unless there's a problem. Then, you process and fulfill the orders at your leisure, or send them off to your fulfillment-services provider.

In addition, the service could take messages for specific people in your business as well as requests for review copies of books and information on workshops, classes, and consulting. A positive here is that you can set standard responses to various inquiries. For example, if someone wants information on classes or to sign up for a free workshop, the caller could get directed to specific pages on your business website, or from the referral information received from the answering service, you could have standard responses to any inquiry prepared in your Outlook Drafts folder, ready to be addressed and sent by e-mail.

- Terminate the number at the number for a fulfillment-services provider that processes orders and payments 24/7, and stores and delivers your products.

G. FAX-NUMBER SERVICES PROVIDER

I conducted an Internet search for providers of free fax services. At this writing, most of these providers, for example, http://www.ureach.com/, offered free inbound fax service, but would only relay the faxes to you as e-mail attachments if you were a uReach.com member, and then only to your member e-mail address. Another drawback in this case is that the uReach.com e-mail address is not POP3 enabled, so it doesn't allow you to receive e-mail from that address through Outlook software. This forces you to go to your e-mail account, open the fax attachments, and print them out while you're online.

Typically, inbound faxes are free, but the charges for outbound faxes are much higher than charges from your long-distance service provider. This appears to be the economic hook that makes the free inbound service possible.

In my opinion, you should not need the outbound fax service, because you will be effectively and economically managing outbound faxes at night through your regular telephone line using WinFax PRO 10.0 from your PC.

For inbound faxes, I recommend using your own machine, and obtaining a dedicated number with a distinctive ring at nominal cost from your local telephone-service provider. In my case, use of a separate fax machine is effective and important:

- As a backup to the computer-based use of WinFax PRO 10.0.
- In freeing the computer from being connected to the telephone line.
- So the computer can be shut down and unattached from the Internet for storm protection and security reasons.
- Because you can leave the fax machine on and connected to your telephone line 24/7.
- By keeping the following rolling in, unaffected by use of your computer and the Internet: incoming product orders containing check payments or charge-card information; completed Workshop Reservation forms from libraries, bookstores, writing organizations, colleges, and universities; and payments and forms from class, coaching, and consulting participants.

Here are a few online fax-number service providers I've come across: http://www.xpedite.com/, http://www.medialinq.com/, http://www.visionlab.com/, http://www.j2.com/. Over the past year, I've noticed many free fax-service providers have left the Internet. This reinforced my decision to retain control of this function.

H. INTERNET-SERVICE PROVIDERS

I suggest choosing an established Internet-services provider (ISP), for example: AT&T, Sprint, MSN, Comcast, or AOL. It should be a cable service, if for no other reason than to free up your telephone line. The extra cost of DSL or cable service pays for itself by saving you the cost of an additional telephone line. DSL providers claim the service is fifty times faster in both directions than regular 56K telephone-line transmissions. Cable service in general is not subject to telephone-line malfunctions, and you never get booted off if the service is busy or for not moving around on the Internet. So far, downtime for cable/DSL service providers has been minimal, usually planned and of short duration.

NOTE: Individuals who work at home without the protection of a secure network often set their computers to automatically connect and stay connected to the Internet for convenience while they work. Many technicians suggest the practice unnecessarily exposes your computer to the next generation of hackers, intrusive information-gathering software, and new viruses against which your detection software doesn't yet offer protection. Accessing the Internet with cable/DSL typically takes only a few seconds. Another common practice is leaving the Internet connection modem on and connected to the computer while it is also turned on. Technicians also see this as dangerous, and recommend unplugging the modem when you are not using the Internet; this can save the computer from hacker technology designed to access the computer without you having instigated an Internet connection.

As a backup ISP, I found Net Zero (http://www.netzero.net) to be very reliable and among the least expensive. It uses a telephone line and a computer's built-in modem. It is still free as long as you don't mind a lot of banners and pop-ups while online. An upgrade, Net Zero Premium, is available at $10/month without pop-ups and with adequate speed. I use Net Zero Premium; I've also copied, pasted, and installed it on my laptop, so that when I travel I can get to the Internet through almost any telephone line by changing the program's local access number to match my location.

One disadvantage in using most of the inexpensive ISPs is that sending e-mail messages from software (for example, Outlook) is not facilitated; the software can only receive. So, using Net Zero for example, you have to go directly to your e-mail accounts to send.

NOTE: Wireless ISPs are beginning to enter the market. The service was not of interest to me at the time of this writing due to limited geographic coverage, subjugation to weather conditions (with satellite providers), and high cost (over $100/month using a cell-phone services provider, plus around $40 for the software *and hardware). Most recently manufactured computers (2001 forward) are set up to connect to this developing technology.*

I. E-MAIL SERVICE PROVIDERS

You will name and organize e-mail addresses for your business using the services of the hosting-services provider you choose to host the website you create for your URL.

Most hosting-services providers allow the definition of five to ten full-service e-mail addresses; for example, at Yahoo! Website Services, my host provider, I'm allowed ten. This includes an "anybody" e-mail address, which is a catchall address for any name that is directed to your URL, for example, anybody@yourwebsitename.com. At my Yahoo! account, I manage these anybody messages by selecting to forward them to one of my named business e-mail addresses; in my case, I used info@gracepublishing.org, an address I created to act as a general-purpose address.

As further examples, I use the following addresses to facilitate the several business purposes of my website: authors@, workshops@, classes@, newsletter@, ancestorseries@, consultingservices@, info@, orders@, reviews@, staff@, and magazine@.

Until you choose a hosting-services provider and launch your website, it's a good idea to establish an e-mail address for business purposes in the interim, one that will act as your backup after your website becomes operational.

Backup e-mail service providers: There are literally thousands to choose from. I chose Yahoo!, http://www.yahoo.com/, as the provider for both my personal and business backup e-mail addresses because of:

- Reliability.
- Service responsiveness.
- Strength of its corporate and organizational partnerships.
- Its useful directory services, for example: clubs, groups, auction, website services, chat, members directory, travel, news, etc.

- Not being an ISP, so it may not be as subject to potential regulation.
- Using its website services to host my business website.
- Having access to Yahoo! from anywhere, whether at home or abroad, no matter what ISP is being used to gain access to the Internet.
- Having send and receive capabilities directly from the e-mail accounts. This allows me to use Outlook to send and receive on my desktop when I'm at home. It also lets me use my laptop when I'm mobile, accessing the Internet through my backup ISP, and going to the accounts to send and receive. In addition, I can use someone else's computer and ISP to get to the accounts.
- Offering many options, such as forwarding to another e-mail address. Enabling forwarding automatically sends messages to another e-mail address. This allows you to avoid reaching the box limit on an account from an accumulation of junk mail when you're not using the account directly. When and if I'm forced to use a Yahoo! backup account directly, for example, using Net Zero through a telephone line at a friend's house, I go into the account and disable the forwarding so I can both send and receive. When I no longer need to use the backup account, I return it to forwarding status.
- Yahoo!'s track record of staying at the technological forefront of Internet-services. In addition, it appears to have proven itself financially profitable, attracting many quality partner relationships.

Free e-mail service providers have started cutting off the capability of sending and receiving e-mail from the accounts they provide when owners use management software on their computers to send and receive. In the case of my Yahoo! backup accounts, for $29.95/year/account, I added this POP service.

CHAPTER VI: Book Production
(Months 25-27)

During these three months, final editing, formatting, and proofing of the book and cover result in sending the manuscript to the printer to print your galley-books; these are books used for the important galley-book review process.

Along the way, you may want to consider developing an alternative means for providing these costly galley-book hard copies by creating PDF e-books for reviewers. It may be beneficial to begin offering these e-books to the general market as giveaways to kick off awareness for the book and build buzz. These promotional concepts are discussed further in Chapters VIII and XI.

During this period, you also establish and organize printing relationships for producing copies of the trade-paperback review-book, and a run of hardbacks if you decide to go that route.

A. BOOK FINAL EDITING AND PROOFING PROCESS (MONTHS 25-27)

The final editing process consists of:

- Revisions based on developmental, style, storyline, and copyediting recommendations of an outside editor.
- Corrections based on outside line-editing/proofing of the revised book, making it ready for printing as a galley-book.
- Additional corrections, last-minute changes, and incorporation of testimonials from reviews of the galley-book. (See the "Galley-Book Review Promotion" in Chapter VIII.)

B. BOOK-PRODUCTION MECHANICS (MONTHS 25-27)

1. SELECTION OF PRINTER(S) FOR YOUR VARIOUS NEEDS

Analyze the print market; the options and prices are changing due to constant technological advances. You may require several different types of print runs at different times in the self-publishing process, for example:

- Galley-books, sent to important reviewers who review 90 days or more from a book's availability through traditional sales channels. I assume a print run of 100 for this simple trade paperback with a blank cover.
- Trade paperbacks, sent to important book reviewers, and to satisfy presales from special offers. In addition, you will want to have an adequate inventory for signings and fulfillment of ongoing sales from your website.
- A first-edition hardback run to satisfy sales at your website of a registered, autographed, collector's edition (RACE), should you decide to offer one.

GENERAL SOURCES

Industry printing quotes can be obtained through http://www.printindustry.com/ and http://www.123printfinder.com/. These organizations offer forms for submitting printing needs to their printer members. There is no charge. You receive quotes by fax or e-mail, as you designate on the submission form, from interested members.

Other good sources are:

- Lists of vendors in the PMA and SPAN resource directories.
- Vendor lists on the PMA and SPAN websites.

- Current advertisements in the PMA and SPAN newsletters.

GALLEY-BOOK

Specialty printing is required to economically produce the galley-book for review. Traditional printers don't usually bother with ultra-short-run, galley work, but I've found a few that do. I suspect with expansion of POD technology and PQN services, more printers will offer economical, ultra-short runs for galley production.

I suggest investigating: http://www.odysseypress.com/, 603-749-4433; http://www.121direct.net/, 866-220-0201; http://www.podwholesale.com/; and http://www.booksjustbooks.com/. Selection of a galley-book printer is related to organization credibility, formatting requirements, delivery time, and cost.

Recently, when I was pricing the galley-book run for my upcoming fiction book, it appeared that 100 copies would cost between $4.50-$6.00 per copy (450 pages—225 sheets both sides—on #50 white paper stock and #10 blank cover stock), plus delivery cost.

TRADE PAPERBACK

Since your trade-paperback run will more than likely require 500-1,000 copies to satisfy the need for review copies, accumulated sales, inventory for signings, and continuing sales at your website, you should consider both POD/PQN printers (not the printer/publisher/distributors) and non-POD/PQN printers. The economic breakpoint with traditional high-tech printing using POD/PQN recently appeared to be in the range of 400-700 copies.

For POD/PQN I suggest checking out http://www.booksjustbooks.com/, http://www.121direct.net/, and http://www.podwholesale.com/. In addition, BookMasters, Inc., now offers small publishers short runs at competitive prices on its new digital printing equipment; go to their website at http://www.bookmasters.com to request a quote. Expect these books to take about three to five weeks for delivery.

For short-run (200-1,500 copies), traditionally printed trade paperbacks, I suggest investigating Morris Publishing, http://www.morrispublishing.com/, 800-650-7888. These take about 45 days for delivery. The website has a cost graph online so you can calculate an estimate for a printing job. For example, the last time I checked, a run of 400 four-color, 210-page trade paperbacks ran about $3.49 each, not including shipping and without a setup charge, assuming you used the publisher's templates for the front and back covers.

The time it takes for setup, printing, and reprinting is also important in selecting printers. The printer must respond quickly when sales make a reprinting viable, especially when you need to fill special orders from traditional and online bookstores.

HARDBACK

Sources: Many of the POD/PQN printers offer hardbacks (see sources suggested above under "Trade Paperback"), and all the major POD Internet publishers now offer hardbacks (for comparisons of services and costs, see *A Basic Guide to Fee Based Print on Demand Publishing Services,* a 25-page e-book offered free by Dehanna Bailee at her website, http://dehanna.com/pod_guide.htm).

I understand that http://www.121direct.net can run up to 1,500 books economically with 10-day delivery once the book is set up. Check out BookMasters Inc., http://www.bookmasters.com/, 800-537-6727, for more than 1,500 copies in a run (expect four to six weeks for delivery). It is a well-known, midsized printing company that manufactures hardback and paperback books, as well as offering the synergistic services of inventory storage, book-project management, and complete fulfillment.

NOTE: BookMasters could be a match for reorganizing your business at a later time, when the level of sales justifies the economics of larger runs, and you want to rid yourself of fulfillment drudgery.

If you're thinking of a hardback, I also suggest checking out the quoting services listed in General Sources above, BookMasters, and the POD/PQN sources discussed above to get a feel for prices, formatting, setup costs, and delivery times.

2. BOOK FORMATTING

Most of the common word-processing programs, for example, Word or WordPerfect, will facilitate page formatting, creation of an index and table of contents, and the inclusion of headers, footers, and pagination.

After your book has been edited and proofed, you will be reformatting it to satisfy the submission requirements of your printers. Book printers are becoming more flexible in the number of file formats they accept for submissions. Many accept PDF and even word-processing files if you pay a small additional fee.

BOOK DRAFTING AND STYLES IN THE WORD PROCESSOR

The comments here apply to Word, and will help you toward mastering the formatting capabilities of the software. They should also be closely applicable to other major word-processing programs. Typically, the format is uniform throughout, so you will establish standard settings for the chapter, front pages, and back pages files. In this example, we start with formatting for an 8.5 X 11-inch page size. This is the size you will use to create e-books in PDF.

- Go to Page Setup in File. Under the Margins tab, set margins at one inch all around. Make checks for Mirror Margins and Gutter Position, Left, and choose This Section in Apply To.

- In Page Setup, under the Paper Size tab, select Letter for Paper Size and Portrait for Orientation.

- Under the Layout tab in Page Setup, select New Page, Different Odd and Even, and Different First Page.

- Then define the Normal style in Format. Select a traditional printing font like Arial or Times New Roman. For my fiction books (6 X 9.25-inch hardback) my Normal style settings are: Arial, Regular, 11 pt., Justified, Window/Orphan Control, Keep With Next, Line Spacing at Exactly 1.25, and 6 pt. Space After for carriage returns if I don't use a tab for paragraphs, or 0 Space After if I use a tab for paragraphs; Tabs at 0.3 inches (the equivalent of 5 spaces) in Tab Set.

- For headings like chapter titles or section names, click on Format and select Style. You can create any number of headings. In Microsoft Word there are nine prenumbered headings. Make your selections for each just as you did when establishing the Normal style.

- You can tinker and test until you get a style right. To have changes you make to a style apply back through the whole document, select Automatically Update. If you use this feature, be sure you go back after you finish an update and uncheck the Automatically Update box; this allows you to make minor changes in a style when you need to without the changes applying to the rest of that style throughout the document.
- Save this standard page-layout document as a Template and name it appropriately, for example, "Title of Book 8.5 X 11 Template." Then, each time you need to start a new document for that size book, you just open the Template document. When you're finished writing, save the document with a different name; the Template document remains, as it was originally on your computer, ready for the next use.

I recommend placing front pages, back pages, and body drafts in separately named files, using a standard page-layout template. In this 8.5 X 11-inch page-size example, the front- and back-cover drafts can be copied and pasted into those files as well (see below for suggestions on a simple, initial drafting process for the cover).

Changes can be made later in the page setup to convert document files from 8.5 X 11-inch page size to trade-paperback or hardback sizes, depending on what you decide to print. Templates of the page layout including margins are often found at websites of printers, for example http://www.morrispublishing.com/ and http://www.books justbooks.com/.

PAGINATION, HEADERS AND FOOTERS

Again, using Word, go to View on the toolbar, and select Header and Footer. The following is an example of the process, assuming you are working with a chapter of a book, and the page numbers will continue through to the last page in the chapter.

Subsequent chapters can be constructed separately in the same way. The file for the body of the book can be put together by copying and pasting, and going into each chapter to create a new section and adjust the numbering of the pages as necessary (chapters usually start on odd pages.):

- First, click on Page Setup in File and the choose the Layout tab. Select New Page, Different Odd and Even, Different First Page, Top for Vertical Alignment, and at Apply To, choose This Section.

- Go to the previous chapter and make sure it ends with an even numbered page—do carriage returns all the way through the next page if your chapter ends on an odd page, until you enter the next even-numbered page. Then, click Insert on the toolbar, select Break, and then Page Break and New Page.

- Then, click on View, Header and Footer. In the toolbar that shows make sure the Same as Previous icon is not enabled—if it is, click it off. This is the first odd page for the chapter and in Word it is called First Page Header (with the section number next to it). Click the Format Page Number icon, and choose the Number Format. At Page Numbering select Start At. In the Start At box, type in the beginning page number; you will have to figure this out from the last (even-numbered) page of body text prior to the new chapter.

- After these formatting selections, choose the font, point size, and characteristics for the text (consider expanded and/or caps). Choose Justify Right from the Standard toolbar, position the cursor at the far right of the header box, and click on the Insert Page Number icon. The page number you elected to start at will then insert (an odd number).

- Then, type the chapter name and enter spaces until you get the chapter name in the middle of the header box and the page number to the far right at the end of the header line. It is my preference to have the chapter name on the odd pages of a book. Many authors put the title of the book on the odd pages.

- Next, select the Show Next icon; this gives you a picture of the next (even) page header. Click on Same as Previous, and repeat the process of inserting the page number (it should be the next page—an even-numbered page) at the far left of the header box by selecting Justify Left in the Standard toolbar. Type in the name of the book and enter spaces until the name is centered. So, on even pages you will have the name of the book repeated.

- Click on the Show Next icon again; this will give you the next page (called Odd Page header in Word). Duplicate the chapter name on this odd page header, inserting the page number at the far right, typing the chapter name, and spacing to get the name to center. Click Close in the header/footer toolbox.
- All the subsequent page headers and sequential page numbers will automatically show to the end of the chapter.
- You can adjust your formatting selections for the different sections of the book to change the headers. For example, the front pages might all just have Roman numerals at the right and left margins of the header, without text, and the back pages might just have a continuation of the page numbering with just the name of the book.

TABLE OF CONTENTS

To create a table of contents for the body of the book using Word, type "Table of Contents" in a selected heading style, and move the cursor to the point in the body text where you want to insert the table. Click on Insert in the toolbar, and select Index and Tables. Select the Table of Contents tab. A Print Preview box will show you how the heading styles you have used in the body of your book (to anticipate setting up the table of contents) will display. Choosing Options in the window allows selection of the number of headings (1-9 in Word) you want to appear in the table. Next, choose how the page numbers appear and choose the format you like for the style of the table. When you're satisfied, click OK at the bottom of the window and the table of contents will appear. It is a good idea to test this function to make sure the table is set up to your satisfaction. To terminate a test and return the document to its previous state, click on Edit in the toolbar at the top and Undo the creation command.

When you are satisfied that the table of contents is complete and correct, define the table as a section, and insert a header/footer that will define the page numbers for the table (these should be different from those in the body, perhaps Roman numerals that continue from where your Front Pages left off).

INDEXING

After the body of the book is edited and proofed and all the formatting is complete, including inserting the table of contents, you are properly prepared to create an index. You will create the index without the front and back pages present, because the text in those pages should be outside the indexing process. The indexing comments and suggestions below use Word as the word-processing software:

- Create a concordance table: Create a new document file containing a two-column table by clicking on Table in the toolbar, selecting Insert, then Table, and completing the screen. I name this file Concordance Table because that's how the indexing Help directions in Word describe it. The left-hand column is used to type in words or phrases that appear in the body of the book, defining the location of information pertaining to index subject names. The index subject names are listed in the right-hand column corresponding to the defining words and phrases.

  The concordance table can be sorted to alphabetically show the subject names in the right-hand column for ease in moving around when you're checking and rechecking. To do this, right click a blank space in the toolbar at the top of the page, and select Database—the database icons will then display as part of the toolbar. Then, select the right-hand column by right clicking the cursor at the very top of the column, and click the Sort Ascending button.

- Tips on typing words and phrases: You must follow some rules that are unavailable through the Help entries in Word in order to make the words and phrases entered in the left-hand column of the concordance table work properly (let's call these entries targets). Specifically, capitalization, punctuation, bolding, and spacing must appear exactly as they do in the book—italicizing doesn't seem to matter. A specific example: If the original target text is: "a tool of the trade," and you enter it as "A tool of the trade," or "a tool of the trade" (without the comma), it won't act as a successful target in the body of the book, because in the first instance you capitalized the A, and in the second instance you left out the comma.

- Format for index subject names: The subject names for the right-hand column in the concordance table should be entered exactly as you want them to appear in the index. One formatting suggestion is to use a colon if you want a subject name to have two or more subheadings. For example, if the subject name is Equipment and you want a breakdown in the index by type, you might use Equipment: Computer and another entry, Equipment: Telephone, etc.

- Test index: I suggest copying and saving a three-page section in the body of the book as a test file. Then create and build a concordance table for it, making up subject names for selected words and phrases. This will allow you to experiment with creating and correcting an index.

- Testing an index: Click on Insert on the toolbar and select Index and Tables. At the bottom of the window, click on AutoMark and select the concordance table you created.

  The program then inserts field marks next to the words or phrases in the text of your document, so you can see if they are successfully marked. If they are, the file is ready for insertion of the index.

  Insert the index in the body document by placing the cursor at the insert location. Then click on Insert and select Index and Tables. Choose a style for the index, select either one or two columns for its display, and click OK. The index subject names will form alphabetically with page numbers corresponding to the location of the field marks that represent targets in the concordance table.

- Deleting the index: Click on Edit at the top, and Undo the index style and AutoMark commands you performed. Now you're back to your original document. Make sure you reverse all index-testing operations. If you don't, and you save the document, the next time you open it up you'll have to remove the fields and index by hand (by going to Edit>Find>Replace>More>Special>Field; the code for "Field" shows in the Find what box. If you leave the Replace with space blank and select Replace All, then the index marks in your document should be removed.

To accomplish this, go to Edit and Find, then select the Replace tab and More at the bottom. Then select Special at the bottom of that screen, and Field from the list. When you do that, the field symbol inserts in the Find What box. Leave the Replace With box blank. Then you execute the replacements.

The index can be removed by clicking at its upper right corner. It will select by shading itself; then press the Delete key.

- Proofing the index: This is a tedious process. You have to double-check to make sure all the subject names in the index have appeared with appropriate page numbers. This means you must check to see if the words and phrases in the body text were AutoMarked where you intended. I print out the concordance table; then, with the body text document open, I place the words and phrases from the left-hand column of the concordance table into the Find box (in Edit) one by one. If an AutoMark is not present at a location, then an error has been made typing in the word or phrase. You should be able to figure out what the error is by examining the format and making appropriate corrections in the concordance table. After testing and retesting, when you're satisfied that the words and phrases you've chosen in the concordance table are correct (that is, that they are marked as going to the places in the body text you intend), your index is ready to insert for the last time.

Be very careful when you originally create the concordance table, and be careful when and if you go back into your body text to make any later editing changes. A general procedure I established after considerable trial and error was to use headings and subheadings as often as I could for words and phrases entered into the concordance table.

3. BOOK COVER CREATION

Several options for book cover creation are open to self-publishers. You can choose a template supplied by your printer (usually part of a package); create a custom design (which costs more money); design one yourself from scratch; or employ a competent illustrator.

TEMPLATE AND CUSTOM COVERS FROM PRINTERS

Internet publishers, as well as many printing organizations that specialize in short printing runs, offer cover templates to facilitate cover design. Typically, the cost of using a cover template is part of a printing/publishing or printing package. To check out examples, go to http://www.xlibris.com and click on Publishing Services, or go to http://morrispublishing.com and click on Designing a Book.

DESIGNING A COVER FROM SCRATCH

A possible approach revolves around acquiring photographs or graphics. Search the Internet for pictures and photographs. Examples of providers are http://www.comstock.com/, http://www.artworld.com/, and http://www.photosource.com/. These sources offer high-quality, unique images, and the cost can run several hundred dollars.

A service at the PhotoSource website provides a form to submit what you're looking for; they publish the information in a daily e-newsletter to their photo-providing clients, who then contact you directly. If you ask, they'll send you a complimentary, hard-copy directory of members, cross-referenced by descriptive words, that describes photographer inventories and gives complete contact information.

You may want to check out the major directories on the Internet like Yahoo! (Photos) to see if the cheaper ($5.95+) images offered there might be useable.

If you're creating your own cover, you'll probably use a page-layout program like Adobe PageMaker 6.5, Adobe InDesign, QuarkXPress, or Corel Ventura, because of the limitations that prevent working effectively with images and overlaying in a word-processing program. Depending on your printer's requirements, you may have to lay out the front cover, back cover, and spine on a single work page and save it as a separate file.

NOTE: It's possible to do an adequate job in Publisher (then copy and paste the image into Word to convert to PDF) or Word by inserting and sizing an image to type over, and using the background capabilities. See "Creating PDF Documents," below, for more on how I created the front and back cover pages for this book to use on my website, and the cover pages for an e-book.

For this book, I used 35-mm photographs that I took myself and had processed as 8 X 10s. I scanned them at 300 dpi and at 75 dpi, and saved them as TIF files. Images at 75 dpi save space on websites and are adequate for a PDF e-book. Printers and media typically require 300-dpi photos.

If your book printer is responsible for these last steps (or a cover designer), you could mail the 8 X 10-inch, 35-mm glossies; or scan them at 300 dpi as TIF or JPG files and mail them on a CD-R along with a file (in Publisher or Word, for example) that show how you want the front cover, back cover, and spine to look.

UTILIZING OUTSIDE DESIGNER SERVICES

Another way to go is to hire an outside designer for your cover. The going rate for high-profile designers appears to be around $1,500. Many capable and successful book cover designers can be found in the PMA and SPAN newsletter advertisements or in their annual resource directories. Or, check out the advertisements in *Writer's Digest* and *Publishers Weekly*. Professional designers work with you and your printer to meet specifications.

For the frugal self-publisher, check out http://budgetbookdesign.com for reasonably priced book cover designs and book formatting.

4. CREATING PDF DOCUMENTS AND E-BOOKS

When I discovered I could create a variety of PFD documents to effectively promote and sell books and book derivatives, I committed to learning Adobe Acrobat and Adobe PageMaker 6.5. I purchased older versions of the software on the Internet for peanuts. Here I've summarized some of the creation mechanics in the two Adobe programs, described how Publisher and Word can work together to create PDF documents, outlined an easy procedure for making a PDF e-book, and mentioned other PDF applications I've found useful.

ADOBE PAGEMAKER 6.5

Adobe PageMaker 6.5 can become your major tool for creating a more complex PDF document, such as a book. The program enables you to place the files making up a book (those created in a word-processing program) into the program and save them as one PDF file.

In PageMaker, you can create headers, footers, page numbers, an index, and a table of contents for the book (as appropriate), and you can bring in images and graphics to size and position. Repetitive items and information can be organized on a master page to display at the same location on every page. Layering capabilities allow you to create text on top of graphics and pictures. The program also enables you to attach the PDF file you create to the original files you imported, causing editing in those master documents to automatically show up in the created PageMaker PDF file.

ADOBE ACROBAT 4.0+

Adobe Acrobat is also a great PDF file-creation program, especially for smaller documents; its biggest drawbacks are the lack of robust editing tools and absence of layering capabilities. You will need to make sure the document is exactly the way you want it, in a compatible creation program like Word, before you create the PDF file in Acrobat. When you do have to make changes to a PDF file using Acrobat 4.0+, the most effect way is to create the document again.

E-BOOK COVERS

The following are descriptions of easy ways to use a picture as a background in a book cover for a PDF e-book, or in other promotional documents, using Publisher and Word software.

I suggest using Publisher when you anticipate needing more flexibility than is available in Word alone. In Publisher, after sizing a picture, click on Arrange in the toolbar and select Send Backward. Then, on top of the background picture (still showing on the page) create and place various text boxes. Then for each text box, go to Format, select Fill Color and Fill Effects, and choose Patterns and the rectangle with the clear symbol inside. The background picture will now show through on the text boxes (of use the keyboard stroke, "Ctrl t"). Then, create the variety of text fonts, sizes, colors, spacing, patterns, and gradients you want in the text boxes.

Now, copy (in Edit, Select All, and then Copy) the page from Publisher and paste it into a standard Word file—the template for a standard book page created for the book in Word. The final step is to convert the Word page to a PDF file using Acrobat. If you have both programs installed on your computer, the Acrobat creation icon will be located in the Word toolbar at the top of the page.

NOTE: Typically, when creating an Acrobat PDF file in other word-processing programs compatible with Acrobat 4.0+, you would either go to File on the toolbar and select Print and a PDF printing option in the Name box, or drag and drop a file onto the Acrobat icon on your computer desktop.

You can create an acceptable cover using Word without Publisher. Insert a picture, adjust its size for your need by right clicking it. In Format Picture select the Layout tab, Wrapping Style, and Behind Text. Now you can format and position text on top of the picture. Should you want to move the picture around underneath the text, you select it with the cursor and nudge it, by holding the control key down and using the arrows on the keyboard.

PDF E-BOOKS

I used the synergism of Publisher, Word, and Acrobat 4.0+ to create my first PDF e-book. The book was a working-paper version of this book—a draft that I offered for sale on my very first website to lists of authors and writers after I completed the first full edit, ten months before I sent the book to the printer. The effort became the precursor to offering PDF e-books as galley-review copies, media-review copies (of the final book), and complimentary promotions to various segments of the market.

Using Acrobat 4.0+ to create a PDF e-book is not difficult. If you're using Word, open each of the standard files that make up your book, for example: front cover, front pages, body (chapters), back pages, and back cover, then click on the Acrobat icon at the top of the page. As you create the PDF files, save them in a book-creation folder in My Documents.

When creating PDF files in Acrobat 4.0+, I suggest making the following choices on the first popup screen: In the Display Options tab, choose the way you want hyperlinks to appear; under the Structure and Headings tab, select Headings; in the Output tab, check all the boxes; under the General tab, choose Use Acrobat Distiller, Print via Distiller's Printer and select Screen Optimization under Distiller Settings. In addition, check all the File options. Then, to create the PDF e-book, open one of the PDF files in Acrobat 4.0, let's say the front cover file (this may be the first page, or maybe you'll have a cover page and document-information pages first). Click on Document in the Acrobat toolbar and Insert Pages. Browse the files in My Documents to select the PDF files (one at a time) to insert where you want them; for example, when you insert a page you will be shown a box with these selections: After Last Page, After First Page, Before Last Page, Before First Page, After A Selected Page Number, etc.

Table-of-contents headings created in Word come into PDF hyperlinked, but surrounded with a visible rectangle. Although I find the rectangles unsightly and permanently imbedded, I leave them as they are rather than copying and reformatting the table of contents back into the Word document so it converts without hyperlinks. You could then hyperlink the table of contents, one heading at a time, within the Acrobat file.

NOTE: Acrobat 4.0+ has its own index, table-of-contents, and pagination capabilities. At the time of publishing this book I had not explored whether or not it would be more effective to use them after the e-book was created.

To complete the e-book in PageMaker 6.5, you place each individual PDF file into its appropriate location in a PageMaker document that you have previously formatted with a specific page layout, with design items on the master page. Essentially, the book is complete when you save the PageMaker file. If there were hyperlinks in the PDF files, they remain.

If you prefer, you can create a table of contents and index within PageMaker that are automatically hyperlinked to page numbers, and paginate the document using the PageMaker master page.

OTHER USEFUL PDF APPLICATIONS

Using the combination of Publisher, Word, and Acrobat 4.0+, you can convert many useful documents and presentation pieces to PDF files for use in promotions and for postings on your website that visitors can open and/or copy to their computers, for example:

- PDF e-books for sale at your website, or available free through promotions at a special page on the site.
- PDF e-books created for the galley-review-book and formal review-book promotion stages in the self-publishing process—available to invited reviewers at your website, by e-mail attachment, or delivered by postal-mail on CD-R.
- Monthly newsletters—the current edition and the archives.
- Articles offered to the media for publishing.
- Booklets (larger pieces than articles) you can derive from your book, representing expansions of important topics or the development of new ideas and concepts.
- General information brochure or flyer designed to display blurbs, testimonials, quotes, and basic book-presentation information.
- All the pieces that make up a PDF media kit.
- Draft news articles and draft book reviews.
- Chapters of works in progress as pre-final-edit drafts.

5. GALLEY COVER PREPARATION

Check with your printer on the formatting required for the cover. Typically it is a layout page of 11.0 X 17.0 inches. Draft, copy, and paste the text you create from the standard text-page template you've been using for the book. I recommend typing key information in black, using a justified-left, outline style for the front and back covers. The text typed on the spine will be basic identification information. A printer can use simple #10, white stock for the galley-book cover.

FRONT COVER KEY INFORMATION

I recommend the following book information neatly typed and centered on the white front cover:

- Title: ....
- "Galley Review-book: Uncorrected Page Proofs."

- Author: ....
- Category: Fiction, Nonfiction, Historical Fiction, Romance, etc. 1st Edition.
- Specifications: Hardcover, four-color dust jacket, 6.5 x 9.5 inches, 436 pages; Trade Paperback ....
- Season: Spring 20XX.
- Price: Hardcover: $xx.xx US, $xx.xx CAN. Trade Paperback: ....
- Numbers: ISBN: 0-0000000-0-0, or "To Be Assigned." CIP/LC pending, or Library of Congress Control Number: 2000-000000.
- Major promotional-plan elements: For example, space advertising, press releases, e-mail announcements, newsgroup postings, organizational announcements, bookstore and library direct-sales offers, direct mail, co-op advertising, writer conferences, trade shows, radio and TV interviews, writing and publishing workshops on a major-city tour schedule, etc.
- Distribution to the trade: "Under Negotiation," or list your vendor of record, which may be your own self-publishing business and/or a fulfillment-services provider, and/or list your distributor, and/or wholesaler relationships, such as Ingram Book Group and Baker & Taylor.
- Publisher's header: Business logo, address, voice-mail telephone number, fax number, business e-mail address, website URL, toll-free customer-service number.
- Business attribution-signature: A paragraph describing your business. This should be the same one you use on promotional materials and communications.

  BACK COVER INFORMATION
- Paragraph on why this book is the greatest.
- Paragraph weaving together all your developed taglines for the book. Using my upcoming fiction novel, *The Mountain and the*

Place of Knowledge, as an example, I'll weave in the following: "The Ancestor Series of sci-tech-mystery-thrillers," "Grounded in plausible reality," "An experiential reading adventure," "The past is not what it seems," "Who are our ancestors?" and "Why are we here?"

- A synopsis of the book.
- Your best review blurbs and testimonials. If you don't have any yet, ask an author or publishing cohort for permission to put his or her name on one you make up. You may want to go to the trouble of asking a book-review editor at a regional newspaper to favor you with an unpublished advance review. Ask your city library director to do the same.
- A short, intriguing biographical sketch of the author.

SPINE INFORMATION

Use black type for the title, author's name, and publisher's name. Including the publisher's logo is optional. The spine is important, so the book can be easily identified if it's lying flat and covered by other books on a review-editor's shelf.

For example, in Word you should be able to paste in the text on the cover-layout page and rotate it into position within the spine dimensions. You have to have an object to rotate in Word, so I create a text box in Publisher and copy and paste it into the Word document, then select the Drawing toolbar, Draw, and Rotate and Flip to rotate the box to 90 degrees. Then I adjust the size, if needed, and move the box into position on the spine.

6. E-BOOKS FOR HANDHELD DEVICES

You may opt to acquire the software necessary to format your book into an e-book product specifically designed for handheld reading devices. In mid-2003 the average retail price (at major online bookstores) was around $7.95 for an e-book, depending on the subject matter; usually business books were priced higher. E-books in these formats can be sold at your website using the same purchase options and charge-card capability as with other products, should you decide to invest the time and money in the e-book creation software.

I don't recommend investing time or money in keeping up with this technology. Book publishing, sales, and distribution-services providers—for example, Amazon.com and Barnesandnoble.com online bookstores—will typically format your books and make them available in the e-book formats seen as practical and profitable. Let them adjust to the changing times.

Jason Epstein reported in an article in the January 24, 2001 *National Post*, that "only 10,000 handheld reading devices are currently in use." He was referring to the first quarter of 2000. At that time, a Stephen King novella was offered to the market as an e-book and sold 400,000 copies at $4.95 in the first 24 hours. That went to show the market that readers were willing to store and read the book from their computers and other devices.

As this book went to press, the e-book market for handheld devices seemed to be fading away, but some professionals think that in ten years or so the inhibiting problems of price, standard format, protection of content, readability, and flexibility will be resolved, and the devices will make a comeback. James Lichtenberg, a communications consultant and president of Lightspeed, LLC in New York City said in the April 2002, PMA newsletter, "...that at some point between 2015 and 2020, handheld e-book readers are going to be as familiar as toasters."

7. E-BOOK INTERNET SALES SITES

The setup costs for e-book sales are nil to nominal at most of the Internet showcase sites offering to format, display, and take orders for e-books. The time it takes to submit and get set up is minimal. A list of e-book sellers is maintained at Midwest Book Review, http://www.midwestbookreview.com/; go to Book Lover Resources and then to E-Book Publishers/Dealers.

For e-books, as well as hard copies, I believe it doesn't make economic sense to invest the time dealing with the smaller bookstore sites that have proliferated on the Internet, unless the book is highly technical or very subject-specific. In that case, consider the sites that have emerged and gained reputations in the market for your subject/specialty. I found the author's share of sales from these relationships ranges from 30%-80% of sales price.

However, as I intimated above, the savvy self-publisher should aggressively develop relationships with the major online bookstores to sell any e-book product format available. Presenting and selling books and book products there offers powerful image identification, the building of publisher and author credibility, and exposure to a large, active segment of the worldwide marketplace that seeks information as well as specific books to purchase. In addition, the relationships don't require consignment inventory or setup costs.

As an example, at Barnes and Noble the royalty to the author was recently 35% for e-books. I favor letting the major sellers keep up with the encrypting and formatting technology. Income from these sources can be seen as windfall gain.

8. E-BOOKS ON CDS

Another practical e-book product has come into being through acceptance by a significant part of our computerized culture that works with CDs on a daily basis, whether as music or data files.

Placing your book on a CD-R in files of several alternative but common formats is easily mastered, for example: Word, Rich Text Format (RTF), PDF, and one or more formats for handheld devices—if you decide to go that route.

You could choose to use the CD-R as a delivery vehicle for review copies of your book and include a complete book presentation and media kit.

Here's an idea of what you'd need, all of which is available at most office and computer superstores, for example: http://www.quill.com/, http://www.officedepot.com/, or http://www.bestbuys.com/; at comparative shopping or wholesalers like http://www.pricegrabber.com/ or http://www.cnet.com/; or at auction sites online like http://www.yahoo.com/, http://www.ebay.com/, and http://www.ubid.com/.

- A good hard-drive CD disk writer is about $100 for one that you have to install in a slot typically available on PCs that don't already have a built-in CD writer.

- A good portable disk writer is around $150. You then have the flexibility of taking it with you to use with your laptop or another PC anytime the need arises; portable disk writers offer a quick and cheap way of backing up the files on your computer using CD-RWs. After formatting, these disks have about a 550-MB of useable capacity.

- Simple CD-creation-kit software that comes with an application device and design library for the CD pasties and jewel kit inserts, at around $20-$30.
- Blank, Avery-type CD-label pasties at about $22/100.
- Compact jewel cases at about $0.05 each for cases of 50.
- Jewel-case insert forms at about $22/100. These are optional; I let the CD-label pasty do the identification job.
- Blank CDs at about $12/50.
- CD mailer pouches at about $5/10.

This capability makes it possible for you to easily place another book product for sale at your website. The cost of producing and delivering (U.S. Postal Service Book Rate is $1.33 each) a CD via an order on your website is under $3 each. Since it's standard practice to require reimbursement from the buyer for shipping and handling costs, at a selling price of $7.95, it makes economic sense to do it yourself. My guess is that you could get processing time down to five or so orders an hour if you had to do charge-card processing, make accounting entries, send e-mail confirmations to buyers, produce the CDs, and fulfill the orders. In this scenario, you would make the disks one by one and do all the processing until volume justified one of the following:

- Employing an outside services provider to duplicate the CDs from a master in runs that make economic sense.
- Purchasing high-speed, CD-copier equipment that attaches to your PC (at about $3,000. Do a search on the Internet).
- Placing the business with a fulfillment-services provider (do a search on the Internet, and see the lists for publisher resources at http://www.midwestbookreview.com).

9. SEND GALLEY TO THE PRINTER (MONTH 27)

The galley-book should now be ready to send to your selected printer. You will tell the printer how many copies you want after you set your

Book Production 113

review objectives in the galley-book review promotion described in Chapter VIII.

CHAPTER VII: Developing the Business Website (Months 25-27)

Your website should be all business. That's not to say it can't have a flavor, but keep it simple, professional, and predictable. You want serious visitors as well as surfers to have an easy, enjoyable experience, and at the same time have their needs met. Use the same theme throughout. This means colors, background, logo, headers, footers, fonts, use of font sizes and font forms (bold, italics, caps, etc.), layout of control forms, and placement of navigational aids.

The website should sizzle with speed without distractions, so eliminate gizmos like characters or symbols that move or direct, distracting music, or video that forces a visitor to wait it out. Concentrate on clarity and navigational simplicity. Make the design easy on the eyes, and don't use dark colors in the background; they eat ink and time when a visitor prints pages. Provide useful, complimentary information in PDF files that can be opened on the spot or easily downloaded to the visitor's computer.

The website should be capable of facilitating all the functions of your business, except those that require your personal appearance. The more time you can save through an effective website, the more time you have to write, promote, and provide services.

In this chapter, I present a generic how-to approach for developing an effective author/self-publisher website. I recommend uploading a temporary home page for your website from day one, announcing the site in general terms, and giving a projected schedule for completion of functional pages. Then add to it as you complete the schedule.

A. PURPOSE AND GENERAL ORGANIZATION

The Internet provides a cost-effective opportunity to establish recognition, credibility, and respect in the world marketplace. The major purpose of your website is to create a professional image and effectively satisfy the interests of visitors you have driven to the site through your promotions.

Effective promotional activities will focus on generating book reviews and published articles, driving product sales to fulfillment, and presenting chosen business services. In addition, the website, as the great facilitator, can act as a gatherer of contact information for useful databases.

Below is a list of suggestions worth considering for organizing an informative, responsive author/self-publisher website:

- Offer readers, media, the book trade, and publishing-industry professionals complimentary book excerpts and chapters, and direct them to return to the website to give reviews and comments on a simple form.

- Write and post PDF articles on topics related to your genre and subject expertise for readers, writers, and the media to freely download.

- Provide creative news ideas to generate media interest.

- Provide extensive author and business background information to support publisher, editor, media, and other research efforts.

- Organize book and book-product presentations, and facilitate sales for different segments of your buying market.

- Package and offer your presentation expertise in ways that generate book sales and promote the business services you've chosen for making a living. For example, I offer organizations in Florida self-publishing workshop/signings.

- Offer a complimentary newsletter and subject-based club for subscription.
- Package and present your chosen business services and offer procedures for inquiry.
- Make it easy to contact staff by e-mail, fax, and contact forms. I suggest eliminating all telephone numbers except those that relate to outside service providers, such as 24/7 product fulfillment.
- Offer to serve the community in ways that tie in to your writing and business services. For example, I offer an Affiliate Author Program and offer to participate in arts and cultural fairs and events in my state of residence.
- Identify supportive people, organizations, resources, and suppliers, and provide links to their websites.

B. EXAMINE WEBSITES OF AUTHORS AND SELF-PUBLISHERS

I recommend gaining perspective by examining other author and author/self-publisher websites. I found the websites of Shirley MacLaine, http://www.shirleymaclaine.com/, and Victoria Strauss, http://www.sff.net/people/victoriastrauss/, to be particularly inspiring and educational. A good way to find author sites is to go to http://www.webring.org/. There is a directory of web rings by subject, and you can search for rings by keywords.

The websites of authors/self-publishers vary across the gamut. For example, mine, http://www.gracepublishing.org/; Danny O. Snow's, http://www.u-publish.com/; Dan Poynter's, http://www.parapublishing.com/; and John Kremer's, http://www.bookmarket.com/, are examples of recognized experts' sites.

C. WEBSITE SOFTWARE

There are many choices of website-development software; the cost is affordable at around $100. I used Microsoft Publisher (98-2002) to create the business website for The Grace Publishing Group, and have continued to use it as I've adjusted and refined the site, without finding significant shortcomings. It is extremely easy to learn and use. Microsoft FrontPage has more capabilities, but it's more difficult to learn, and I was committed to simplicity. I've heard from several authors that Dreamweaver is excellent.

NOTE: I elected to stay with Microsoft products for the synergistic capabilities between programs; the quality of free support offered at their website, http://www.microsoft.com/; and availability of download updates to keep older programs almost the equivalent of new software.

Many hosting-services providers have their own tools for creating adequate websites that you can use online at no charge (Yahoo! site-building tools are available as downloads at no charge to use off line).

In my view, the decision of which way to go revolves around control and flexibility. I didn't want to work on my website online, preferring to use my own computer and software. I decided it was important to learn the basics about this critical form of doing business, and not be dependent on a technician or a remote ABC program offered by a host. In addition, if I learned how to do it, I would be able to teach someone else when the time came.

D. HOSTING SERVICES

A website-hosting service is a very important business relationship. There are literally thousands to choose from. Do a search on hosting services for a picture of the current situation. If you go to Internet Lists at the top of the home page at http://www.internet.com/, you can search for available hosts by category. For additional perspective, take a look at two well-known organizations offering website hosting and management tools in packages: http://www.buildit.sitesell.com/ and http://www.monstercommerce.com/.

My advice is to choose an experienced, financially stable hosting-services provider, one that offers levels of service at affordable prices and flexibility, for example, Yahoo! and Earthlink. They offer free write-ups on relevant subjects, answers to frequently asked questions, and listings of facts and figures to educate the novice about website construction and management. In the case of Yahoo!, where I elected to place my website, go to Yahoo!'s main page, http://www.

yahoo.com/. Click on More Yahoo! near the top, or scroll to the bottom of the page to find your way to Business Tools and Web Hosting. I suggest exploring the levels of hosting services they offer to get an orientation. Recently, Earthlink offered free test use of website-creation tools at their website, http://www.earthlink.net/. I found this a useful way to get oriented, develop confidence, and acquire general knowledge.

Consideration could also be given to experienced organizations that specialize in books, and/or your subject matter or genre; for example, SFF Net, http://www.sff.net/, for established science-fiction authors who want simple webpages and synergistic networking opportunities. Major factors in choosing a specialized host server are support, costs, synergism with your subject and/or genre, reputation, and site traffic.

Setup costs charged by hosting-services providers typically range from little or nothing to around $400; the design and development of the site is your responsibility. Monthly costs appeared to be around $8-$80, depending on factors of site size, capabilities selected, and traffic generation at your site.

Many hosting-services providers offer free services, for example, Yahoo! GeoCities. As with most low-cost service providers, these usually prohibit commercial sales and post random advertisements and sales banners on your site. In my opinion, any such distractions to visitors you are trying to impress with your professionalism is unacceptable.

I chose Yahoo! web hosting for my website. For a $15 setup charge and $14.95/month, you get a relatively robust Business Starter package. At the time of going to print with this book, some of the services and capabilities were:

- Free domain registration (a domain is your site name, or URL), if you haven't already registered it elsewhere.
- 50 MB of disk space and 20 GB of monthly data transfers (for uploading changes). As I went to press with this book, my website had 70 pages and was under 11 MB in file size.
- 10 e-mail accounts, unlimited e-mail forwarding, and POP access, managed from a web console for your account.

- A web console (control page) that allows you to administer all your account information and quickly go to additional services, resources, and Yahoo! staff help.
- website statistical reports over any period back two weeks or less.

The clincher for me was that the Yahoo! packages supported FrontPage Extensions, which included accommodating a website created in Microsoft Publisher.

I figured I could learn for a year or so, produce an adequate site, maintain control and flexibility, make changes to the site 24/7, afford the cost, and have access to more complexity through Yahoo!'s continuing efforts to remain at the forefront of the market.

E. CREATION MECHANICS

It took me a solid five weeks from start to finish to create the first 20-page Grace Publishing Group website, thoroughly pretest it in Publisher, and upload it to Yahoo!, my website hosting-services provider.

1. MASTER PAGE

Key information needs to be repeated on every page. I found it useful to create a master page in Publisher by using the Background button in the View menu. I designed this page, placing text, images, logos, headers, and a column of navigation buttons (shapes I created) hyperlinked to major website pages. These items will then appear at the same location on every page of the website. I've listed details on some of these items below:

- Business identity and logo: This is the header information at the top, confirming for arriving visitors they are at the right place and presenting an initial business image.
- Navigational buttons: In creation software, these buttons are usually available as templates. They can be stacked under the business header at the top of the page and directly under the last of the text at the bottom, or in a column at the right or left of the page, or both. It's a design preference. These hyperlinked buttons take visitors to the major subject pages on the website.

Navigation buttons can have drop-down description boxes that offer further subject breakdown, depending on the complexity of your site and the templates offered in your creation software.

You can also create or place shapes, add descriptive text, hyperlink them, and place them anywhere you want.

- General business contact information: Place the business name, mailing address, general contact information (telephone voice-mail, toll-free number, fax number, and e-mail address) below or at the side of the business identity and logo at the bottom of the page. Also include an e-mail address for the webmaster, webmaster@yourbusiness.com, at the bottom for website inquiries, and a copyright notice, for example: © your name 2000-2004.

- Group and association memberships: Organize their hyperlinked names and logos at the bottom of the page. These acknowledgement links establish business credibility.

- Borders and design elements: Place borders, logos, lines, images, and any other design feature you want to appear in the same place on every page.

- Right and left columns: You can dedicate space on every page for important changing information. For example, defining and using a column at the left for news enables you to easily edit it in one place.

2. HYPERLINKS AND PAGE CONSISTENCY

Set up hyperlinks after the text at the bottom of every page to assist navigation. In Publisher, you type in the text, for example, "Go to the Top" and "Return to the Whatever Page." Then at Insert on the toolbar, select Hyperlink and name the page number for the jump.

In most word-processing programs, formatting the appearance of hyperlinks is accomplished by selections made in the Style for the hyperlink found at Format in the toolbar; for example, you can select appearance features such as font, size, color, underlining, etc.

Every time a hyperlink takes a visitor to a new page, there should be consistency in how the page looks. I suggest titling all pages with the same look. When you need to continue information because of running out of space on a page, use the main page name and then a subtitle. For example, a major page called, Authors and Books might contain a book presentation and author media kit with hyperlinked lists of content. The hyperlinks would take visitors to subtitled pages containing the specific content information.

To let visitors know where they may have come from—and related spots to return to or go to—when they click around your website, you might consider posting a generic, hyperlinked backtracking route at the bottoms and/or at the tops of pages, for example, Authors and Books>Book Presentation>Synopsis.

3. CONTROL FORMS

Create various forms to transact business and to facilitate communications. Two generic form types are the order form for products or services and the special-purpose form. Tailoring the use of these two types by adding specific form controls available in your website-creation software and combining them with creative text entries will be useful for many purposes on your website.

See reputable vendor sites for examples of order forms and special-purpose forms. For instance, surf http://www.amazon.com/ to research different ways individual form-control elements can be organized to gather and process information. Remember, all forms serve as valuable sources of contact information in building databases.

In Publisher, there are six form-control types: option buttons, text boxes, command buttons, check boxes, and list boxes. These forms are found in the Insert menu by clicking on Form Controls. From these choices, in combination with text, functional forms can be created. Below are some examples of using these forms in Publisher:

OPTION BUTTON EXAMPLE

Insert two option buttons next to questions you type on a webpage or in a form. Then, create two small text boxes and type the answers, Yes and No, next to the option buttons. An individual completing the form clicks the option button of choice, corresponding to the yes or no answer to a question, causing a check mark to appear in the option button circle. The option button, like all the form controls, is formatted so the actions elicited are transmitted when the form is submitted.

Developing the Business Website

NOTE: To format a form control, double click it; a window appears for labeling the information to be transmitted when the form is utilized and submitted. Typically you may designate whether an entry is required in a control form in order for the whole form to process when it's submitted. When a form is submitted at your website, if required entries are absent, error messages appear to explain what boxes need attention.

SINGLE-LINE TEXT BOX EXAMPLE

You can use single-line text boxes next to descriptive text that explains what information you are requesting, for example: name, organization, e-mail address, fax number, charge-card number, expiration date, total cost, tax amount, shipping amount, etc.

COMMAND BUTTON EXAMPLE

The command buttons are the square Submit and Clear boxes you insert at the end of all forms you create. After insertion, double clicking allows you to designate the e-mail address where information submitted in the form is to be sent, as well as the description of the form, for instance: Class Registration and Payment Form, Book-Order Form, Guest Book, Workshop-Reservation Request, Newsletter-Subscription Form, PDF Review-Book Request, etc.

CHECK AND LIST-BOX EXAMPLES

Like the option button, a check box can be used to indicate a response to a query. For example, you may type into the control form next to the box, "Let me know if you don't want to receive my monthly XYZ newsletter by e-mail." A list box provides space for you to type in a list of items, and a visitor may select one from the list.

ORDER FORM EXAMPLE

Any time I construct an order form for purchases of products or services, I insert purchase-option explanations and completion directions above the form. I also have standard phrases that help explain the use of information. As examples, I have listed some quotes from those explanations and directions that appeared on my website in 2003:

- Complete a copy of the form and send it by e-mail, fax, or postal-mail, along with your check or charge-card information, to The Grace Publishing Group.
- For charge-card telephone orders, call in the information on the form using the toll-free customer-service number.
- Fill out the order form here at the website if you are comfortable with entering your Visa or MasterCard information for the purchase. Or, click on the hyperlinked PayPal logo to purchase by charge-card, using secure processing at PayPal's website (no charges to purchasers).
- Purchase payments received will be confirmed by e-mail or fax (only) on the day payment clears, and will include an estimated delivery time. Another confirmation will be sent on the day the order is shipped.
- Please make a copy of this order form for your records.
- Charge-card information may be sent to an unsecured server where it may be viewed by others.
- Notice: All contact information submitted on the website by customers, clients, and friends of The Grace Publishing Group is considered confidential and will not be provided to any outside party unless by legal writ—Jonathan and Peter Brown, Publishers.
- This form will not process without completion of these items.
- If you copy and send the form information by postal-mail or fax—and are ordering by charge-card—make a signature line and sign it.

SPECIAL-PURPOSE FORM EXAMPLE

All the special-purpose forms I've constructed for my website were derived using the form controls in Publisher. For example, the Contact Us page until recently contained a General Contact form that allowed visitors a more intimate means of asking questions. It consisted of a list of single-line text boxes for entering visitor information and then a multi-line text box for a query to a specific person. The names, titles, and functions for the people involved with the business were outlined at the top of the webpage, and I added hyperlinked icons for visitors to click on to send e-mail direct. At the end of the form were two command buttons to Submit and to Clear (start over).

Other examples of forms I developed for my website include: Guest Book, Newsletter Subscription, Request for PDF Review Copy, General Feedback, Workshop-Participant Reservation Request, Class-Reservation Request, Workshop-Hosting Request, etc. I am constantly designing forms to process responses to different promotions, for example: Complimentary PDF E-book Order Form and Ancestor Series Chapter-Acquisition Form.

4. ORIGINATION OF MASTER CONTENT FILES

When developing content for website pages, it is often necessary to first create master content files in a word-processing program like Word or WordPerfect. Many of these content files, for example, Author Credits, Draft Book Review/Article, Reviews and News, Frequently Asked Questions, etc., will also be used for other promotional purposes, such as putting together a media kit or a brochure.

In creating website pages, you will often insert images and text from different content files, and reformat the results to conform to your webpage style. Having master content files lets you go to one place to update information; then you can copy, paste, and rework the updated information into website pages and other appropriate documents to keep them current.

For larger files, when you don't want to detract from webpage impact by taking up space for the information, you can place a hyperlinked icon on the page for visitors who desire to open the file then, or copy it to their computers for later review. The universal format for these files on websites is PDF.

F. MAJOR PAGES

Design pages on the website to be responsive to the needs of anticipated visitors. The objectives are to get them quickly to what they're looking for and entice them to take the actions you desire. The major pages will have titles; the same titles will appears on your hyperlinked navigation buttons. The outline below represents my vision of a dynamic website for an author/self-publisher. In some cases I give examples from my websites that were in use prior to release of this book. I hope the outline will assist your thinking as you develop your own personal approach.

1. HOME

This page accomplishes the following:

- Presents a business introduction.
- States the major purposes of the site.
- Gives specific directions to expected visitor types to meet their needs.
- Puts visitors on notice that surfing the website is proof of understanding and agreement to caveats and policies you've posted at the Policies page. Include a Policies page hyperlink right there.
- Authorizes copyright release for all information contained on the website. This is particularly important for news media and publishing-industry professionals. This statement of release can be tied to registration, using a guest form. I allow and encourage copying of files I place on the website that contain proprietary information, such as draft articles, draft book reviews, draft interviews, newsletter archives, promotional pieces, and free chapters and excerpts. This statement of release would also appear at the Policies page. The statement in use for The Grace Publishing Group as this book was completed was:

    For members of the professional media, The Grace Publishing Group and Marshall Chamberlain hereby grant permission to reprint or quote written information posted on the website, so long as it is not authored by others, and so long as such use is accompanied by acceptable literary credit, or an attribution-signature appropriate in the industry, to recognize its source. For any reprint or large quote, we respectfully request that you register in our guest book.

- Contains the keywords determined important as sensitive search-engine registration data. At the time of writing this book, Yahoo! had a good article by Paul Graham at its website that focused on this important topic: "Generating Sales from Search Engines." It could be found at http://www.store.yahoo.com/ by clicking on Learn More and using the Search Yahoo! Store window to search for "Graham." The website http://www.selfpromotion.com/ explains the topic as part of its registration services.

2. MEDIA ROOM

This is a very important page. Many different visitor types will come here (because you have driven them and because they surf), but media editors from newspapers and magazines searching for news stories and book-review background are the most important. This is where the dedicated self-publisher has the unique opportunity to create credibility and win significant exposure to the marketplace without expending financial resources.

Benefits to your business will accrue only if you are successful in serving the interests of these important visitors. The information on the page needs to be concise, professional, compelling, and provocative. At the top of the page I say, "Welcome Editors and Publishing-Industry Professionals." Then I reiterate the hooks and taglines used to lure them to the website. I explain that if they register in my guest book, they have copyright permission to utilize any information found on the website.

These important visitors need to quickly find key information about you and your book, so place hyperlinks on this page to pages containing the book presentation, author media kit, review-copy acquisition form, draft articles, etc., where supportive data you have created is organized for viewing on the website, and/or in PDF files for copying to their computers.

3. LIBRARY ROOM

This page welcomes the librarians who respond to your promotions. The page should:

- Reiterate the promotional hooks and taglines that brought the librarian to the website to investigate.
- Display your most compelling library review quotes and testimonials.

- Provide hyperlinks to send them to appropriate pages of support information, for example, the book presentation and author media kit.
- Define the terms of purchase, including: shipping and handling costs, purchase and payment options, identification of special offers in effect, applicable taxes, and the need for a tax ID number and statement of tax-exempt status.
- Offer a hyperlink to a convenient book-order form.
- Provide contact information (and offer hyperlinked logos) for any distributor, wholesaler, or vendor of record relationships you have established to process sales of your book.

In my case, I designed an explanation and Host Workshop query form for libraries in Florida that respond to my promotional invitations to organize self-publishing workshop/signings.

4. BOOKSTORE ROOM

This page welcomes bookstore owners and managers who respond to promotions or who are filling special orders from their customers. Bookstores will typically find vendor-of-record contact information (your self-publishing business, fulfillment-services provider, exclusive distributor, and/or wholesalers) through their computer-software tie-ins to *Books in Print*.

Access to input forms for *Books in Print*, published by R.R. Bowker, is a free service provided to publishers. Changes can be made to the *Books in Print* database 24/7 from account-update forms at its website, http://www.bowker.com/. This information is added daily to the *Books in Print* database/software used by its book-trade clients worldwide.

Like the Library Room, the Bookstore Room should:

- Reiterate the promotional hooks and taglines for the book and contain your most compelling review quotes and testimonials.
- Provide hyperlinks to send viewers to appropriate pages of support information on the website, for example, the book presentation and author media kit.
- Define the terms of purchase, including: shipping and handling costs, purchase and payment options, identification of special

offers in effect, applicable taxes, and the need for a tax ID number and statement of tax-exempt status.
- Offer a hyperlink to a convenient book-order form.
- Provide contact information (and offer hyperlinked logos) for any distributor, wholesaler, or vendor-of-record relationships you have established to process sales of your book.

In my case, I designed an explanation and Host Workshop query form for bookstores in Florida that respond to my promotional invitations to organize self-publishing workshop/signings.

5. READER ROOM

The objectives with reader/visitors are to sell books, increase curiosity, develop positive buzz, develop loyalty and brand recognition, and create an image of unique style and story for the books that are coming.

In accomplishing these objectives, the page presents:

- A brief description of the book (and any book-derivative products) for sale and hyperlinks to more information and book order forms.
- Book taglines and the hottest testimonials about the book and author.
- Directions to invitees of reader promotions for obtaining complimentary PDF e-books. This includes hyperlinks to Complimentary E-Book Acquisition forms.
- Directions for readers responding to promotions for obtaining complimentary PDF files of upcoming book chapters. I set up a separate page containing a schedule of chapter releases (pre-final-edit drafts) for book projects I was working on, and presented a Chapter Acquisition form that led readers to the Chapter Download page.
- Directions to returning readers of draft chapters for posting review comments and a hyperlink to a Chapter Review form.

- A list of hyperlinks to pages that provide appropriate supportive information, for example, the book presentation and the author's media kit.
- Descriptions of a complimentary newsletter and supportive group/club (fan club), complete with hyperlinks to pages of information and the subscription forms.
- Directions to participate in any other promotional concepts you have creatively designed, for example: to view and purchase t-shirts or coolie cups, or to register to win something.

NOTE: As this book went to the printer, I was designing several styles of t-shirts around my fiction-writing themes, taglines, and logo. I will establish a fan club for the Ancestors Series of sci-tech-mystery-thrillers—all well (12 months) in advance of the first book's release. It's part of establishing a new brand in the marketplace.

6. BUSINESS ROOM

Design this page to satisfy the potential interests of publishers, literary agents, film agents, film and TV producers, book-catalog publishers, book-club publishers, foreign-rights interests, serialization editors, and visitors who represent any other special sales situation.

Here you provide:

- A general explanation of the interest you have with these business segments.
- A specific contact person and e-mail address for queries. It may even be appropriate to have a telephone number available on this page.
- Directions (and hyperlinks) to appropriate pages of support information, for example: the book presentation, media kit, and special pages for downloading works in progress.
- A hyperlink to the Contact Us page for staff introductions, individual e-mail addresses, and a Contact form for inquiries.

You might consider offering book-sales figures, applicable business policies, an outline of the marketing/promotion program(s) for books under publication, and a picture of what's planned for the business in the one- to five-year range.

7. RADIO AND TV ROOM

Radio and TV producers and hosts, driven by your promotional efforts and word of mouth, should find proof that an author interview or guest appearance would be newsworthy, entertaining, and of value to audiences. Later in your promotional planning, you will execute a contact program using every ploy of creativity you can muster to woo this important source of free publicity.

Suggestions for accomplishing this:

- An interview based on a list of frequently asked questions— questions you would like to be asked that let you define elements that make your book (or the story around the creation of your book) interesting news. You could weave in biographical and author background information, book taglines and sales hooks, directions to major market segments for buying the book, and offers of valuable giveaways.

  If you are inclined, you could place an audio and/or digital video interview files on the website page. You can create an audio file with the Sound Recorder program available in most Windows operating systems, as long as you have speakers ($15) and a microphone ($6). Go to Start>Programs> Accessories>Entertainment>Sound Recorder. These days adequate video recordings (even with audio) can be made using some mid-priced digital cameras (around $400) or video recorders.

- Hyperlinks to the book presentation and author media kit for complete background. I suggest listing the contents of the media kit.

- Descriptions of the radio and TV appearances you have made (if any).

- Hyperlinks to pages on your website that facilitate ordering a review-book in PDF and downloads of sample works under construction.

8. AUTHORS AND BOOKS

On this straightforward page, you could have hyperlinked icons to pages or websites for any affiliate authors of your business. At a one-author business website I suggest organizing the Authors and Books page into two categories of information, the book presentations and the media kit, displaying their contents and hyperlinking the content pieces to other pages on the website where you have plenty of space to present the information.

As mentioned previously, the master content files should be created as individual files in word-processing software, so they can also be used for other purposes than as webpage content. In the section on the Media Kit Master PDF file, below, I've given an example of how the individual master content files are brought into pages on the website.

Also included below is a brief description of an author activity-calendar concept you may find useful and appropriate for this webpage.

BOOK PRESENTATION AND CONTENT

Most of your visitors will be coming to this page to look at your book presentations. The primary objectives of the page are to generate impulse sales from reader/visitors and to meet a variety of needs for book and background information, especially for media professionals developing reviews of a book or articles where the book and/or author add elements of newsworthiness.

To accomplish this, I suggest you include a short description of each book product you have available for sale, with hyperlinks to purchase information and order forms to satisfy impulse buyers. For example, I offered a PDF e-booklet, autographed trade paperbacks, and e-books as products.

For a master book presentation, I suggest creating the following content pieces (master content files), listing them, inserting them (and reformatting) on separate webpages, and hyperlinking them from the list to the pages:

- About the author: A relaxed story written by the author about his life experiences, present motivations, and plans, both personal and professional.
- Front and back covers: Color drafts (you don't need exact

sizing here) with superimposed text at 75 dpi.
- Table of contents.
- Synopsis: Include this if the back-cover information is not sufficient.
- Reviews: A copy-and-paste layout of the best testimonials, blurbs, and article excerpts. I suggest using a two-column format that resembles newsprint.
- Excerpt or chapters: PDF files for opening and viewing or downloading to a visitor's computer. Any sharing of these complimentary excerpts or chapters is free publicity, so I don't add document-security features when I create the PDF files in Acrobat 4.0+.
- Schedule of free chapter releases: You always want to invent new ways of bringing people back to your website. When a book reaches the editing process (edit number three for me), I set up a schedule page of chapters, so I can begin introducing the book to potential buyers through e-mail promotions that drive them to the new book's home page. There they can fill out a Chapter Acquisition form, submit it, and return to a page that lists the chapter titles ready to open or be downloaded. On that page, I also include a list of all the chapters in the book and estimated dates for completion. In addition, the page offers readers an opportunity to return and fill out review forms—to help me write a better book.
- Book-order forms: Explanations of purchase options and forms to order books and book products.

NOTE: Generally, if master content files would take up more than two pages on my website—for example, in the case of an excerpt or chapter—I create PDF files for them that can be opened on the Book Presentation page or downloaded for later review.

MEDIA KIT AND CONTENT

The author media kit will be the primary destination for media and publishing-industry visitors. It should contain all the information expected of an author presenting his or her works—and more. Like the book presentation, list the elements (either hyperlinked to other pages on the website or PDF files to open or download.

Above the list, direct visitors to the bottom of the page to download the entire media kit as a PDF file (see next section).

Suggested media kit contents include:

- Book information: Description of the book, for example: trade paperback, number of pages, ISBN, Library of Congress number, publisher, author, distributor, wholesalers, vendor of record, and summary of promotional plan.

- Bio-sketch: I chose to draft this in written form as a quasi-interview with an outside author/interviewer.

- Author credits: A concise, uncluttered listing of writing accomplishments and related experience.

- Author interview: If you don't have a transcript of an actual interview, you could include written, audio, and/or audio-video dummy interviews, perhaps starting with the written and working up to the other formats.

  The interview should be designed to include all the questions (and answers) you would like to have asked, as well as those you think interviewers and audiences would like to hear answers to. A list of frequently asked questions can be an interim effort to fill this need (see below).

- About the author: A relaxed, first-person story written by the author about life experiences, present motivations, and plans, both personal and professional.

- Reviews and news: A layout of the best short testimonials and blurbs, article excerpts, and news announcements. I suggest using a two-column format that resembles newsprint.

- Book reviews and articles: Here you could offer the best longer excerpts from published reviews and articles or, if nothing has as yet been published, you could draft an example review/article.

Also, you could consider creating a PDF archive file for all the reviews and articles (adding to it as new ones are published) that could be opened on the page or downloaded.

- Book covers: I used photographs as background for both the front and back covers of this book, inserting images created at 75 dpi in Publisher and drafting text on top.
- Book table of contents.
- Excerpts and/or chapters: PDF files you create to be opened there on the page or downloaded.
- Book synopsis.
- Author photo gallery: I placed 35-mm pictures, including headshots, on the webpage(s). The purpose is to give a down-to-earth flavor to your lifestyle. I suggest that the pictures be in color at 75 dpi in TIF or JPG format to maximize usefulness and limit file size.

NOTE: *If a media editor wants something different, he or she will contact you. You can scan and resize the images at the needed resolution, save them to the file types required, and send them by postal-mail on floppy disk, CD-R, or as glossy prints.*

- List of speaking topics: List of topics for speaking engagements you offer to organizations, supported by an explanation of your expertise, experience, and contact information.
- Press releases: In addition to your most current press releases, you could create a PDF archive file to be available here.
- Draft news stories: I recommend drafting several of these as differently slanted stories to give editors some ideas and raw material to work with. You may need to create a PDF file for them.

NOTE: These news stories should contain timely core information that news editors can use in developing stories based around current events.

- Professional activities and work in progress: A description of the author's day-to-day professional activities, such as workshops, classes, consulting, and writing modus operandi. It should include the status of the work(s) in progress, including short-form synopses, excerpts of books, book products, and articles.

- Appearances: A chronological listing of radio interviews, TV-show appearances, organization presentations, and event participations.

- Frequently asked questions: List of questions you would like to be asked. The questions should be formed to: elicit information that makes your book, or the story around the creation of your book, interesting news; reveal unusual author background information; insert book taglines and sales hooks; give book-buying directions to major market segments; and facilitate offering valuable giveaways.

MEDIA KIT MASTER PDF FILE

The content files that make up your media kit should originate from master content files created in a word-processing program.

I create the Master Media Kit PDF file by individually converting the master content files I want to include in the media kit to PDF, and then inserting them, one by one, where I want them, in the Master Media Kit PDF file.

Specifically, you start by opening one of the PDF content files in Adobe Acrobat. Then click on Document in the main menu at the top of the page and Insert Pages. Following the directions, you select the PDF content files from your hard drive and copy them (insert them) to where you want them in the Master Media Kit PDF file.

The next job is to create About This Document and Table of Contents files in your word processor, convert them to PDF, and insert them in the proper place in the Master Media Kit PDF file. The Table of Contents file is simply an attractive layout of the titles of the content files. The About This Document file explains any document security features you might have enabled for the document (in Acrobat 4.0+), how to get around in the document using Acrobat features, and any use caveats you want to state.

The last task is to use the functions in Acrobat 4.0+ while you're in the Master Media Kit PDF file to hyperlink the titles of the content files in the table of contents to appropriate pages in the media kit.

Now you can offer the entire media kit on the website for media and publishing-industry professionals to download for later review. See my media kit as an example at my website, http://www.gracepublishing.org/.

NOTE: *If you're sending your book to reviewers as a PDF e-book on CD-Rs by postal-mail, the same Master Media Kit PDF file can be included on the CD-R for added impact.*

ACTIVITY CALENDAR

The concept is to develop a simple way to summarize an author's schedule of professional activity, as well as point out his availability. The calendar could show, month by month, day by day, the author's scheduled commitments. For example, you could use simple calendar templates found in Publisher to show your scheduled commitments by creating a legend for the types of activities, such as: VA means vacation, WR means writing, WS means workshop, SP means speaking engagement, CF means conference, TS means tradeshow, DO means dates open for booking, etc.

9. BUSINESS SERVICES

This page of your website is dedicated to listing and explaining the activities and services you and/or your business offer that directly or indirectly generate income or provide some other form of satisfaction. For example, you might be interested in teaching through a school; presenting at workshops; editing; proofreading; ghost writing; authoring articles for syndication or for sale to magazines; screenwriting; writing commercials; collaborating with other authors; speaking for organizations; writing columns for magazines, e-zines, or newspapers; designing websites; planning book promotions; etc.

If the explanations are lengthy, hyperlink them to other webpages for the details. You could also define major navigation buttons for the most important activities.

I chose to include the following activities and services that are personally rewarding and allow me to help people while I promote and sell my works:

THE AFFILIATE AUTHOR PROGRAM

The Affiliate Author Program is for mentoring aspiring authors/self-publishers. It provides guidance, affirmation, and discipline in the design and execution of creative self-publishing plans. By sharing expertise, business resources, and the costs involved, authors can be empowered to sustain the motivation required to successfully complete self-publishing plans. The relationship promotes effective use of time, helps to ameliorate the debilitating effects of working alone for extended periods of time, and it lightens the workload on my own business.

Acceptance as an affiliate author is a determination I make personally by reviewing an author's proposed works and other writing, acquiring a sense of the degree of commitment that must be present, understanding how the person views his or her life challenges, and discovering whether we have a synergistic mesh of personalities.

On the website page for the program, which can be found using its navigation button in the right-hand column of every page, I provide an Inquiry form to get the process started.

SELF-PUBLISHING WORKSHOPS

This service is my primary personal-appearance and promotional activity. After wrestling with several workshop ideas, I settled on offering workshop/signings to writing and arts organizations, libraries, bookstores, colleges, and universities. Authors/self-publishers have double expertise to share.

I gave my self-publishing workshops a major page on my website, with its own navigation button, to explain how workshops are presented and what's needed from host organizations. A Workshop Reservation Request form and specific contact information were also provided to get the process started. I use e-mail and fax to announce the workshop opportunity, and let my website perform the explanatory functions.

To help participants who wanted to reserve spots in scheduled workshops, the Self-Publishing Workshop page offered hyperlinks to a Workshop Information flyer they could print out, and to a Participant Workshop Reservation form for them to complete.

For more detail go to my website, http://www.gracepublishing.org/, and click on the navigation button for Self-Publishing Workshops, and see the "Workshops" section in Chapter X.

OTHER SERVICES I OFFER

Information about the following additional services can be found on pages at my website by clicking on their navigation buttons: self-publishing classes, individual self-publish coaching, and consulting services. These services add to the mix of earning a living while promoting. The pages gave descriptions of services, provided forms for reservation requests and payments, and listed specific contact information for direct inquiries.

10. NEWSLETTER

Consider setting up a page offering subscription to a free monthly e-mail newsletter. This way you can share your expertise and present cutting-edge concepts, ideas, news, and general information to help readers and writers interested in your subject or genre. My page was called Self-Publishing Newsletter, and it explained the philosophy and objectives of the newsletter, *Tips, Tricks & Scoop,* offered an archive download of previous issues, and presented a Newsletter Subscription form.

I also presented a hyperlinked newsletter logo box on my website master page. The box was displayed in the left-hand column on every website page as a convenient reminder, and was hyperlinked to the Self-Publishing Newsletter page.

11. INTERNET CLUB

I created a free Self-Publishing Club at http://www.lycos.com/ and hyperlinked the Lycos Communities logo in a Club box on the master page of my website; so like the newsletter logo box, it also appeared in the left-hand column on every website page.

The page on my website was entitled Self-Publishing Club and contained the same information posted in the founder's message at the club site on Lycos.

Most of the major Internet directories (for example: AOL, MSN, Lycos, and Yahoo!) offer the free service of organizing a club or group.

12. BUSINESS LINKS

Consider giving promotional consideration to supporting organizations that have proven of professional value to you or your business by displaying their hyperlinked logos and offering a short explanation. For example, you might consider: printer(s), fulfillment-services provider, wholesalers, vendor of record, distributor, website host, ISP, publishing partner, illustrators, designers, photographers, copy editors, proofreaders, special co-op organizations, organizations where you maintain membership, important writing/publishing resource sites on the Internet, other business-services providers, etc.

As you go along, you can increase the page's effectiveness by reorganizing these link listings into categories, adding links to synergistic businesses that offer reciprocal links to increase traffic to your site, and including affiliate/associate programs, such as Amazon Associates to earn additional income. (See http://www.amazon.com for more information on this program.)

13. FREQUENTLY ASKED QUESTIONS

Construct a page of frequently asked questions as a method to promote as well as inform. Invent the questions you would like to have asked, and include your answers. I organized a list of the questions on this page and hyperlinked each to the page where the answers were posted. Consider designing your questions and answers to accomplish the following objectives of:

- Presenting interesting biographical and author background information.
- Revealing book taglines and sales hooks.
- Providing book-buying directions to major market segments.
- Facilitating promotional giveaways.

- Bringing out information that makes your book, and/or the story around creation of your book, interesting news.

14. CONTACT US

On this page, list names, e-mail addresses, telephone numbers (if you want to go that far), fax number, mailing addresses, and specific functions for everyone involved in your business. For example, list yourself, your virtual staff, affiliate authors, special support people and advisors, webmaster, and key outside services providers like wholesalers and/or a vendor of record. Hyperlink the e-mail addresses and websites (if you create the website in Publisher, a hyperlinked e-mail address brings up an Outlook Express form for sending a message).

NOTE: Just a tip, if you post your personal telephone number, you may get so many calls that you never have time to write. Your website should answer 90% of all questions and needs for information. E-mail and fax should do the rest.

In addition, I suggest you place the following general contact information in a footer on the master page of your website, so it displays at the bottom of all pages alongside the hyperlinked logos of your organizational memberships: logo, URL, business name, mailing address, business voice-mail number, business fax number, toll-free customer-service number, and general e-mail address.

15. POLICIES

For this page, I suggest reviewing the websites of credible organizations for privacy policies, disclaimers, and any other information designed to protect a website and its business; then, based on these examples, draft your own. Cover any other policy issues, for example: permission for use of website content and use of contact information supplied by visitors to your site on various product-purchase and information forms.

G. TESTING AND UPLOADING THE WEBSITE

Testing the working features of your website is typically a feature found in creation software. You can test the pages one by one or the whole site at once by uploading to a browser, for example Windows Explorer or Netscape. You then view the page or site as if it were live and operating on the Internet at the host server. This allows you to work out the kinks and make sure that all the hyperlinks, posted PDF files, and control forms are functioning properly. In Publisher, this test is performed by going to File and selecting Web Page Preview.

NOTE: In Publisher, the program alerts you to formatting problems on the pages as it uploads, for example, a control form may be overlapping a text box, or a hyperlinked file is linked to an incorrect location on your computer.

Uploading the website to a chosen website host server is usually the easy part. Website-creation software normally has this function built into File in the main menu. For example, in Publisher you save the file (your constructed website) by selecting Save As Web Page. That act sends you to a window with a box where you fill in a file name or select a previous file to replace—in this program you must use your actual URL as the file name—and then you click OK. The saving process sets up the website file to be sent to a website host server. In Publisher, you have to click OK again, without being prompted; for some inexplicable reason the screen just sits there without any prompts. Then the file starts the process by first showing a Percentage Complete screen to track the upload process, and then a screen asking for account and password information for your host server. Each time I make changes to my website, I repeat the process and select the file, http://www.gracepublishing.org/. If you have DSL or cable, it takes 3-20 minutes for the upload/replacement process, depending on your computer and the size of the website. For my 11 MB website, it takes about five minutes for the 2 GHz, 256 RAM computer to do the job through my cable connection.

Before I start work on a website revision, I save a copy of the old site to my Old Websites folder in My Documents, and change the name by adding the date. Then, I send a copy to a backup ZIP disk or CD-RW. It's good business practice to have a record of what you've presented to the public.

NOTE: With a 56K modem and a telephone connection, uploading my first site was a disaster. It took three and a half hours, and several attempts due to telephone line or ISP problems popping up during that time period. There were also quirks in Publisher that only trial and error taught me how to overcome.

H. SEARCH-ENGINE REGISTRATIONS

For search engines to generate any significant traffic for you, your website—or information leading to the website—must display on the first or second page of search results when surfers look for you or your works. Development of identity taglines that link to your works, business, and you as an author is very important. You will need to learn about keywords and where to place them on your website in order to maximize the success of the periodic registration work that should be carried out. Most of this education will come during the registration process provided by search engines and/or registration-service providers. The website http://www.selfpromotion.com/ offers a quick orientation to this constantly changing subject.

The self-publisher has several options to choose from to effectively register with search engines. The whole idea is to maximize traffic to a website by making it possible for people to find you even if they start with incomplete information. The basic options are to:

- Pay for site-registration services.
- Buy registration software and do it yourself.
- Use free registration services.
- Register directly with the search engines one by one.
- Use a combination of the above.

Hiring a competent site-registration service can be accomplished online with little cost by filling out forms. Do a search for search-engine registration. If you search using http://www.google.com/, the right-hand side of the page shows paid ads for service providers.

Services typically cost around $7-$20 per registration for 20-1,000s of search engines at a time, with discount packages for a schedule of multiple registrations. Be aware that most of the website hosting-services providers will offer, amongst other service add-ons, levels of registration services, and most of the site-registration services are through organizations that offer hosting. Total website-hosting and site-management services should be checked out as part of the selection process for your hosting service. For example, Monster Commerce, http://www.monstercommerce.com/, offers a basic package for $80/month with a one-time setup fee of $80, and http://www.sitesell.net has an all-inclusive website-management approach.

An example of registration software is TrafficSeeker, available at http://www.trafficseeker.com/. For $99, you can automatically register with 6,000+ search engines anytime it's convenient; a download demo version is offered at the website. For more options, search for registration software.

Or, you could investigate free registration services, for example, http://www.uswebsites.com/submit or http://www.promotingonline.com/. These sites, like many others that show up in a general search, are often tied into many other website performance- and sales-enhancement services, as well as offering some form of free registration. As mentioned above, http://www.selfpromotion.com/ offers a quick introduction to the registration topic as well as a free registration service.

Or, register yourself. For assistance, see Midwest Book Review's URL Submission List for Publishers at http://www.midwestbookreview.com by clicking on Publicity and Promotion. At this page, about 60 of the major search engines are listed with links directly to their submission-form pages. Using this list can save a lot of time. This website also maintains a current list of web search engines.

But don't be overwhelmed by the number of search engines. In a posted article, "Generating Sales from Search Engines," Paul Graham on the Yahoo! Store webpages at http://www.yahoo.com/ stated, "There are hundreds of search engines and indices, but only eight that matter: Yahoo!, AltaVista, Excite, WebCrawler, MSN, Infoseek, Lycos, and HotBot. All the others might account for 1% of your traffic, combined." The article appears a little dated; I would add Google and AOL.

I ended up using a combination of free registration services at http://www.submitwebsite.com/, selected direct registrations with search engines specializing in my business subject matter (for this book), and direct registration with Goggle at http://www.google.com and the Open Project Directory at http://www.dmoz.

com/.Submitwebsite.com claims to have been around the longest, and they allow you to come back periodically to reregister at no charge. A month or so after registering with Google, my website showed up second when I searched for self-publishing. That was two years ago; recently I found the first reference to my website buried in that big topic area on the seventh page, so I went through the process of re-registered as I've outlined.

I. DEVELOPING KEYWORDS

For an author/self-publisher, important keywords and phrases could be book titles, taglines for a work, sub-genres you make up for your work, name of the author, business name, business services, etc. Determining these keywords or phrases is similar to the process you would go through in creating your website—picking keywords as part of the data entered in the software to attract the web crawlers of search engines. In Publisher, for example, keywords to associate with your website are entered by going to File and selecting Web Properties.

H. REGISTERING KEYWORDS

Another important tool for increasing traffic to your website could be to utilize a service provider for registering keywords on the Internet. Surfers using a search engine and your keyword are taken immediately to your website. Do a search for keyword registration to research this topic. Before May 2002, http://www.realnames.com/ provided the premiere registration service for this dynamic activity—the next generation in search-engine effectiveness. Rumors seem to indicate that Microsoft may have withdrawn support for the activity, which triggered closure of this viable business. Realnames.com had provided:

- Online keyword-registration services.
- Education on use of the concept in the marketplace.
- Different registration packages, for example, $49/year for basic registration of a keyword.
- Assistance in defining keywords for your own particular business.

As a substitute, an effective practice is to registers your keywords as separate domains, URLs that you own and control. For example, at the domain-services provider I presently use, a domain registration costs $11.95/year. To me, this is a small cost to ensure that surfers who use my well-chosen keywords will come directly to my website, or even exact pages (URLs) on my site. A specific example is the theme name for my fiction writing, the Ancestor Series. I registered the domain, http://www.ancestorseries.com, and paid an additional $5.95/year to have the name forwarded to http://www.gracepublishing.org/page4.html, the page on my website that serves as the home page for the Ancestor Series of sci-tech-mystery-thrillers. This technique appears to be the most cost effective for guiding surfers looking for you, your works, or your business services to specific information at your website. You maintain ongoing control of that power through the ownership of domain names.

CHAPTER VIII: Phase I Promotion (Months 28-29)

The day you upload your first completed website, you are in business. At this point, your carefully laid-out website should contain all the facilitating mechanisms and information necessary to begin phase one of your promotions. Now's the time to launch your business and begin establishing credibility and awareness in the marketplace for you, your coming book, and the business services you have selected for making a living and promoting. It is also time to invite review of your galley-book.

A. BUSINESS-CONTACT FILE SYSTEM

It's useful to organize a system of recording contact notes. I use the Contacts folder in Outlook to organize contacts, information about contacts, and my actual contact notes. To do this, create contact records in a sub-folder you create under the Contacts folder. I call my sub-folder Business Contacts. After I enter basic contact information in a contact record form, I assign the contact a descriptive category, for example: major galley-book reviewers, review-book reviewers, librarians, bookstores, Florida newspapers, magazines, authors, newsletter subscribers, etc.

I log summary information into these contact records of important e-mail, postal-mail, and fax messages sent, as well as notes I accumulate from face-to-face meetings, telephone contacts and research. If I ever want a hard copy of a contact record, I open the contact record in Outlook and print it out.

B. BOOKS AND BOOK-RELATED PRODUCTS FOR SALE (MONTHS 28-29)

The creation of book-related products is only limited by your imagination. These products, along with your book, should be posted for purchase at your website. I've used my own generic approach as examples of product creation.

1. REGISTERED, AUTOGRAPHED, COLLECTOR'S EDITION

I will offer a registered, autographed, collector's edition (RACE) for each of my fiction books well in advance of the printing; it will be a limited-edition (1,000 maximum) hardback with each book identified by an autographed, numbered registration seal on the copyright page. The RACE will be a unique book available exclusively through the publisher (me), and I'll create credible reasons for ordering the book well in advance of delivery. Creating this product gives me opportunities to promote to specialty sectors of the market, for example: book collectors, first-edition bookstores, my Individual Potential Buyers list, and online auctions such as those at http://www.yahoo.com/ and http://www.ebay.com/. Setting up a schedule of ongoing auctions for the RACE is a creative sales-promotion tool with nominal costs up-front and small commissions (3%-7%) when products are sold.

2. PDF E-BOOK

The creation of PDF e-books is a marketing tool that makes it possible to—in advance of hard copy availability—offer potential buyers an opportunity to get a jump on the rest of market, and at the same time provide you with advance sales. I priced the pre-final-edit PDF e-book for this book at $7.95 on my website. I posted it for sale almost eight months ahead of the first printing of the trade paperback. As this book went to the printer, I was planning to re-edit the PDF e-book, hyperlinking websites and e-mail addresses, to offer as a promotional giveaway at my website.

If you have a functional website up and operating earlier in the time sequence than I've laid out in this book, you could consider offering a PDF e-book that would be a working-paper version of your book. Although only a draft version, its early creation (perhaps 12 months in advance of a pre-final-edit book, assuming the book is nonfiction) offers you an opportunity to promote it as a product of significant value to those who see advance information in rough form as important. So, for a business book, it might be appropriate to charge $10+ for the working-paper version.

3. AUTOGRAPHED BOOKS

As a self-publisher, you can offer autographed books on your website, available exclusively through your publishing business. These can be hardbacks (the same book as the RACE) or trade paperbacks. You can offer discounted (or nondiscounted) books to individuals, libraries, and any other source you come up with for presales as much as 6-12 months before your final manuscript goes to the printer and way before the official publication date (OPD), which is typically four months after the first printing. Because you control this special form of the book, you can promote it anytime you want without affecting any fulfillment or wholesaler relationships.

4. OTHER PRODUCTS

The potential products you can develop to support personal promotion, build image, and make the most out of your book are unlimited, for example: t-shirts, coolie cups, autographed pictures, other theme-oriented products, etc. If your book is nonfiction, perhaps the most significant use of creativity is multipurposing. Subjects covered in your book can be expanded to appeal to specific specialty market segments. For instance, if your book is on gardening, taking coverage on a certain plant or technique and expanding it might appeal to clubs, groups, and organizations formed around interest in that plant or technique.

In multipurposing this book, I extracted the last chapter and added a few guerilla-marketing concepts I'd like to try out, ideas that were not appropriate for including in the book. So, I created a PDF e-booklet entitled, *My 20 Favorite Creative Self-Publishing Promotion Concepts*, available for sale at my website for $10.95. Its creation will enable me down the road to present twenty more concepts, and so on, as the self-publishing road reveals new marketing ideas.

C. PROMOTIONS TO GENERATE ADVANCE SALES (MONTHS 28-29)

Advance book sales add to the economic feasibility of larger print runs. Even the galley-book review promotion later in this chapter can be viewed as an opportunity to make contacts that could potentially produce advance sales to individuals, libraries, catalog and book-club organizations or premium buyers.

1. MASTER PROMOTION LOG

If you haven't done so already, now is the time to organize a master promotion log for recording every promotional action you initiate. This can be a hard copy, for example, a three-ring binder with support sections containing a chronological record of actual copies of faxes, e-mails, and postal-mail.

Or, you can organize copies of the content files on your computer into a Master Promotion Log folder. A master promotion log (file) would be a page for recording important summary information, for example: data, entries for list identification, number of recipients, delivery means, subject heading, date sent, and code number (embedded in the communication for tracking responses).

2. FIRST SALES OFFERS TO LIBRARIES

By e-mail and then by fax, offer libraries a 10%-20% discount (for example, 20% for five or more copies; you pay shipping) for paid book orders placed through your website prior to a certain date. After that date, you could extend the offer, reprice it for another promotion, or just make it applicable to autographed copies.

In addition to potential sales, making these inexpensive library sales offers will be worthwhile because you'll be:

- Building recognition and a credible image for you and your book with library directors and selection/acquisition librarians.
- Paving the way for offers through participation in upcoming PMA co-op marketing programs to libraries.

- Providing an opportunity to invite library directors to review your book, via the galley-books prepared for the galley-book review process. (See the "Galley-Book Review Promotion" below.)

Design an 8.5 X 11-inch folding flyer for your book (you will use a similar approach for the flyers required for PMA's co-op marketing programs). Deliver it to the following lists: major national public library systems, state of residence public library systems, state of residence libraries of higher education, state of residence high-school libraries (if appropriate for your book), military base libraries, libraries with special collections.

If you have the resources, you could consider purchasing the *American Library Directory* database on CD, now available through its new publisher, Information Today, Inc., http://www.infotoday.com/ (previously published by R. R. Bowker). Recently, it cost $499 and was available by calling the customer service number, 800-300-9868, or 609-654-6266; traditionally, new editions have been published annually in June.

3. FIRST SALES OFFERS TO INDIVIDUAL POTENTIAL BUYERS

This is the first of many scheduled e-mails to lists of individuals you have previously compiled, including friends and relatives.

NOTE: Development of your Individual Potential Buyers list(s) is an ongoing project of surfing the Net for genre- and subject-oriented clubs, groups, and organizations and culling e-mail addresses, and/or purchasing lists of opt-in buyers.

With due diligence to your current non-spam operating procedures (see "Toward Non-Spam Standards for E-mail" in Chapter X), draft crafty, concise e-mails to potential buyers.

The subject line is the most important part of the message. What you say on that line must convince the recipient to open your communication, for example: "Readers Need to Know," "XYZ Club... Organization Name," "Reading Announcement," "Serious Readers of Science Fiction," "Gardening," "The Sci-Tech-Mystery-Thriller Has Arrived," etc. Your intention is to drive interested prospects to your website to receive complimentary chapters and/or other giveaways. (See "Sales Offers to Potential Individual Buyers" in Chapter X.) A dynamic giveaway example is a complimentary PDF e-book for a limited period. Acquisition of the book would take place through a form at your website, and delivery could be by attachment to e-mail or a download at a special page on your website.

If your website is effectively laid out, the purchase of books or other products, or investigations of your business services will be ancillary results of the promotion.

Tell your friends and relatives. When you e-mail them, attach a copy of a press release or the general sales flyer and subtly indicate you look forward to seeing their names on the purchase forms they fill out on your website. Ask them to help you by going to local libraries and bookstores to put in requests for the book.

NOTE: One of the interesting characteristics of the Individual Potential Buyer list(s) you've compiled, for example, from Yahoo! reading clubs and groups, is that 10% or so of the contacts are from countries other than the United States. A well-conceived e-mail promotional program has the potential to produce a snowball effect worldwide.

4. FIRST ANNOUNCEMENTS TO ORGANIZATIONS

Send tailored fax or e-mail announcements of prerelease book offers to organizations where you maintain active membership, requesting inclusion in the member news section of the next newsletter and/or websites.

Send e-mail announcements to your lists of book-related organizations; included in these lists are appropriate book clubs and catalog organizations, newsgroups, e-zines, newsletters, subject- or genre-interested membership organizations, and other clubs and groups you've tracked down. (See the compilation of the Book-Related Organizations list in Chapter IV.)

These announcements of your book's availability for sale under special offers should present news, sales-oriented hooks, perhaps a list of articles available on your website and an appropriate, limited-time giveaway.

5. FIRST INTERNET ANNOUNCEMENTS

Post announcements at the following Internet locations:
- Website message boards of clubs, groups, and organizations you have joined.
- Websites of book-related organizations that facilitate direct posting.
- News release/announcement sites (services) you choose to utilize.

These announcements should be concise, offer a giveaway, and send interest to specific fulfillment locations, for example, special pages on your website.

This will become an ongoing activity in the continuing creative promotion plan discussed in Chapter X.

6. SUBMIT THE BOOK PRESENTATION TO AMAZON.COM

Recent observations at Amazon.com indicate that they will post your book presentation with a delivery date as far out as three months. This is huge, free exposure, and a promotional bridge of credibility for you, your book, and your publishing business. Go to http://www.amazon.com/ and search for Publishers' Guide or Bookseller Services. If you have elected to absorb their 55% discount terms, having your books for sale at Amazon.com at this stage in the self-publishing process could be a major coup. You have the option of discontinuing the relationship at any time if results aren't in line with your objectives.

7. SUBMIT TO SPECIALTY INTERNET SITES

There are hundreds of Internet posting sites claiming various degrees of exposure to a variety of market segments. While compiling important lists in Chapter IV, you selected genre- and subject-oriented sites for posting your book presentation and researched their submission requirements to prepare for this action.

Consider the following organization sites for credible exposure to the publishing industry and reader market at reasonable costs; submission procedures were offered at the sites:

- http://www.authorlink.com/: This may be the premiere site for publishers and agents to surf for the best new work ($105-$220/ year). Inquiries from your page on the site come directly to AuthorLink and then to you.
- http://www.authorsden.com/: According Matt Miller, the president, early in 2003 this site began as a "100% free author community... bringing authors and readers together. The site has grown to become... the largest and still the fastest growing author and reader community on the Internet." Recently it still offered a free author page, as well as a variety of promotional services at reasonable costs.
- http://www.authorshowcase.com/: Another site for getting your book in front of the publishing industry, at a cost of $70/year.
- http://www.jlbooks.com/: A nicely laid-out posting site at a cost of $30 for two years. If your book is sold by charge-card through their site page, they take a 10% administrative fee.

Some organizations (not necessarily those above) allow hyperlinks to locations for additional information, for example, pages on your website for other product-purchase information (perhaps a PDF e-book, autographed books, multipurposed pieces of your book, t-shirts, or chapters of upcoming work).

D. POST AND PROMOTE YOUR BUSINESS ACTIVITIES (MONTHS 28-29)

1. POSTING

Now is the time to launch the business-activities element of the personal promotion program. (See the "Personal Promotion Program" in Chapter X.) These business activities will be events and services you create. Consider posting your events and services (for example: workshops, classes, seminars, and speaking topics) for free at prestigious Internet organizations like:

- http://www.zulu.com/.
- http://www.shawguides.com/.
- The Authors Highway, http://www.publishersweekly.com/.
- The Events Calendar, http://www.bookwire.com/.

Consider posting your availability as an expert speaker with one or more of the more credible service providers on the Internet, for example:

- http://www.guestfinder.com/ ($249/year).
- http://www.talion.com/expert_source.htm/ ($49/year).
- Guest Yearbook at http://www.expertclick.com/ ($495/year).

Consider joining a major speakers bureau, such as a local chapter of the National Speakers Association, http://www.nsaspeaker.org/ (about $300/year), or http://www.toastmasters.org/. As a member of the National Speakers Association, you can post your availability as a speaker on their website, and both these organizations offer a wealth of training opportunities at reasonable costs.

2. PROMOTING

Send your first announcement of business services to individuals interested in your subject or genre; use your Potential Individual Buyers list(s), and sort by individuals located in your market area.

Also, send announcements to organizations in your market area that have interest in your subject or genre; for example, I offer free self-publishing workshop/signings to libraries, bookstores, writing and arts organizations, colleges, and universities as my primary promotion activity.

NOTE: *These promotional efforts will be repeated periodically as part of the personal promotion program outlined in Chapter X.*

E. PARTICIPATION IN PMA CO-OP MARKETING PROGRAMS (MONTHS 28-29)

Now is the time for contacting the PMA to participate in their marketing and direct-mail programs to public libraries and book reviewers. The programs are delivered 45-60 days after the submission deadlines. Participating in these two programs at this time in the promotion process will reinforce the credibility of your direct approaches to libraries, and enhance the effectiveness of the review-book promotion program outlined in Chapter IX.

In general, one or more PMA marketing programs go out each month to libraries, bookstores, book reviewers, and defined target markets. The mailings have copy deadlines and submission requirements. There are two types of submissions: flyers and information blocks for catalogs.

From 3,500 to 4,300 two-sided, 8.5 X 11-inch flyers are required for the various library co-op mailings. The flyers can be elaborate or simple; it's up to you. PMA will send you samples of recent flyers as well as catalog pages; send an e-mail request to info@pma-online.org/. You can reformat the flyer information to create a one-page general information brochure as part of the review-book presentation suggested in Chapter IX.

An information block is required for inclusion in newsletter-type color catalogs mailed to bookstores, book reviewers (with return cards that come directly to you), and defined target markets such as fiction/mystery, business/career, travel, lifestyle/men's and women's issues. The information block consists of a 100-word description of your book, a 300-ppi cmyk (a color separation option in most image creation software) TIF file of the front cover at two inches tall, and book information, including ISBN, price, number of pages, and distributors and wholesalers.

Each program is sent at least four times per year; the costs range from $180 to $330. This is the most punch for the buck in the marketplace. PMA is respected, at the top of its field, and in business to perform for the small guys—you and me.

Current details about the programs can be found at PMA's website, http://www.pma-online.org/, or in the midsection of their monthly newsletter.

F. GALLEY-BOOK REVIEW PROMOTION (MONTHS 28-29)

This is show time, and a very important promotional step. The primary purpose is to obtain significant review blurbs to place in the final book before it goes to the printer.

Remember, book reviews, articles, even brief mentions are the single most important objective of any promotion plan, and they are free.

Even mediocre comments in print can often be used to add impetus to your book's success through crafty insertion of bits and pieces in your different promotional efforts. The good blurbs and testimonials are priceless as unbiased market barometers, and can be candidates for inclusion in the front pages of your book, and/or the front and back covers.

Secondary purposes of the galley-book review promotion include cultivating professional relationships, developing general market exposure, continuing to explore interest in book-club and catalog sales, and obtaining promotional ammunition to help sell your book to different market segments such as libraries. If you choose, this is the time to expose your book to agents and editors in the publishing industry.

The eight-week process calls for designing creative invitations, e-mailing and faxing the invitations to promotional lists, following up by telephone, and creatively packaging your galley-book for review.

1. PREPARE AND DELIVER GALLEY REVIEW INVITATIONS

Prepare the galley-book review invitations and deliver them to appropriate lists first by e-mail and then by fax. I set 100 galley-review commitments as the objective for this promotion. The cost of the invitation process is miniscule, and your success will be in proportion to your construction creativity and follow-up persistence.

THE PROCEDURE

Schedule group e-mails and faxes in your master promotion log for appropriate lists you've compiled. Assigning a code number to each promotion, and inserting it in the subject line of e-mails and faxes and as an extension of the zip code in your return mailing address, enables tracking of the promotions even when respondents elect to use postal-mail.

DRAFTING

Draft the review invitations in your word-processing software and save the files. Later, copy and paste them, or import them directly, into Outlook and WinFax PRO 10.0 for sending to contact lists you have imported into those software programs.

NOTE: In the case of Word, the fax and e-mail invitations can be sent directly by selecting File>Send to>Mail Recipient (or Fax Recipient). The communication goes directly into a new e-mail window in Outlook, or fax window in WinFax PRO (if you have that software), ready for you to select recipients from your imported lists.

CONTENT

The faxes and e-mails should be concise, professional, and provide real news as well as the invitation to review. The subject line is vitally important. It is the first item read, and in the case of e-mail it must cause the reader to open the message or read the two-line thumbnail at the beginning of the body. It's common practice for editors to enable the thumbnail for inbox messages in their management software. So, this makes the first two lines in the body of the invitation the next most important consideration. In the remaining body of the invitation, include expansion of the news angle and hooks, your best testimonials to date, and other key book information.

Keep the invitation to one page for e-mails. For faxes, I suggest using only the cover page; it's less expensive to send and eliminates the possibility of pages subsequently being separated. I've outlined an example below:

- Subject: I like to link the review invitation to a short news zinger or book tagline or hook, for example: "Galley-Review Invitation—Cancer may be finished," "Galley-Review Invitation—Where Did We Come From?" "Galley-Review Invitation—The Garden That Saves Lives."

- Thumbnail: Place the heart of the news angle, your most powerful book tagline or hook, or your best review testimonial in no more than three lines at the beginning of the message body.

- Remaining body (before the book information): After the thumbnail, expand on the news angle, weave in all the book taglines and hooks in a riveting fashion, quote testimonials, and tie in applicable author credentials.

- Book description: Title, author, publisher, distributor, wholesaler, vendor of record, format (trade paperback, hardback), number of pages, projected official publication date, price.

- Galley-book format and delivery: Here you define the galley-book format alternatives and delivery options to be selected. (See the "Format and Costs" section below.)
- Instructions for replying: At the bottom of the message, above the request form, direct the e-mail recipients to select Reply, fill in the request form, and send. Instruct fax recipients to fax or mail back the completed request form. Don't forget to list your mailing address.

  As an option in both the e-mails and faxes, offer a special webpage URL for a request form for the galley-book. In the e-mail, the URL can be hyperlinked.

- Galley-book request form: Include lines for the reviewer's name, title, organization, fax number, confirmation telephone number, e-mail address, mailing address, and selection boxes for format and delivery alternatives.
- Attribution-signature: Insert or copy your attribution-signature at the end. This contains direction to your website for important background support. (See Chapter X for an example attribution-signature.)

NOTE: *Learning how to draft creative promotional pieces, such as announcements, press releases, review articles, book reviews, sales offers, review invitations, newsletters, agent and editor query letters, is an important part of a self-publisher's education. Do your homework so you know the structuring, content, and drafting techniques that have worked for others in the past. The references and resources I use on a day-to-day basis are listed in Chapter II.*

E-MAILING

The first mailing is to all the contacts with e-mail addresses in lists you've compiled and selected. It took me the better part of a week to import the lists into Outlook one at a time, and execute broadcast e-mails. The amount of time it takes you will be based on any restrictions your e-mail services provider places on the number of recipients allowed per e-mail and the total number of e-mails you may send in a given (usually 24-hour) period. The following are generic instructions for preparing to send a broadcast e-mail using Outlook:

- Create a folder named Temporary as a sub-folder of the Contacts folder by right clicking on the Contacts folder for the option.

- Import a prepared, comma-separated text file, Access file, or Excel file into the new Temporary sub-folder by going to File, selecting Import Export, and following the wizard instructions.

- Then, when the list is finished importing, you are ready to choose this new Temporary folder when you select the BCC header line for inserting contacts in the broadcast e-mail.

- Create your e-mail message (or select one you have previously drafted and saved in the Drafts folder) for the list you've imported into the Temporary folder. Select (click) the BCC header for the message. This causes all the contacts folders and sub-folders to show as selections. Choose the Temporary folder—the names will then display in the window. Then select the first name and hold the shift key down as you scroll the list until you've selected the number of names you want. The names will be outlined. Then click on Add and OK. When you do that, you return to your e-mail message and the addresses and/or names show in the BCC header.

- Now you're ready to send the e-mails. Each contact will receive a personal e-mail.

In preparing for a broadcast e-mail, I draft tailored e-mail messages to each of the different lists I plan to import into Outlook. An easy way to do this is by customizing the subject line and first two lines of the body, leaving the rest of the body standard. Draft messages can be saved in the Drafts folder of Outlook, waiting for you to edit and send them out, by closing (saving) the draft at the top right X on the page, or in File—without clicking on the Send button. The draft e-mail goes automatically to the Drafts folder.

To help keep the messages organized, you can enter a descriptor in the "To" line of a message so it further identifies itself in the Drafts folder. Sub-folders to house draft messages by topic are easily created by a right click on the Drafts folder. By right clicking messages, you can move them to other folders. Later, you delete the descriptors and edit the subject line when you add addresses to a draft message.

If you send e-mail to a large list, you may have to use the same e-mail message many times, especially if your e-mail provider has limits on the number of recipients for individual messages and/or limits on the total number of recipients you can send to in a given day. Copies can be easily made of messages in Drafts folders by highlighting a message, going to Edit, copying, and pasting—or by right clicking the message, selecting Copy to Folder and then selecting the same Drafts folder.

NOTE: In Outlook, if you elect in Tools>Options>General tab>Mail Format to check the box for using Microsoft Word to edit e-mail messages, you'll have access to the broader formatting capabilities of Word for creating e-mail messages.

FAXING

A week later, begin faxing to your selected lists. Create the lists by sorting out the contacts who have fax numbers. This can be done directly in an Outlook Contact folder by clicking on the Fax Number header at the top of the information page; this sorts the contacts that have fax numbers all together so you can select those contacts, right click, and Move them to a sub-folder you've created in Contacts.

Lists and sub-lists you've organized in Outlook Contact folders, or have ready as comma-separated lists from another location on your computer, are imported as phonebooks in WinFax PRO. When you are ready to send a fax, you select the appropriate phonebook for the recipients.

WinFax PRO allows you to schedule faxes at night while you sleep. So, if you are sending to 20 lists totaling 5,000 faxes, and you're organized, it should take about ten days to get all the faxes out. My current cost of faxing is around $0.05/minute out of state, using the services of my long-distance provider, http://www.americom.com/. From my experience, a one-page fax (a well-designed cover page) takes under a minute to complete. So 5,000 faxes would cost about $250.

2. COMPILING THE GALLEY-BOOK REVIEW LIST

The Galley-book Review List is compiled by adding invitation responses to an Automatic Deliveries List, and supplemented by successful results from the telephone follow-up program outlined below. The list should contain: name of the reviewer, organization affiliation, e-mail address, mail delivery address, telephone number, and fax number.

The Automatic Deliveries List is comprised of your list of super major reviewers and contacts sorted by importance-indicator (indicating automatic mailing of the galley-book review presentation and/or the review-book presentation—see the next chapter) from the lists you compiled in Chapter II of major distributors, wholesalers, syndicated reviews and feature writers, magazines, book clubs, catalog organizations, and publishers. For this book, the automatic deliveries list totaled 84.

3. TELEPHONE FOLLOW-UP PROGRAM

The purpose of the telephone follow-up program is to generate galley-book review commitments and awareness by the most important book-review editors, media editors in your local market, experts in your subject and/or genre, and executives of major membership organizations involved with the subject or genre of your book.

Test your telephone techniques in the local market first, and make adjustments before you take on the rest of the telephone-call program. (See the next section for telephone techniques.)

My objective is to generate 50 firm review commitments from the following:

- Automatic deliveries list.
- Local market-area media organizations.
- Genre/subject industry movers and shakers.
- Major authors and experts in the genre/subject.
- Other major organizations.

Before initial telephone contacts, visit websites to verify contact names, gather related contact information, look over appropriate submission guidelines, and get familiar with these organizations and key contacts so you will be knowledgeable when you call (I create contact records in Outlook and take notes).

AUTOMATIC DELIVERIES LIST

Call on all the organizations defined in this list (see above).

LOCAL MARKET AREA

Identify the major newspapers, magazines, organizations related to your book subject or genre, and major library systems located in your state of residence (about 40 for this book in Florida). As a local, you should have an advantage in securing reviews and articles.

NOTE: In my state of residence, calling on individual library systems and writing organizations also allows me to introduce my free, self-publishing workshop/signings.

MOVERS AND SHAKERS

These key industry individuals should be identified in your list of book-related organizations by an importance-indicator data-line. For this book, I identified 25—and 45 for my upcoming fiction book.

MAJOR AUTHORS AND EXPERTS

Out of 100 contacts in my Major Authors list for my upcoming fiction book, I only found 4 telephone numbers and 26 mailing addresses. For this book my list was shorter, about 25 author/experts, and I had telephone numbers and addresses for them all because they were business professionals involved day to day with the activities of self-publishing.

If you have telephone numbers, call them. Alternatively, mail a personal note, referencing your previous invitation, and politely ask them to e-mail back or telephone you with the information you need to deliver the galley-book review presentation.

Acquiring e-mail addresses, let alone telephone numbers for major authors, is almost impossible without persistence with personal notes (use creative envelopes), a little luck, and a few referrals you can stumble on by asking questions whenever you're networking.

MAJOR PUBLISHERS

Including major publishers in your telephone-call program can be an interesting opportunity to see if you can hook somebody's attention. The chances are not with you, but who can tell? It might behoove you to try several very senior people in each organization with a variety of approaches to attempt to stimulate interest in your book. Tell them succinctly what they are missing. What do you have to lose? Whatever the outcome, send a provoking e-mail or postal-mail follow-up message, and of course, try to drive them to your website. I identified about 28 publishers for my upcoming fiction book and four for this book.

NOTE: These contacts are set up in my list of publishers to receive automatic galley-book and review-book copies of my upcoming fiction book whether the invitations or telephone calls are successful or not.

OTHER MAJOR ORGANIZATIONS

Other major organizations that review books deserve attention in the quest for galley-book review commitments. If they have interest, most of the media suggested here will probably be more receptive to the actual book when it's available for review. (See the next chapter for this promotional phase.) But it's positive PR to make these contacts now, and lay the groundwork for follow-up when the review-book is ready. I include the following organizations interested in books: the Associated Press; UPI; CNN; ABC; AARP; National Public Radio; appropriate TV shows, for example: C-SPAN, C-SPAN 2, Oxygen, and major talk shows; the 50 largest daily newspapers in North America; and the 20 largest library systems in North America.

4. TELEPHONE TECHNIQUES

It will likely be difficult to get to the right person quickly or on your first attempt. Be patient and persistent in winning opportunities to introduce yourself. Some techniques to consider in developing a successful approach—success meaning the opportunity to speak to the right person and completing the call—are: grabbing attention, delivering a gripping 30-second tell-and-sell, knowing when to courteously sign-off, establishing rapport with support personnel, and keeping contact notes for future reference.

GRAB ATTENTION

Tailor approaches to individual contacts. You will probably start out talking to voice-mail or an assistant. Here's an example of a voice-mail approach:

Hi, Mr. Jones, this is so and so. I write sci-tech-mystery-thrillers (your compelling tagline). It's about receiving my galley-book. My invitation to review must be in your slush pile. I know you're busy, but I ask you to grant me 30 seconds to go on stage. Please favor me with a call back at 000-000-0000.

If you leave other voice-mail messages, make them completely different, and keep trying. In the case of the New York and Los Angeles newspapers, Dan Poynter tells us in *The Self-Publishing Manual* we may have to sharpen up our begging skills.

If you have to get through to people who are screening calls, one technique I've used is to refer to something outside of the book-review business to get attention; for example—and I only mean these to spark your own creativity: confirming lunch, or the meeting; picking the person up; verifying receipt of the tickets; etc. Make up your own recipes for unusual messages that get through, but with just enough coquettish creativity that you don't spark alarm or animosity.

If by chance you get a return call from your unorthodox and semi-devious techniques, you should be prepared to mend the inevitable wound, for example:

I apologize if I misled you. I so much wanted just an iota of your time. I know how busy you are and harassed. I thought I needed to be outrageous to compete for your attention. Please accept my apology and allow me go on stage with my 30-second spiel.

Once you've got your quarry on the line and get an okay for the 30-second tell-and-sell, you can relax, knowing you have been given the go-ahead to do it your way and quickly.

DEVELOP A 30-SECOND TELL-AND-SELL

This is a summary of what you want to get across; you should be prepared with this on your first call, just in case you get who you're after the first time you call. This spiel is something you will find of value in day-to-day conversation, media interviews, and speaking engagements.

The spiel should weave in your developed taglines and sales hooks, answer the key question of why your book is so important that people should buy it, and include the storyline (30-word plot description). If your conversation gives you more time than the 30-second tell-and-sell, be prepared to bring up three presentation points expanding your answer to the key question—points that are supported by facts, stories, analogies, and direct experience—to convince the potential reviewer that you and your book are news. Practice your delivery to take full advantage of opportunities to present.

SIGN OFF QUICKLY

As soon as you finish your spiel, ask for the review. If yes, confirm delivery information and format for the galley-book review presentation (see discussion of alternative formats below), and get an e-mail address for sending a shipping notification. Say goodbye and thanks in a memorable way. You want the reviewer to remember your name or the name of your book. Parting ideas might be to say: *Please watch for our notification e-mail; it will have xxxxxx (something quirky) in the subject. We should be able to get it out tonight. I'll wrap the CD with a green ribbon and send it Priority Mail.*

Immediately send the galley-book review presentation by the means and format agreed; never lose momentum.

RAPPORT WITH REVIEWER ASSISTANTS

It can be important to develop rapport with an editor's secretary or assistant, the person who screens the editor's postal-mail, faxes, even e-mail. As soon as you succeed in obtaining permission to send the galley-book review presentation, call the secretary or assistant, introduce yourself, instill awareness of the format and delivery method for the requested galley-book review presentation, and make the person realize that the editor is expecting delivery. It's a good idea to verify the following key information, making him or her feel responsible, important, and vested in the process:

- Correct spelling of the full names of the editor and the secretary or assistant.

- Special department or floor number as part of the mailing address.
- Fax number.
- Private telephone numbers for both the editor and the secretary or assistant.
- E-mail addresses of both for delivery notification.

NOTE: Should you run across contacts that don't review galleys, make sure you deliver a pitch for receiving the finished book for review as soon as it's available (about three months). If the editor agrees to review at that time, go to the secretary or assistant and request the same information as above—then e-mail the editor and the support person periodically, short one liners restating the delivery date; this will keep this important "yes" fresh.

FOLLOW-UP NOTES

I suggest following up all telephone contacts the same day with short, personal e-mail and/or postal-mail notes of thanks—something upbeat but professional—even to the negative ones. I suggest sending them to the editor as well as the support person. The e-mail note can be in the form of a card you design, or you can use one of the free greeting card services available through the Internet, for example: http://www.greetings.yahoo.com/, http://www.bluemountain.com/, and http://www.e-cards.com/. For more, search the Web for free greeting cards.

Follow-up notes are another prime promotional opportunity to create positive image and continue to develop relationships. Sending both e-mail and postal-mail spreads out the contacts by a few days, adding positive reminders of your call.

5. GALLEY-BOOK REVIEW PRESENTATION

Galley reviews are critically important because of the need to add testimonials and positive blurbs to your book during final edit. This makes the content and packaging of the galley-book review presentation important. Consideration of format options, other than hard copy, and associated costs will be important for self-publishers on limited budgets.

DELIVERING THE GALLEY PRESENTATION

Preparing and delivering the galley-book review presentations takes place as you go through the invitation process. Some of the super major reviewers will automatically receive the presentation as soon as it's ready. Other presentations will be delivered as you receive accepted invitations or successfully complete telephone follow-up calls.

Remember, book reviewing is a business. This is what professional reviewers do to make a living. They have to be turned on—motivated—to review a book; this is your job, to turn them on. It's not the time to be shy. It's a time to be creative and persistent, but with respectful courtesy. You will not be refused in the end. You may be rebuffed, but if you keep coming back, no matter how many times, with a humorous or light-hearted slant, never leaving sour notes, the door will open. Send flowers if you have to.

Also, remember that review of self-published books by most of the super majors, like *School Library Journal, Library Journal,* and *Kirkus Reviews* has not been commonly practiced. But this is changing; and it will change all the faster by the positive impact you make through professional and creative communications.

CONTENTS

Besides the book, the galley-book review presentation should contain a cover letter, a general information brochure, and photographs.

COVER LETTER

Create a short (no more than one page), concise cover letter to the reviewer/editor that:

- References your telephone follow-up call to the review invitation—whether or not one actually took place (I use a "Re:" line for this).
- Gives thanks for the coming review.
- Reintroduces the book, taglines, and hooks.
- Reiterates the book/author tie-ins to news values, and restates the book's importance to readers.

- Offers your personal telephone number and e-mail address for questions.
- Drives any need for more information to your website and names the most important background support, for example, your media kit.
- Requests a clip of the article/review by e-mail, fax, or postal-mail (that contact information should be part of your stationery header and/or footer).

GENERAL INFORMATION BROCHURE

The general information brochure (flyer) I create is black and white, on 8.5 X 11-inch, 100 bright, #24 white stock, folded on the short side one time (four working sides—sometimes called book fold in the Page Setup or wizard choice in some word-processing programs and in most design software). I create this piece in newsletter/column format, using a wizard or template in Publisher.

The brochure can be derived from the flyers prepared for the PMA co-op library mailing programs, and should be included in your media kit and presented on your website. This brochure/flyer can be an extremely cost-effective, general sales piece, for example, as a handout at workshops or a mailer insert. I suggest the following content:

- Book information: page count, cover, binding, size, ISBN, Library of Congress PCN, price.
- A summary of your promotional plan.
- Quarter-sized, black-and-white pictures of the front and back covers.
- The best review blurbs and testimonials to date.
- All the book taglines and sales hooks you've dreamed up.
- A short-form synopsis.
- Author bio and picture.
- Description of the book's importance to readers and tie-ins to current news and trends.

- Publisher and author contact information.
- Purchase sources, for example: distributor, wholesalers, vendor of record, online bookstores and posting sites, and your website.
- Direction to your website for background information (list the primary topics).

The cost is minimal. Have the two-sided brochure/flyer printed and folded at a local print shop for around $70/1,000. Put a couple of brochures between pages of the galley-book.

PHOTOGRAPHS

Enclose 4 X 5-inch, black-and-white or glossy color photographs of the book's front and back covers and author headshot. Consider adding a full body shot of the author—editors like to have a picture that shows personality. Recent quotes at local printers were around $90/1,000.

If the number of presentations you intend to deliver is relatively small, you could order duplicate 4 X 5s from the negatives at a local photo-processing center.

PACKAGING MATERIALS AND CONSTRUCTION

I use free U.S. Postal Service Priority Mail envelopes. They come in various sizes of cardboard flats and boxes; or you can elect to pay for packaging envelopes.

To accomplish the goal of getting recipients to open the galley-book review presentation package, I use an 8.5 X 11-inch, Priority Mail cardboard mailer, strapped with colored tape like a Christmas present. I design catchy stickers (Avery 2-inch diameter) in Publisher to identify and resell the contents, and put one on each side of the packet. I use large, 4 X 6-inch address labels designed in Publisher with my business logo, header, and the same border I use in all the promotional materials. I address them individually by hand with permanent-color ink markers.

FORMAT COSTS AND DELIVERY

The galley-book review presentation can be:

- Hard copy, with a trade paperback as the galley-book in the presentation, and delivered by postal-mail.
- Computer files, created in word-processing programs like Word, and delivered as Word and/or PDF files attached to e-mail messages, or placed on a special page of your website for download by requesting reviewers.
- Computer files and/or PDF files written on CD-Rs and postal-mailed.

Total costs and delivery by U.S. Postal Service Priority Mail vary from about $4.60 for a CD-R to around $9.35 for a hard copy. I recommend the additional cost of Priority Mail service, because as Dan Poynter says in *The Self-Publishing Manual*, "...if you do not attach some importance to your package, you cannot expect the reviewer to."

HARD COPY

I recently priced a trade paperback galley-book run of 100 for 144-450 pages at $2.50-$5.00 per copy, including delivery to my address. (See the section on the galley-book in Chapter VI.) Using a free Priority Mail envelope, and allowing $0.50 for the costs of stationery, the general information brochure, colored strapping, two photos, two stickers, and an address label, the total cost of a galley-book review presentation should be in the range of $6.85-$9.35, assuming you use Priority Mail (currently $3.85 each for under a pound).

COMPUTER FILES AS ATTACHMENTS TO E-MAIL OR POSTED AT YOUR WEBSITE

To date, sending galley-books or support documents like media kits, book presentations, flyers, and photographs to reviewers as attachments to e-mail is not acceptable practice unless the reviewer has made a specific request.

This delivery means is inhibited by many factors, a few of which are:

- Many free e-mail service providers restrict e-mail attachments, for example, the maximum attachment size at Yahoo! was recently 1.5 MB. With the purchase of a premium service at a nominal cost, for example, $4.95 per month at Yahoo!, the limit could be upped to 5.0 MB.

- Recipient network restrictions or personal computer settings may restrict receipt of attachments altogether.
- The increasing sophistication and proliferation of viruses discourage many users from downloading attachments.

My galley-book review invitations offer reviewers the contents of the galley-book review presentation as a PDF file download located on a special page at my website. The file has a hyperlinked table of contents. When I receive a review request from an invitation or a positive response from my telephone follow-up call program, and the reviewer has elected to download the presentation at my website, I send a confirmation e-mail. The e-mail contains the password for opening the PDF file, a hyperlinked URL to the special page, and a note that the media kit is also available there for download.

The good news is that the cost of using this delivery method is limited to the time it takes to organize and set it up on your website. The bad news is that editors may perceive it as more of a hassle than a time saver.

CD-R DISCS

Using CD-Rs is another delivery option for the galley-book review presentation. Most personal computers are now sold with CD-RW drives for writing to CD-Rs and CD-RWs. If your computer doesn't have one, exterior CD-RW hard drives cost around $150 at office-supply stores and even less online.

Designing labels for CDs and jewel cases is typically a capability offered in software that operates a CD-RW drive. But if you prefer, you can buy a simple CD kit at an office supply store for around $25, or use Publisher to design labels. The cost per CD is about $0.22 for the CD label, $0.18 for the CD case (I use the compact slim cases at about $18/100), $0.10 for an ID label, and $0.25 for the CD-R—totaling about $0.75 each plus postage ($3.85 U.S. Postal Service Priority Mail).

A CD-R contains around 700 MB of useable space, more than you will probably ever need for a galley-book review presentation. I write (copy) the master PDF file of the galley-book review presentation, the media kit PDF file, and a Word file of the cover letter on the CD-R.

Deliver the galley-book review presentations using Priority Mail and the free, 8.5 X 11-inch cardboard Priority Mail envelopes (not a CD-sized mailer—they can get lost or stolen easily). Use colored wrapping tape, stickers, and labels to draw attention just as I outlined for the packaging of a hard-copy presentation. The only other item in the packet beside the CD-R will be a hard copy of the cover letter, and perhaps a front cover photo, to make sure your reviewer becomes quickly oriented.

6. TELEPHONE FOLLOW-UP TO GALLEY-BOOK DELIVERIES

Follow up with telephone calls to each recipient. Be polite, and ask only for confirmation that the presentation has been received. The more polite you are, the more impact your follow-up call will have on a reviewer's memory. Most of these organizations have some sort of "Received Galley" log. If you've adhered to the plan, then except for some of the super majors, chances are good you've already spoken with the reviewer and a support person once. In all cases, I recommend you persevere until you have a confirmation of receipt.

G. BOOK REGISTRATIONS AND LISTINGS (MONTHS 28-29)

During these two months, make the following applications and submissions as part of the accepted processes in printing and announcing a book to the publishing industry. Much of the information in this section has been condensed from *Document 112, Poynter's Secret List of Book Promotion Contacts*. A current edition is available at nominal cost from Dan Poynter at his website, http://www.parapublishing.com/.

1. ISBN AND SAN

The International Standard Book Number (ISBN): Order a block of ten ISBNs from the International Standard Book Numbering Agency, an R.R. Bowker business, 121 Chanlon Road, New Providence, NJ 07974. Telephone: 800-521-8110 or 908-665-6770. Fax: 908-665-2895. Request a Title Output Information Request form, their standard instruction sheet, and *Major Issues in the Implementation of the ISBN*. The cost for the ISBN block is $225. Expect a three-week delivery time.

You may complete the application forms and order online by charge-card at http://www.isbn.org/. If you opt to transact this business online, the receipt of the ISBNs comes in a few days by e-mail.

The ISBN is printed on the copyright page of the book and at the bottom of the back cover or jacket, above or below the bar code, in OCR-B typeface. You will need to assign an ISBN to your book to submit to PMA co-op marketing programs or post a book for sale at Amazon.com and other online bookstores, so get your block of numbers in plenty of time.

It is important to realize that ownership of the ISBN defines an author/self-publisher as a real publisher. Publishers who own ISBNs control the information that's available to the book trade about a book through a free account established at R. R. Bowker's website, http://www.bowker.com/. Click on Add/Update in *Books in Print* and then Publisher's Authority Database. By establishing an account at the website, you can create, add, and edit publisher and book information using input forms on the site. The information you provide on the forms goes immediately into the *Books in Print* database available online to Bowker book trade clients worldwide. This service is utilized by a majority of bookstores and libraries worldwide to access information about a book, find a distributor, vendor of record, wholesaler, and direct publisher contact information in facilitating book purchases. The information is also automatically inputted into Bowker's monthly hard copy and CD updates to *Books in Print* provided in other services to the book trade and publishing industry.

The Standard Address Number (SAN): The SAN for your publishing business is a seven-digit, universal industry address identifier. The issuing agency suggests that it become a part of your business address, appearing at the top left above the business name in all communication modes. The cost is $150, and further information and purchase forms are available through http://www.bowker.com/.

2. BAR CODE

After receipt of the ISBN block, order a Bookland, EAN/13 bar code with price extension—order the small one—at a cost of $10-30 from one of the following:

- Fotel: 41 West Home Avenue, Villa Park, IL 60181. Telephone:

Phase I Promotion

800-834-4920. Fax: 630-834-5250. Fax-on-demand: 800-815-5885.

- Film Masters: 2301 Hamilton Avenue, Cleveland, OH 44114. Telephone: 800-621-2872 or 216-621-2633. Fax: 800-230-3456.
- General Graphics: P.O. Box 3192-A, Arnold, PA 15068. Telephone: 800-887-5894. Fax: 412-337-6589.
- Precision Photography, Inc: 1150 North Tustin Avenue, Anaheim, CA 92807. Telephone: 714-632-9000.
- PMA, http://www.pma-online.org/, and SPAN, http://www.spannet.org/, both have discounts in place for members purchasing bar codes. (See the "Member Benefits" pages on their websites.)

The bar code is incorporated into a book's back-cover design, on the lower half, usually at the bottom on the right-hand side for hardcover and trade paperbacks. The bar code comes to you in 3-5 days as a print and/or a negative (see if you can get both at the same cost). Downloads are now available online at some service-provider websites.

Many provider websites post information on this topic to keep publisher and printer clients up to date. Or, you can order a copy of *Machine-Readable Coding Guidelines for the U.S. Book Industry* ($7.50) from The Book Industry Study Group, 160 Fifth Avenue, #604, New York, NY 10010. Telephone: 212-929-1393 or 212-989-7542. Fotel (above) may provide a free copy.

3. ABI AND *BOOKS IN PRINT*

Advanced Book Information (ABI) Form: Call the ABI Department of R.R. Bowker Co., 800-521-8110 or 908-464-6800. Request an *ABI Guide Book* and half a dozen ABI forms; they're free. This form is for required information inputted in the publication of *Books in Print, Guide to Books in Print, Forthcoming Books,* and several other specialized directories published by Bowker. *Books in Print* is published annually in October. Bowker will send a computer-generated ABI checklist every other month to keep listings up-to-date; these must be filled out accurately and sent in each time to keep your business and books from being de-listed, even if there have been no changes.

NOTE: It is unclear at this writing as to whether the online information forms accessible at Bowker's website are automatically utilized in updating these publications.

In the *Self-Publishing Manual*, Dan Poynter suggests submission of the ABI form six months prior to the book's official publication date. But he indicates self-publishers may be better off waiting until a book goes to the printer because of the many little delays typical of the first time around—and you don't want to get into the Bowker system prematurely.

4. LIBRARY OF CONGRESS CATALOG CARD NUMBER

Contact the Copyright Office, Library of Congress, Washington, DC 20540. Call 202-707-6372 and ask for two free publication/applications: *Procedures for Securing Pre-assigned Library of Congress Catalog Card Numbers* and *Request of Pre-assignment of the Library of Congress Control Number (LCCN)* (Form 607-7). Or, you may now download these from the Library of Congress website, http://www.loc.gov/.

The LCCN is assigned to the work itself, not the edition; it appears on the copyright page of the book. Be advised that you can't complete the application until you have an ISBN. There's no charge for this service. Worldwide, 20,000+ libraries subscribe to the catalog card service and to *The National Union Catalogue,* issued four times/year by the Library of Congress. Many libraries order all the Library of Congress catalogued books, making it important to acquire the LCCN. However, most small publishers and self-publishers can't utilize the process described above, but can use a new program discussed below.

CIP/PCN programs: Go to the Library of Congress website, http://www.loc.gov/, click on Search at the top of the home page, and search for CIP/PCN programs. Check out the eligibility requirements for the CIP (Cataloging in Publication) and PCN (Preassigned Control Number) programs. Both programs are fully facilitated with application procedures on the website.

Self-publishers and most small publishers who publish works by only one or two authors are ineligible for the CIP program. However, self-publishers can apply for the PCN Program; the whole process takes about a month. It includes:

- Applying to enter the program online at the Library of Congress website.
- Issuing by the Library of Congress of an ID and password sent to you by e-mail.
- Using your ID and password to enter the Library of Congress webpage to fill out a PCN Application.
- Waiting for the Library of Congress to e-mail you an assigned Library of Congress Control Number (LCCN).

This relatively new processing system appears to replace and vastly simplify the old procedures. You can even get your PCN prior to assigning an ISBN to the book.

5. PUBLISHERS DIRECTORY

Request an application form for a free listing from the Gale Research Company, 27500 Drake Road, Farmington Hills, MI 48331-3553. Telephone: 313-961-2242.

6. SMALL PRESS RECORD OF BOOKS IN PRINT

This publication of books in print by small publishers is published as a CD-ROM. Request an application form from Dustbooks, P.O. Box 100-P, Paradise, CA 95967. Telephone: 530-877-6110. It's free. If you're a member of Publishers Marketing Association, Dustbooks automatically sends you the form in the mail.

International Directory of Little Magazines and Small Presses: Request an application from Dustbooks, also free.

7. PUBLISHERS TRADE LIST ANNUAL

This is an R.R. Bowker publication used by the publishing industry to announce books. For information and a rate card, call R.R. Bowker, 800-521-8110 or 908-464-6800.

8. PUBLISHERS, DISTRIBUTORS AND WHOLESALERS OF THE UNITED STATES

Contact R.R. Bowker (above) for listing information requirements; this is also free.

9. PUBLISHERS' INTERNATIONAL ISBN DIRECTORY

This is published by K.G. Saur Publishing Company (Bowker subsidiary), 121 Chanlon Road, New Providence, NJ 07974. Telephone: 800-521-8110 or 908-464-6800. When a publisher purchases a block of ISBN's, it is automatically included in the directory at no cost.

10. ABA BOOK BUYER'S HANDBOOK

You need to have three books published to qualify for listing. This handbook is used by bookstores to find publisher shipping, discount, STOP (cash with the order: a Single Title Order Plan used by bookstores), and return policy information. For an application contact the American Booksellers Association, 828 South Broadway, Tarrytown, NY 10591. Telephone: 914-591-2665 or 800-637-0037. Fax: 914-591-2720. Listings are free.

11. LITERARY MARKET PLACE

Published by Information Today, Inc. You must publish at least three books a year to get a free listing. Request an application (see http://infotodayinc.com/ for information).

12. CONTEMPORARY AUTHORS

Published by the Gale Research Company (see above for contact information), this directory contains some 91,000 biographical sketches. Call for the application. Listing is free. Write as much detail as you like because they print everything you write. Keep a copy as an effective, credible, handout.

13. POLICIES OF PUBLISHERS: A HANDBOOK FOR ORDER LIBRARIANS

For listing requirements, contact Scarecrow Press, 4720 Boston Way, Lanham, MD 20706. Telephone: 301-459-3366.

CHAPTER IX: Phase II Promotion (Months 30-31)

During these two months you should: send out your second sales offers to individuals and libraries, invite reviewers and syndicators to review your final book or write news articles around its story, post the book for sale at major online bookstores, organize your fulfillment supplies, and begin the continuous process of delivering review copies and fulfilling book orders.

A. SECOND SALES OFFERS TO INDIVIDUAL POTENTIAL BUYER LISTS (MONTH 30)

Change the subject line of your first e-mail offer and the slant of the short message in this second offer to your Individual Potential Buyer lists. I suggest offering—for a limited time—a discounted, autographed copy of the book, along with a complimentary e-book (PDF file you create—see below), or other writing products you've created. Cite reasons to go to your website for other giveaways; for instance, offer free PDF chapter-downloads of an upcoming book, a subscription to your newsletter, a free coolie cup, or a discounted t-shirt.

B. SECOND SALES OFFERS TO LIBRARIES (MONTH 30)

Using the same approach as you did for the first offer to libraries, send e-mails and faxes to the directors and selection librarians. These limited-time discount offers on autographed copies should also include another invitation to review the book, but this time it will be the final book (you could offer the PDF e-book on CD-R, or the actual trade paperback, depending on your budget).

I design the e-mail to include a hyperlink to a general information brochure on my website, a similar piece used to participate in the PMA co-op marketing program to libraries. (See Section E, Chapter VIII.) For the fax, I keep it to one page and include as much of the zip from the general information brochure as space allows.

Large numbers of book sales are not anticipated from these prerelease offers. It's an opportunity to solidify the professional image of the book, author, and publishing business, and to reinforce the recent arrival of the PMA co-op marketing flyer for the book. It may also generate positive review testimonials for posting on your website or inclusion in future library promotions.

I recommend telephone follow-up with a dozen or so major library systems in North America, and all the library systems in your state of residence, to help bolster and cement recognition of you and your works, increase the potential for sales, and give you a chance to re-offer the book for review. Each library sale to good-sized library systems will give you increased promotional power. For me, in my state of residence, it's also an opportunity to continue promotion of my free self-publishing workshop/signings.

C. FINAL BOOK EDIT, ORDERING AND RECEIVING BOOKS (MONTHS 30-31)

Select the best reviews and testimonials from the galley-review process, and along with any other editing changes, produce the final manuscript. Proofing and coordinating with the printer will stretch over the two months covered by this chapter. Your objective is to get your hands on the printed book as soon as possible. The need to deliver review-books will start building up the moment you begin sending out review-book invitations as part of the review-book promotion outlined below.

For example, the number of trade paperback books I anticipate ordering for the first printing of my upcoming fiction book is about 700 based on:

- The objective of 400 review-book presentations generated from the review-book promotion outlined below.

- An inventory level of 100 established for additional review-books as promotion continues to these all-important sources of publicity.

- Fulfillment of sales from posting the book for sale on my website well in advance of availability (50).

- A conservative number set for future sales from my website and workshop/signings (150).

There will be two initial printing runs, one for a second edition trade paperback to satisfy the above requirements, and the second for the first edition hardback (estimated at 200) to fill presales and establish inventory for future sales from my website of the registered, autographed collector's edition.

NOTE: An example of how the economics might work to your benefit with advance sales of a hardback collector's edition is as follows: At a discounted sales price of $24—discounted from the full cover price of $27.95—plus $1.50 each for packaging and shipping, if you sold 250 copies in advance, you could pay for a run of 500 (estimated cost of short-run digital printing of $11 each for a 450 page book), leaving you with 250 books in prepaid inventory plus around $125 in cash.

For the 450-page, second-edition trade paperback to satisfy the 700-book requirements listed in the above example, the cost from the printer at today's prices would be about $4 each, including packaging and shipping. This will probably be my largest out-of-pocket promotional expenditure, assuming I don't contract any catalog or book club sales for the trade paperback.

D. REVIEW-BOOK PROMOTION (MONTHS 30-31)

You will find it said over and over in this book, and hammered home universally by publishing professionals, that reviews are your single most important source of promotional publicity. For the financially strapped self-publisher, this is great news because access to review sources can be literally free using e-mail and at reasonable costs through faxing. It is strictly up to you and your creative abilities to catch the attention of reviewers.

Although I indicate that two months are allotted for this promotion, generating book reviews and articles is the most important ongoing promotional effort during the first year or so after a book is universally available for sale.

This promotion is similar to the galley-book review promotion; it includes sending review-book invitations, compiling the Review-book List, a telephone follow-up program to selected invitees, and preparing and sending out the review-book presentations. In addition, you will post the book for sale at the online bookstores you've selected and organize your fulfillment system.

1. SENDING REVIEW-BOOK INVITATIONS

E-mail and then fax invitations to all the reviewer lists you have compiled. If you have the funds, I recommend a postal-mailing as a third mode of contact to just the major media and reviewer/syndicators.

Like every promotional communication you send, the invitations are opportunities to create credibility for yourself, your business, and your book. Invest the amount of time necessary to create a positive and professional impact.

Use the same procedures outlined for the galley-book review invitations, designing, logging, and coding all your broadcast e-mails, faxes, and postal-mails in a master promotion log.

REVIEWER LISTS

You will use most of the same lists employed for the galley-book review invitations. For example, I include the following lists discussed in this book: national daily and weekly newspapers, national magazines that review books, major publishers, traditional book reviewers and syndicators, Internet book reviewers, catalog and book-club organizations, major paperback publishers, foreign-rights publishers, alternative newspapers, major wholesalers, major traditional publishers, print newsletters that review books, general book-related organizations, film producers and film agents, literary agents, and movers and shakers.

CONTENT OF THE E-MAIL AND FAX INVITATIONS

The content should be created and organized like the galley-book review invitations. Because this promotion is to the broad reviewer market and the hard-copy trade paperback is so expensive, I offer the review-book presentation in three different formats and delivery means as follows:

- Trade paperback and support background information delivered by postal-mail.

- A PDF e-book, and the supporting background information organized into a PDF media kit, delivered as downloads at a special page (URL) on my website.

- The PDF e-book and media kit files on a CD-R, delivered by postal-mail.

Depending on your financial resources and which list you utilize, your invitations could offer one or more of these format/delivery alternatives; for example, in the case of a general list like my Internet book reviewers list (with 700+ contacts), you might consider offering the review-book presentation only as PDF downloads from your website, or perhaps by CD-R. Or, in the case of the initial review-book list (described below) of the major reviewers, your invitation might offer all three format/delivery alternatives.

In all cases, you will develop a review-book reply/order form within the e-mail, fax, or postal-mail for providing review/editor contact and delivery information and for facilitating selection of the presentation format and delivery means.

NOTE: It bears repetition that your objective in all invitations is to drive recipients to your website where you've designed all your creative support information. There, editors can conveniently satisfy their needs, and then return to your invitation to complete and send back the review-book reply/order form by e-mail, fax, or postal-mail.

POSTAL-MAILER

Building solid relationships with the major book-review sources is a worthwhile investment, so I recommend a simultaneous postal-mailer to your initial review-book list (see the next section on its compilation) as another avenue for getting your name and message in front of this important world of reviewers. Draft the same concise, catchy content for the cover letter as you did for the e-mails and faxes. You can do a mail merge from your word-processing program for the letters and the envelopes—although I prefer to hand-address the envelopes and embellish them with stickers I design.

Along with the cover letter, enclose a general information brochure, and include a postcard version—without postage—of your review-book reply/order form. (See the "Review-Book Reply Card" discussed below.)

If you don't hand-address the #10 envelopes, I suggest putting time into an interesting, attention-getting label. For example, designing 3 or 4 X 4-inch mailing labels in Publisher allows you to include your business header information, logo, and a powerful tagline or sales hook. Using Avery-brand, one-inch-diameter stickers designed in Publisher and printed out in sheets of 12 to a page, can draw attention to the envelope front and back.

For additional identification impact, you could state "Book Review Invitation" (or any other custom wording) on the envelopes in an unusual colored font at the bottom left on the front. I use Publisher to do this by selecting the #10 envelope in Page Setup, placing the attention-getting text where I want it, and printing out the number of envelopes I need.

The postal-mailer should weigh in for the $0.37, first-class U.S. Postal Service rate. For my upcoming fiction book, the postal-mailing to my initial review-book list should end up around 420 pieces at a cost of around $155 plus the cost of contents.

2. COMPILE THE REVIEW-BOOK LIST

Compile a review-book list for contacts who will receive the review-book presentation by first sorting out all the major media editors and book reviewers identified by importance-indicator data-lines assigned to contacts in your data lists at the time you compiled them. Copy and paste them into a new comma- or tab-delineated text file or a new Access database file. In compiling this review-book list, you may find it useful to create an identifier data-line labeled Type, and make the following entries:

- P for contacts from Dan Poytner's list of majors previously cited from his booklet, *Book Reviews From Pre-publication Galleys Through a Continuing Review Program*.
- R for other major media editors and reviewers.
- OR for respondents to your invitations.
- Any additional letter-identifiers that seem helpful.

The review-book list will grow as editors and reviewers respond to the review-book invitations and the telephone follow-up program discussed below.

NOTE: Review-book invitations will be periodically repeated to nonrespondents from your lists over the next year or so as an important activity in the continuing media promotion program outlined in the next chapter.

3. TELEPHONE FOLLOW-UP PROGRAM TO INVITATIONS

I recommend beginning a disciplined telephone follow-up program to all the contacts in the review-book list, starting from the time of the first e-mail invitations. The procedure becomes an important element in the ongoing, long-term media promotion program outlined in the next chapter.

The procedures are basically the same as those utilized in the telephone follow-up program for the galley-book review invitations. Just as I suggested in that program, open your contact records in Outlook and note all calls made and actions taken.

4. PREPARING THE REVIEW-BOOK PRESENTATION

The reviews you hope to receive from these vital book-review media contacts are free; the promotional value of published reviews by the professional media is incalculable. Because of the reviews' importance, the review-book presentation must be great. The exterior should stand out as unique, compelling the editor/reviewer to open it. Assume he or she will not remember any contact you have previously made. Use your imagination. I've outlined my own approach to give you ideas and perspective. The scale of your program and method of delivery can be adjusted to fit your time, energy, and capital resources.

MATERIALS AND DESIGN

For my upcoming fiction book, *The Mountain and the Place of Knowledge,* I'll use a white, corrugated, self-seal, 7 X 10-inch mailing packet, and design an eye-catching, 5.83 X 8.27-inch Avery shipping label with business header and color logo; and I'll use the outer edges of this large label to lay in taglines and sales hooks in different colorful fonts, for example:

- Book I of the Ancestor Series.
- A sci-tech-mystery-thriller.
- Grounded in plausible reality.
- The past is not what it seems.
- The future is at risk.
- An experiential reading adventure.

The actual mailer packets cost about $67.50 for 250. Search for packaging solutions on the Internet. The Avery #3059 shipping labels are about $20 for 200.

For label design, I use Microsoft Publisher. Most word-processing programs are not adequate for this task. Some trial and error is usually required to get labels to print out properly; I ended up practicing with copy paper until I was sure the positioning would be right when I put in the real sheets of labels. You can use most common color printers to print the sheets of labels from design software. After you print out the designed labels, I recommend hand-addressing the labels with a permanent-color ink marker to increase the personalized effect.

A nice finishing touch is to put a round, 1.5-inch diameter Avery sticker on the back over the leading edge of the mailer's sealed flap as well as somewhere on the free space in the front. The sheets of stickers cost about $20 for 250; design them with clip art and text, and print them out. I want to have something attractive, unique, and attention-getting on both sides of the packet. You could even go to the extra effort of adding other artwork or lettering by hand on the mailer packets.

CONTENT

The review-book presentation consists of: the book, review slip, cover letter, general information brochure, prepublication review sheet, review-book reply card, long-form draft of a generic review article, and useful photographs. A courtesy statement requesting a copy of a review or article via e-mail, fax, or postal-mail, should be placed conspicuously on each content piece. If you don't include the statement in the piece itself, I suggest designing a sticker and placing them on the backs of the pieces or in blank spaces.

BOOK

Review-books are commonly trade paperbacks from the first run of your first edition. Buy a stamp that says something with pizzazz to indicate a review copy, and stamp the outside page edges on all three sides, as well as inside on the back of the front and back covers.

REVIEW SLIP

I use a 5.33 X 8.27-inch Avery shipping label pasted on the inside front cover of the book for the information usually required by reviewers, for example:

- Notification that the book is a review copy.
- Name of the book.
- Author's name.
- Publisher and author contact information.
- ISBN.
- CIP/Library of Congress identification number or LCCN.
- Indication whether the book is a hardback or trade paperback.

- Size and page count.
- Price in U.S. dollars.
- Season of the year.
- Official publication date (about four months after the bound book date—the first printing).
- Rights status (summarize any that are under negotiation, for example: catalog, book club, serialization, or condensation).
- Distributor.
- Wholesalers and/or vendor of record.

Reviewers are accustomed to finding this standard information inside the front cover. Using the label gives you flexibility if you need to make additions or changes, and insures the information stays permanently.

COVER LETTER

Like the cover letters for the galley-book review presentation, these cover letters should be concise. Introduce the taglines and sales hooks you've developed, and quote your best blurbs. You should convince reviewers that readers need the book, and cite legitimate news and human-interest angles having to do with the author and the book. Itemize the enclosures, and specifically request the review-book reply card be returned. Refer the reviewer to the Media Room page of your website for directions to more detailed author and publisher background information and PDF downloads of your media kit. Courteously request a copy of any review or article, and sign off by offering direct access numbers for the author and publisher. Full contact information should appear in both the header and footer of a hard-copy cover letter.

GENERAL INFORMATION BROCHURE

The general information brochure (flyer) was part of the galley-book review presentation (see Chapter VIII).

PREPUBLICATION REVIEW SHEET

Make a composite of all the good reviews and quotes you've received so far. I suggest organizing it in newspaper-column style, using both sides of common, white, 8.5 X 11-inch paper, and having black-and-white copies printed for about $34/1,000. The design can be effectively created using most word-processing software; I use Microsoft Publisher. This review sheet should also be on your website and included in your media kit.

NOTE: *It's a good idea to keep reviews and articles on your website for researchers and editors to explore and/or download. A website page can easily be organized and updated with listings by title, source, and date, including hyperlinks to other pages on the website for the full text, or hyperlinks to PDF files of full text that can be opened or downloaded. You could also create a master archive file in PDF—adding to it periodically—and place it on the page for download.*

REVIEW-BOOK REPLY CARD

You can create these standard postcard-size cards in design software, such as Publisher, and use Avery postcard stock commonly available at office-supply stores to print them out (in black-and-white or color) from your computer. I suggest you take the time to make the card professional and unique.

I type "REVIEW-BOOK REPLY CARD" at the top of the picture side of the card; the remainder of this side can be a design, a picture of your book cover, a piece of clip art with a quote, your business logo with taglines, or some other image.

I neatly place the name of the book and publisher/author contact information at the top of the left-hand half of the address side of the postcard (under the return address). Then I draft a fill-in form for the reviewer's name, organization, job title, e-mail address, fax number, and telephone number. At the bottom of the left-hand half, I leave lines for indicating the date(s) the review or article will be published, and for comments and/or requests. This is the piece you hope will be returned.

I include two review-book reply cards in case one gets lost, or the editor/reviewer wants to retain one or share it. No postage is included; typically editors place their correspondence in an outbox and someone else processes the mail.

LONG-FORM DRAFT OF A GENERIC BOOK-REVIEW ARTICLE

Draft a great 350-word review of the book, using the editorial style, formatting, and column sizing of book reviews in a major newspaper like *USA Today*. On 8.5 X 11-inch, 100 bright, #24 white stock, center four columns of text, so they can easily be edited into final copy for insertion into the newspaper. Label the piece a draft, place the article title across the top of the columns, and insert one or more photographs as examples. This draft book review article should be a part of your media kit and should appear on your website.

PHOTOGRAPHS

Take 35-mm photographs of the book cover, front and back. Compare local photo-lab batch pricing of 4 X 5-inch prints. Search for "photo prints" on the Internet for sources. You will need perhaps 1,000 of each. Quotes I received from local printers at the time this book went to press were around $135/1,000 on glossy stock. It was the same cost for 500 as it was for 1,000. These photos are print-ready quality for the media.

I also suggest including an author headshot at 2 X 2 inches, and a 4 X 5-inch photo of the author in a personality revealing activity. If you're in luck, these photographs will be used by an editor/reviewer in putting a review article together.

NOTE: I post a variety of photographs on a photo gallery page on my website, so that editors can have further options if they see something they like. These pictures on the website are at 75 dpi to save space. In my cover letter I mention the gallery page's URL and note that editors can request 300-dpi glossies. I also include a photo gallery as part of my media kit.

5. COSTS OF THE REVIEW-BOOK PRESENTATION AND DELIVERY

Below I've briefly brought together some general observations and costs for the hard-copy, CD-R, and PDF-download delivery options.

USING HARD COPY

The content cost and mailing the review-book presentation will probably be the most expensive promotion you will undertake. Recent printing costs for a run of 500 trade paperbacks—four-color, 150-450 pages, including shipping—ran around $3.50-$6.50 per book, utilizing the POD/PQN digital technology increasingly available in the print market.

NOTE: For POD/PQN printing organizations, I suggest checking out http://www.booksjustbooks.com/, http://www.121direct.net/, and http://www.podwholesale.com/. Usually a one-time setup charge of around $100-$200 is required.

Currently: The U.S. Postal Service Library (Book) Rate is $1.35 for up to a pound and $1.75 for one to two pounds. Mailing packets are $67/250 ($0.27 each). Labels are $20/250 ($0.08 each), as are stickers. Add $0.40 per mailer for the cost of four photos, two review-book reply cards, and stationary, and it turns out to be around $9.08 each for a 450-page book, assuming the mailer weighs between one and two pounds.

USING CD-RS

You may want to consider including a CD-R of all the files that make up the review-book presentation and your media kit together with the hard copy presentation you send by postal-mail. The cost is small, and you then have provided everything an editor could want right at his fingertips.

As an alternative to an all-hard-copy presentation, CD-Rs can be delivered immediately; there's no waiting for the hard copy of the book. After sending the final manuscript to the printer, a PDF file of the finished book can be created and placed on the CD-R along with the other content pieces of the review-book presentation. The CD-R has plenty of space for everything, including photos at 300 dpi for direct media use.

For a 450-page book, you could save the difference between $9.08/presentation, using all hard copy, and around $2.02 for the CD-R (about $0.40/CD and label, $0.27 for the mailing packet, and $1.35 for Book-Rate U.S. Postal Service postage).

The CD-R format may also help the reviewer by not cluttering up his notoriously chaotic work area, making it more likely he or she will notice the CD among the books stacked all over the office, and place it conveniently with other CDs near the computer.

USING PDF FILES ON YOUR WEBSITE

An even less expensive approach that could work well might be to invite reviewers by e-mail and fax to review your book by offering the review-book presentation as a master PDF file at a special page on your website. In the invitation you could send review editors directly to that page to complete a simple acquisition form, allowing you to keep track of who downloads the presentation.

FLEXIBLE ALTERNATIVES

When offering your review-book presentation as a PDF file on your website, if you discover a reviewer is reluctant to go to the website to download the file when you follow up the review invitation in the telephone follow-up program, you could have the CD-R and hard-copy presentations ready to deliver. It's possible the reviewer will accept the CD format delivered by postal-mail.

6. SPREADING OUT BOOK REVIEWS

Reviews and articles about you and your book will not come all at once. This process has the benefit of spreading promotional news and reviews over time and from widely separated locales, and is an aid to keeping the book fresh. It also gives you a feel for market response, where and when sales are taking place in relation to the publication of reviews and articles.

You will continue to fill requests from respondents to your invitations and telephone follow-up program on an ongoing basis. Constantly seeking reviews is a key part of the continuing creative promotional plan discussed in Chapter X.

E. POST THE BOOK FOR SALE AT THE MAJOR ONLINE BOOKSTORES (MONTHS 30-31)

The moment you send the final book to the printer, it's time to submit the book for sale at the major online bookstores (Amazon, Barnes and Noble, Borders, Books-A-Million, and Indigo and Chapters in Canada) according to the submission requirements found at their websites or available by e-mail request. It can take 4-12 weeks to go through the hoops to get your book presentation operational, depending on the bookstore, your patience level, and your diligence in filling their requirements.

As pointed out in the previous chapter, at one or more of the online bookstores you may have already posted your book for sale several months in advance of availability.

NOTE: You may choose to post your book for sale at other online bookstores, depending on your genre and/or subject. It is also worth noting here that posting a book for sale at the major online bookstores is a decision based on the tradeoff between giving up significant profits (because of the 55% discount given to the bookstores) and the credibility and promotional value you associate with the relationships. Self-publishers also need to recognize that giving a large discount to the online bookstores opens a potential problem area for you: random discounting of your book online. The discounting could undermine your sales promotion efforts that will be based on full cover price or small discounts.

1. SALES PRESENTATION

It's important to make sure your book's sales presentation at online bookstores is as good or better than those of the major publishers. To accomplish this, you can examine endless examples online and crib from them, inserting your own brand of creativity.

2. ORDERS

The initial order with these bookstores is usually one or two books; this consignment cost is affordable and controllable. Since these bookstores only respond to paid orders from customers, you need to be prepared to quickly deliver orders to their distribution warehouses.

In the case of Amazon.com's Advantage Program for publishers and authors, if you provide an initial stocking level of 1-5 books, a book will be displayed as available to be shipped within 24 hours. This is a powerful sales statement; readers don't want to wait.

NOTE: This program has changed substantially over the writing period for this book, so I recommend exploring the current situation at Amazon's website, http://www.amazon.com/.

3. COSTS AND PROFITS

To date, little direct cost is associated with organizing books for sale through the online bookstores. This is one of the principle benefits in creating these relationships. It's the fulfillment of the frugal self-publisher's dream of convenient universal availability at no out-of-pocket cost; however, coming directly to these bookstores as a self-publisher typically requires a 55% discount off the cover price, and you have to absorb the cost of shipping.

As far as practical economics are concerned, sales through online bookstores may be at best a break-even situation. At 55% off cover, with high printing costs on small runs, and paying shipping on the orders, you will be lucky to break even until and unless your book takes off and you can afford to contract larger printing runs at significant unit-cost reductions. For example, assuming a cover price of $29 on a 450-page hardback, $9.50-$11.00 for the cost of printing (POD/PQN at 50-250 at a time), $1.75 U.S. Postal Service 1-2 lb. Book Rate for shipping a single book, and $16.40 as a discount (55% of cover), your profits could be flat. Another fact to keep in mind is that it can be in excess of 90 days after sales for you to see a check from the online bookstores, so it also will cost you the time value of that money.

NOTE: However, a benefit often overlooked by authors who are interested in self-publishing is that some of the Internet publishers in today's marketplace have negotiated around a 40% discount with the online bookstores. If a publishing/printing/distribution/fulfillment relationship with an Internet publisher passes on a fair part of this discount saving to an author, it could be a significant factor in considering the most beneficial framework for launching a self-published book.

4. OTHER VALUES

Even though the profit margins are exceedingly small for a self-publisher relegated to short printing runs, justification for selling through online bookstores can be strongly influenced by the intangible values from credible exposure. Major online bookstores play a significant part in today's marketplace, and the availability of your book in their systems converts into instant credibility for self-publishers. This, combined with dynamic book promotions, should help increase sales, and relationships could become more profitable through the increased size of print runs.

Major online bookstores are continuing to develop acceptance and credibility in the market, and perhaps as many as 90% of searching readers who buy books on the Internet buy at these locations. In addition, these readers go to the online bookstores to obtain information about books, to see what's happening. So, for taking the time necessary to get up and running at the majors, with no up-front cost, your book will have worldwide exposure.

Remember, major publishers and literary agents are looking for ways to eliminate their risks. What could be better than a self-published book selling well at online bookstores? In addition, you are normally not locked into a contract, so you can pull your book from these stores at any time for any reason.

5. E-BOOKS

E-books are also sold at most of the online bookstores. For example, Barnes and Noble currently pays a 35% royalty and takes care of all the formatting work; this includes keeping up with formatting technology. The online bookstores have submission requirements and agreements posted at their websites, and they post contact numbers or e-mail addresses for inquiries.

NOTE: *This market has yet to prove itself, and many professionals believe its inevitable success is still 10-15 years away. At this juncture it's an insignificant segment (only about 10,000 handheld units in the marketplace at the end of 2000—and a leveling off of sales in 2001). So, I'm in favor of letting the online bookstores do what they will for now with e-book presentations and sales; it costs me nothing.*

To add a positive note to involvement with e-books by self-publishers, in a mid-2002 telephone discussion with me, Danny O. Snow, a well-known self-published author and CEO of Unlimited Publishing, LLC, indicated that recent studies showed about 20% of people who purchase an e-book end up buying the hard copy.

F. SET UP YOUR FULFILLMENT SYSTEM AND FILL ORDERS (MONTHS 30-31)

Prepare to fulfill book orders by designing an effective fulfillment system in advance. The system should include: order handling, invoice creation, order processing, record keeping, receiving and storage, packaging, finishing and labeling, and shipping. The pure self-publisher will perform all the fulfillment functions; consideration of a professional fulfillment service can take place at the point when sales make it economically feasible.

I have relied heavily on the information and experience expressed by Dan Poynter in his *Self Publishing Manual* to summarize information on receiving, storing, packing, finishing, labeling, and shipping.

It's impossible to outline all the accounting and processing details. In the next three brief sections, I present a general picture of the procedures I've developed and used, so you'll have an initial handle on how to organize your own fulfillment system.

NOTE: The section on references and Internet resource sites in Chapter II contains publications that cover the fulfillment topic. In addition, many fulfillment-service providers are members of the Publishers Marketing Association (PMA is a "must" organization for self-publishers to join.); access to the membership list is provided free at PMA's website, http://www.pma-online.org/. Many fulfillment organizations advertise in the monthly PMA Newsletter and in Publishers Weekly magazine. Dan Poynter has authored a special report entitled, "Book Fulfillment," available at his website, http://www.parapublishing.com/.

1. INITIAL ORDER HANDLING

The following are some generic order-handling processes:

- Send confirmation e-mails or faxes upon receipt of all orders. These standard responses should be ready to select from drafts you've prepared, for example, in Outlook and WinFax PRO 10.0.
- Orders received by fax, e-mail, postal-mail, telephone, and through your website that contain charge-card information should be processed for clearance and payment by your

- Facsimile check payments with fax orders containing required order information should be deposited directly to your bank account, and clearance obtained. I understand deposit acceptance by banks of check-payment forms received by e-mail is not too far in the future.

merchant-account services provider. You may want to consider incorporating the charge-card processing services of an Internet organization like PayPal.com on your website as a payment alternative offered on your order forms.

- Save original envelopes, copies of the original fax, e-mail, postal-mail, and verbatim written copies of telephone order messages. Make copies of order confirmations you send. These purchase-order source documents should be bundled and stored by date—to be joined by copies of paid invoices you will send later—as prudent record keeping and in anticipation of possible problems.

NOTES: When I ordered my toll-free order number for customers, I initially terminated it at my business voice-mail number, which gives callers options, one of which is for taking order information. As volume justifies, I'll switch termination of the number to an answering service or a fulfillment-services provider.

In the beginning, unless you decide to risk your capital, accept only prepaid orders, except for online bookstores. Dan Poynter indicates in his "Self-Publishing Manual" that even Baker & Taylor will pay up front if requested.

When you receive purchase orders without checks or charge-card information, just turn them around, apologize for the delay, and indicate that cash, check, or charge-card payment must be included with the order.

2. INVOICE CREATION AND ORDER PROCESSING

Using the software of your choice, for example, QuickBooks, you should be able to:

- Design custom invoices for sales to different customer categories, for example: individual, library, bookstore, wholesaler, book club, premium, catalog, business services,

etc. Typically, the templates available in the software allow you to customize all the contact, product, payment, shipping, and delivery information, as well as create spaces for standard blurbs, tags lines and thank-you notes. These invoice forms are then available to call up when you're ready to process an order.

- Define product types, for example: e-book title, report booklet title, book title, speaking fee, workshop fee, consulting fee, t-shirt, etc. The product types are then available to select during the creation of an invoice.

- Develop customer profiles as you receive orders, including business name, key personnel, shipping address, postal-mail address, e-mail address, telephone number, fax number, shipment information, applicable discounts, sales tax if appropriate, state resale number (for resellers), and any notes you think appropriate. This is an effective method of record keeping, and allows you to insert customer information into invoices you create in the program.

- Complete paid invoices for all orders paid by checks and charge-cards that clear bank processing, including bank-account clearance date or charge-card payment-authorization number, and print out two copies.

  In QuickBooks, the clearing of charge-card payments is accomplished through the program and your Internet connection. You can batch invoices and send them all together or individually. Charge-card approvals are received by e-mail. The capability is just a click away after a merchant account has been set up through QuickBooks. Go to http://www.quickbooks.com/ for details.

- Add one printed copy of the paid invoice to the bundle of purchase-order source documents for the order.

- Put the second printed copy of the paid invoice in a Ready for Delivery file; this copy will be included with the book as a packing slip when the mailing packet goes out.

- For orders you choose to give credit, complete unpaid invoices with terms of payment and print out two copies.

- Place unpaid invoices in the software's accounts receivable file, and a printed copy in a hard-copy accounts receivable file.

- Put the second printed copy of the unpaid invoice in the Ready for Delivery file, to be included with the book as a packing slip when the mailing packet goes out.

- Send the unpaid invoice by fax or e-mail right from the accounting software to the purchasing customer. This becomes an invoice sent for payment, containing an estimated shipping date, so your customer knows when to expect delivery. Depending on the situation, you may have to send unpaid invoices by postal-mail.

- When payment is received, mark the copy of the unpaid invoice from the accounts receivable file as paid, and add it to the purchase order source documents (hard copy record) for the order.

NOTE: As an alternative means of processing charge-card payments, you could utilize the e-mail request for payment service provided (free) when you establish an account relationship with PayPal.com. Go to http://www.paypal.com/ for information.

3. RECORD KEEPING

If you haven't done so already, since you will now be generating regular income, it's recommended that you keep track of income and expenses, as well as converting all your current-year expenses, using an accounting-software program. In my case, I'd been keeping track of income and expenses using Excel worksheets and attaching them to Form C when I filed annual income-tax returns. It took two days to set up the accounts necessary in QuickBooks to manage the business properly; part of that process was to transfer eight months of income/expense data from the current year's Excel worksheet.

NOTE: The QuickBooks tutorials in the Help menu walked me through the business-organization process. An added benefit was an introduction to basic accounting sufficient for understanding how to provide necessary information for an outside accounting service.

The accounting software will convert your data entries into complete accounting records, and act as your customer- and product-information database, including setting up accounts receivable for follow-up. Outside of the invoice copies for processing orders, the paperwork is eliminated. On days when I work in the program, I copy the QuickBooks files to a backup CD, just like all the major files and folders I work on in a given day.

4. RECEIVING AND STORING BOOKS

Direct your book manufacturer to shrink-wrap in twos, box and seal your cartons, and ship books to you palletized and banded. Cartons should not weight more than 40 lbs. If you start your business at home, store the book inventory in unbroken cartons on top of each other, like the overlapping bricks in a wall, out of the sun, and off the ground with air space behind. As soon as it's economically feasible, either transfer your inventory to commercial space where the atmosphere is regulated and you can obtain insurance, or employ a fulfillment-services provider.

5. PACKAGING

Purchasers must receive books in good condition. One way to ensure this is to keep them clean and immobile in the carton. I recommend taking Dan Poynter's advice from the fulfillment section of *The Self-Publishing Manual:* Use the plastic-bubble Mail-Lite ® bag (Sealed Air Corporation, Palatine, Illinois. Telephone: 800-789-1331.); it's clean, lightweight, heavy-duty, and waterproof when heat-sealed. These are used for individual books up to 6 X 9 inches.

For multiple books less than full carton size, you can use variable-depth boxes; these are cartons you cut down to any size you need to keep the books tight rather than using stuffing. A good source for shipping and packaging supplies is Uline Shipping Supplies. For information and ordering go to http://www.uline.com/, or call 800-295-5510 to inquire and receive their catalog.

When you're just starting out, you can usually find used book cartons behind major bookstores. Even though they throw them away, it's a good idea to ask permission. You can customize them to size by cutting down the corners and trimming the flap panels.

According to Dan Poynter in *The Self-Publishing Manual,* you will need the following equipment and supplies:

- A 0-2 lb. letter scale.
- A 0-50 lb. scale for the larger cartons (a rule of thumb is don't exceed 40 lbs./carton).
- Address labels (Avery 3 x 5-inch labels in sheets) you design with your business and return address information.
- Stamps for the following information: "Printed Matter—Books," "Forwarding and Return Postage Guaranteed," "Special Fourth-Class Book Rate," or "Library Rate," "Air Mail. Check with the post office to make sure the terminology is up-to-date.
- 4.5 X 8.5-inch, clear packing slip envelopes; for example, stock #45-3-23, offered by the Associated Bag Co., 400 W. Boden Street, Milwaukee, WI 53207. Telephone: 800-926-6100.
- Handheld dispenser, and rolls of cheap, one-inch-wide, non-reinforced, low-mil, plastic sealing tape (don't use cheaper brown tape you have to put through a wetting device; it's a pain). This tape is used to seal box and carton edges and flap closure points.
- Half-inch, reinforced glass strapping tape for cartons.
- Cellophane tape to seal the clear packing slip envelope and attach it to cartons and boxes.
- An assortment of cheap plastic bags for wrapping books inside cartons to doubly insure airtightness.
- Heavy-duty stapler or heat-sealer for the individual bags.

6. FINISHING AND LABELING PACKAGES

Use the non-reinforced, clear-plastic sealing tape to seal all the carton edges and flap closures. Place the 5.5 X 8.5-inch clear packing-slip envelope—containing a copy of the invoice folded and placed inside to be read as the mailing address and serve as a packing slip—over the flap closures of a carton or on the front of the Mail-Lite ® bag. Seal it with cellophane tape, and tape it to the carton or bag face. Band the cartons with half-inch reinforced tape in two directions over the packing slip envelope to protect it from chafing loose. There's no need to use the reinforced tape to band the Mail-Lite ® bags or the severely cut-down cartons; use cellophane tape crisscrossed over the packing slip envelope for extra protection.

7. SHIPPING

Go to the post office and get up-to-date domestic and international rate schedules. Up to one pound, the U.S. Postal Service Library Rate is currently $1.35; 1-2 pounds is $1.75; 4-5 pounds is $2.95; for 5-70 pounds, you need a chart. U.S. Postal Service, two- to three-day Priority Mail is $3.85 up to one pound on flat rate envelopes (you can get 3-4 books in the envelope); over one and up to 70 pounds, you need a chart. The U.S. Postal Service has library rates for Canadian and other foreign destinations as well; the required packaging and customs forms will consume additional time.

Library-Rate packages can take 3-30 days depending on the time of year and how smart you are. You can save as much as 2-6 days by delivering the packages to a central postal facility.

Simple economics and delivery-time requirements will dictate when to consider using a non-U.S. Postal Service carrier.

CHAPTER X: Continuing Creative Promotional Plan

This last chapter outlines the development of a long-term promotional strategy, using a programs approach to organize an effective plan. This approach leaves you plenty of room to tailor-make your own plan. Along the way, I introduce some creative concepts for your consideration. The implementation of the programs will span a year or more.

As an introduction, I've summarized the major promotions to date and presented my views on developing non-spam ground-rules for drafting the all-important e-mail communications that announce and promote the business interests of a self-publisher.

A. SUMMARY OF MAJOR PROMOTIONS TO DATE

To this point, you have promoted your work every time you communicated with another human being about writing, your business, and your book. Direct promotion to the marketplace began when you:

- Purged contact lists (tested the fax numbers and e-mail addresses) as you compiled them.
- Offered a PDF e-book, working-paper version of the book to your Individual Potential Buyers list.

- Sent galley-book review invitations and galley-book review presentations.
- Placed the book for sale at your website.
- Completed your submission to the PMA, cooperative marketing mailings to libraries and reviewers.
- Posted book announcements at Internet news, writing, and other book-related organizations.
- Announced first offers for sale to libraries and individuals by fax and e-mail.
- Announced second offers for sale to libraries and individuals by fax and e-mail.
- Posted the book for order at Amazon.com and a variety of Internet book-posting sites.
- Sent review-book invitations and began delivering review-book presentations.

You have now launched your book, and it's still about four months prior to the nebulous official publication date (which is typically three to four months after the first printing).

B. TOWARD NON-SPAM STANDARDS FOR E-MAIL COMMUNICATIONS

The Internet is the most dynamically effective information and marketing vehicle ever created, so it's worth investing time to develop standards for e-mail communications that are both effective and acceptable in the marketplace. This section presents some concepts for consideration.

A 100% non-spam goal is probably not realistic. In general, the Internet is unregulated, but federal and state laws that touch on the subject of spam are changing rapidly. In addition, the attitudes of people regarding spam are in favor of controls. It appears likely that changes in Internet operations, more robust consumer software, and new legal regulation will produce more and more control in the near future.

If you send unsolicited e-mail communications, no matter how hard you try to be nonintrusive, you are likely to irritate many recipients, even when you restrict your messages to those that have a demonstrated interest in what you have to say or offer.

Perhaps there's a need for a term that defines acceptable commercial communications; for example, value-added communications (VACs), meaning potentially useful communications, offering something of tangible value, sent to individuals, groups, or organizations that have demonstrated interest in what is being offered.

There is no safe harbor. But designing e-mail communications to your market that always offer substantive, complimentary value may be the safest way to preserve a professional image and remain effective. In other words, you have to be willing to give away something of real tangible value. Besides that standard, I have listed some elements and principles below that may help e-mail messages escape the spam label:

1. USE RICH TEXT FORMAT

If you use Rich Text Format (RTF), you can insert hyperlinks to your website, use colored fonts, add backgrounds, and use variable paragraph formatting. If recipients have limited their incoming messages to Text format, the formatting lost from the conversion to Text from Rich Text should still render the message readable.

2. IDENTIFY THE SENDER

Connect a responsible individual to each business e-mail address you use for sending promotions. You can do this as part of setting up outgoing e-mail accounts; for example, in Outlook, go to Tools and Accounts and fill in the Name under User Information. I suggest setting up several e-mail accounts, each for a specialty activity such as a newsletter@, authors@, publishers@, staff@, info@, workshops@, consulting@, speaking@, etc., and each associated with a responsible sender.

3. BULK E-MAIL SOFTWARE OR A SERVICES PROVIDER

Consider using bulk e-mail software that sends from its own server; or use a credible outside services provider when you send e-mail to lists. These are ways to insure that any complaints don't reach your regular e-mail service provider (search the Internet for e-mail mailing services).

4. SUBJECT LINE

E-mail services and management software like Outlook will always show recipients the subject line of messages, so, it's critical to make it short and to include the value-added hook or the specific purpose, for example:

- Until June 1st: Complimentary New Age, Teen-Controls Article.
- Please Review a New Writing Style/Genre, the Sci-Tech-Mystery-Thriller.
- New Complimentary Cave-Exploring Newsletter.
- Complimentary Copy of the Newly Released…
- Complimentary Quilting Workshop in…
- Invitation to Review the Galley-Book…
- XYZ Mystery Club T-shirts Are Here: First 10 Member Sign-ups are Complimentary.
- Seniors in Action: 84-Year-Old Author Releases Unique Fiction Novel.

5. FIRST THREE LINES

Many e-mail services and message-management software programs allow you to set the inbox so that the first three lines of the e-mail are displayed under the heading information; for example, in Outlook go to View and select Auto View. Many computer-literate individuals and professionals apply this feature to their e-mail inbox, so it's imperative to use those first lines effectively to maximize chances that a message will be opened.

First line: Address recipients directly in the first line of the communication. Use the actual name if you have it, or use a title and/or interest descriptor—or tie them both together, for example, Dear:

- Mr. Daniels, *EFG* Editor.
- Fiction Book Review Editor.
- Fellow Author.
- Mystery Reader.

- XYZ Club Member.
- Mrs. Jones, Acquisition Librarian.
- Workshop Coordinator.
- Quilting Enthusiast.

Second and third lines: Hook the recipient with the giveaway or value definition, for example:

- To acquire your complimentary copy, please go to http://www.yourwebsite.com/pagenumber.html.
- Mary Smith's new book is entitled, *XXXXXXXXXXXX*. A draft story about Mary and the book is included in her full media kit (PDF file) found at http://www.yourwebsite.com/pagenumber.html. A short review-book order form is provided for you at the website's Media Room.
- Don Jones, Director of the Big City Library says, "This book should be on the shelf of every library in the country." Please visit the Library Room at http://www.yourwebsigte.com/pagenumber.html for the book presentation and author media kit.
- Writer organizations may schedule free workshops facilitated by Mary Smith, author of *XXXXX*, by going to the following special page for information: http://www.yourwebsite.com/pagenumber.html.
- For a subscription to the free *Caving Enthusiast Monthly Newsletter*, edited by Mary Smith, members should go to: http://www.yourwebsite.com/pagenumber.html.

6. BODY OF THE E-MAIL

Many e-mail services and message-management software programs allow you to set the inbox so that when the e-mail message is highlighted, the first ten lines or so of the e-mail are displayed at the bottom of the inbox screen; for example, in Outlook, go to View and select Preview Pane. I use this preview as a last screen in deciding to open or delete messages. The size of the pane can be adjusted, and you can scroll the message without opening it.

Keep the e-mails simple: no images, no gizmos, no attachments. Ideally, through no more than 10 lines tactfully, sincerely, and concisely present a message that continues to explain the giveaway or tangible value, sends recipients to your website, or generates a return e-mail for you to fulfill. For example:

> I just finished an article entitled, YYYYYYYYY, derived from my book, XXXXX, which is on its way to syndication. I've placed it on my website for (group members, my list of writers and self-publishers, my listserv members, members of the organization, members of the gardening club, my list of parents who care, my fellow romance readers, members of the XYZ club) to download until XXXX 30th. There's a review form at http://www.yourbusinesswebsite.com/pagenumber.html; I'd appreciate your comments.

Or one a little longer:

> Mary's Smith's novel of desperation and stark terror takes readers into a world of chaos, cruelty, and confrontation as seen through the experiences of a naïve, recently widowed 68-year-old woman.
>
> Mary's 60+ years of writing experience are poignantly brought to bear in creating an exciting, uplifting tale about a dependent, senior lady suddenly thrust into a world of harsh realities after the sudden death of her domineering husband. Every reader will find great satisfaction, and greater empathy for what life may hold, in becoming riveted to this story of conflict, confusion, and the danger of going it alone. In this adventure, readers will meet the hero within.
>
> We believe readers will identify strongly with this beautifully written success story, set against the modern background of the greater terrors that surround us all in today's world.
>
> Should you decide to favor Mary with a review or article, please send us a copy at: (your contact information). Extensive background information is available at: http://www.yourwebsite.com/.

7. CLOSING AND ATTRIBUTION-SIGNATURE

I am convinced that closings are important. I suggest careful and appropriate selection, for example: Respectfully submitted, Cheers, Regards, Happy hunting, Good luck, Sincerely, Sincerely yours.

I use a standard signature for my name, typing it first in a special-colored font that looks like a real signature, for instance, Brush Script MT, and then again on the next line in the font used for the e-mail.

Add a double space after your closing and signature, then insert a 4-6-line attribution-signature, using fonts one level smaller than those of message. To draft alternative attribution-signatures for insertion into e-mail, see the Help tab at your e-mail account on the Internet and/or check out this capability in your message-management software. I use Word as my e-mail editor in Outlook to create various attribution-signatures for use with e-mail.

8. ACTION FOR REMOVAL

Directly after your attribution-signature, cite a specific action for the recipient to be removed from further communications, for example: To be removed from our contacts, please click on "Reply" and type "Remove" on the first line or in the subject line.

9. CITE CURRENT LAW

Cite a summary of the current law at the bottom of messages, and include a statement of your objective to comply, for example:

> *It is our intention to comply with current laws (perhaps more detail here) and go the extra mile to maintain professional decorum in our communications. Please send constructive criticism or suggestions to: KeyPerson@yourbusinesswebsite.com/.*

NOTE: Look at the bottom of e-mail advertisements you receive daily from major organizations for changes in disclaimer terminology, summaries of the current law, and ideas for courtesy.

C. DESIGNING A LONG-TERM PROMOTION STRATEGY

1. CORE ADVICE

As far as traditional advertising goes, we would do well to take Dan Poynter's advice from the *Self-Publishing Manual* and not spend money on display ads, in favor of concentrating on securing book reviews from the media and networking in the market through personal appearances. I suggest special effort directed at obtaining radio and TV exposure, an activity that most publicists agree is the biggest sales generator.

Dan Poynter, in the foreword for Barbara Gaughen and Ernest Weckbaugh's book, *Book Blitz: Getting Your Book in the News,* tells us, "Book reviews take three months to three years... The secret of savvy book promotion is to keep up the pressure: Keep sending out the packets and keep making those phone calls."

Gaughen and Weckbaugh tell us that even if you have a publisher, "... when it comes to promotion ... the publisher won't do it ... unless you happen to be one of the top .... Which means, if you want your book to sell, it's your job ...." These two knowledgeable publicists and writers tell us further, "Book promotion isn't about (just) convincing people to buy your book. It's about knowing when (and how) to find the people who are waiting for it."

The core advice from the experts for successfully promoting books is to spend your precious time on the media. Part of the beauty of this advice for self-publishers is that to follow it requires little capital. Instead, it takes planning, drive, commitment, creativity, and time.

2. DATABASES

To generate reviews and articles you will need to communicate with the media. Having come this far in the promotional process, it may be wise to invest in a major media database on CD-ROM to expand book-review promotions (see the print-media promotion program discussed below). One of the best databases for the money appears to be the

Continuing Creative Promotional Plan

Publicity Blitz Media Directory on disk ($295) by Bradley Communications Corp., http://www.rtir.com/, 800-989-1400. It contains over 20,000 newspapers, magazines, syndicates, and radio/TV/cable talk shows. The investment makes sense now, when you'll need current, editor contact information.

You may also want to consider purchasing the *American Library Directory* CD-ROM, available through its new publisher, Info Today, Inc., htttp://www.infotoday.com/ (previously published by R.R. Bowker), for $499 by calling the customer service number, 800-300-9868 or 609-654-6266. The directory comes out annually in June. It will enable you to reach selection and acquisition librarians by e-mail and/or fax at over 30,000 libraries in North America.

Consider buying one or more of the bulk e-mail lists of categorized addresses available on the Internet (do a search for e-mail lists). I discuss this briefly below in the sections on testing opt-in e-mail lists and testing random e-mail lists.

3. PROMOTIONAL AND ADVERTISING PIECES

I don't recommend expending resources on written promotional and advertising pieces, except for simple brochures, enclosures in test postal-mails, and promotional documents converted to PDF files for your media kit and website. However, I do recommend considering business cards, bookmarks and postcards. You can design and print them out yourself; they are inexpensive, easily carried, have multiple handout uses, and can be easily and quickly edited and reprinted when changes are necessary.

BUSINESS CARDS

See Chapter V, section B.

BOOKMARKS

I create bookmarks in Publisher. Most printing organizations can set up the print run from a Publisher file (or a Word file you copy and paste in from Publisher). You can use black-and-white or color and have the bookmarks economically printed by the thousands. I suggest including business-card information plus front and back book covers, taglines, sales hooks, your best review testimonials, and book-purchase information.

For printing sources, check out the following quoting services: http://www.printindustry.com/, http://www.123printfinder.com/, and http://www.printusa.com/. One recent industry-newsletter article mentioned U.S. Press, Inc. in Valdosta, GA, http://www.uspress.com/, as having the most competitive bookmark pricing and excellent service.

POSTCARDS

Postcards are another useful vehicle for presenting key promotional information. They're also great for thank-yous. I include a cover picture on the front, and use the space on the other side under the return address for promotional text, a short note and my attribution-signature.

D. DEFINING PROGRAMS IN THE PROMOTION PLAN

Consider creative promotional ideas that are compatible with your time, energy, and financial resources. Because most self-publishers are virtually alone in carrying out publishing functions, it's important to select affordable promotional directions you are capable of executing.

If you're a frugal self-publisher without a staff, you must plan carefully. Below, I've listed the programs I believe should be considered in developing an effective ongoing promotion plan, a plan that is low-cost, technologically manageable, and flexible enough to customize to available resources and desired life-style:

- Print-media program to continue sending review invitations to the general media.

- Telephone follow-up program to major media communications to generate book reviews and feature articles.

- Radio and TV program to gain newsworthy interviews about you and your writing.

- PMA co-op marketing programs to produce credibility in the marketplace, generate book reviews from the media, and generate product sales from libraries and appropriate niche markets.

- Personal program to earn a living while promoting and selling writing products.

- Internet testing program to experiment with creating and delivering effective messages to potential individual buyers for your writing products, and to post information about you and your works in appropriate directories and subject lists.

- Direct-sales program to generate book and writing-product sales from the most lucrative market segments for your works.

- Internet advertising program to develop exchange of website links with organizations involved with your book's subject or genre, join appropriate Internet affiliate/associate programs, and to negotiate opportunities for exchanging publication of your articles for advertising space in genre and subject-appropriate newsletters.

- Foreign rights program to place the availability of your book in view of potential foreign publishers.

1. PRINT-MEDIA PROGRAM

Because of the importance of reviews and published articles, and because they're free, this continuing program may be the most effective use of your precious promotion time.

PERIODIC COMMUNICATIONS

About every 4-6 weeks, e-mail and fax book-review invitations to media editors in your reviewer lists that haven't yet responded to previous invitations. Send e-mails first, then if you get no response, send faxes. Record the communications in your master promotion log.

An effective approach might be to do one state at a time and follow up by telephone with the larger media organizations (see the telephone follow-up program below); for example, in Florida there are around 25 newspapers and magazines with circulations of 50,000 or more.

MEDIA APPROACH IDEAS

Each time you begin the e-mail invitation process over again, you will need to come up with different promotional pieces that are news-oriented and/or grab attention. Consider current events, business trends, the time of year, and upcoming holidays—even the obscure ones. I suggest using the general guidelines in message format and design used in the original review-book invitations discussed in the section on review-book promotion in Chapter IX.

The creative possibilities are endless. For example, to build a story around a holiday, you could go to the following reference books at the local library: *Chase's 2002 Calendar of Events, Holidays, and Anniversaries of the World,* by Gale Research Company; and *The American Book of Days,* by H. W. Wilson Company. For more ideas, go to the Internet and look into http://www.holidays.net/ and http://www.holidayfestival.com/. Or, you could create your own holiday and submit it to holiday-directory databases.

Another creative promotional idea might be to offer media editors who publish a book review or article permission to include a complimentary PDF e-book in the review/article. For a limited time, interested readers could be directed to a special page on your website to fill out a request form, and the e-book could be delivered as an e-mail attachment. Or the special page could provide a PDF download of the e-book.

POSTAL-MAIL MINI-MEDIA KIT TEST

Consider conducting a postal-mail test promotion by mailing a mini-media kit to daily and weekly newspapers with circulations over 100,000, and to your reviewers and syndicators list. You could start out with a test of 100, or perhaps cover one state, and expand the program if the results are good. The mailer should contain:

- A cover letter to a specific editor on business stationary. These can be created using the mail merge features of your word-processing software. Pattern the content after previous e-mails and faxes, and direct the editor to appropriate pages on your website for more information.
- Your general information brochure.
- Two un-stamped, self-addressed review-book reply cards, one to be kept by the reviewer/editor. (See the "Review-book Reply Card" section in Chapter IX for content.)
- A draft of a generic review article you've written as a captivating news story.
- Photographs of the book cover, front and back, and two of the author.

NOTE: *All of these pieces should be available from your stock; they were part of the review-book presentation developed in Chapter IX.*

I suggest employing the same design techniques recommended for the review-book presentation packets discussed in Chapter IX. U.S. Postal Service mailing cost should be about $0.71 each (First Class, weight under 2 oz., and a $0.11 charge for the special-sized envelope), and about $0.15 for the paper and photographs, making the total around $0.86 each.

Response to this kind of mailer may be relatively high. According to Dan Poynter in his booklet, *Book Reviews From Pre-publication Galleys Through a Continuing Review Program,* "A mailing to 1,000 reviewers may bring a response from 200 or so." He was speaking about sending out an effectively designed book-review package.

2. TELEPHONE FOLLOW-UP PROGRAM

If you've stayed with the plan in this book, the largest financial investment you will make, outside of printing runs, will be the mail-out of the review-book presentation. You've spent considerable effort to generate requests for your presentation; so once delivered, it's important to immediately follow-up personally by telephone. The objective is to make one-on-one contact with editor/reviewers to introduce yourself and confirm receipt of the presentation. Using any previous contact notes, be prepared to tweak an editor/reviewer's memory. Have your best taglines and an original news event/trend tie-in ready to throw out. Don't try to engage reviewers further. Thank him or her for the time and wish them a good day. Worst case is that you may be asked to send another review-book presentation, which you will immediately do by Priority Mail with a direct follow-up call to make sure it arrives safely.

If you can afford it, I recommend hiring a senior citizen in your neighborhood to help you make the calls. You take the majors and give the rest to your helper. Any time you are able to speak with a key editorial contact, send a short, postal-mail thank-you/reminder; use off-size stationery, or a postcard you created (see above).

3. RADIO AND TV PROGRAM

Like the print-media, this industry is looking for news and entertainment for its listeners and viewers. Many prominent publicists agree that national television exposure is the most powerful activity for generating sales. I created a Radio and TV Room page on my website to strongly support my promotional communications to this important media sector.

Using your national list of radio and TV talk shows, make a concentrated effort to snag attention from hosts and producers through creative communications, using e-mail, fax, postal-mail and the telephone. You have nothing to lose and everything to gain, so go for it.

For the 40-50 majors and the shows in your state of residence, you'll have the best shot at success if you study each program/show carefully to discern the feel and attitude, the personal delivery style of the host, how the staff members are integrated into the show, and how the host pulls information (the performance) from his or her guests. Search the Internet for show websites, and confirm and expand the contact information (names, titles, e-mail addresses, fax numbers, and telephone numbers) you have for potentially important contacts.

The objective of your promotion program is to sell yourself as an interviewee or guest. To effectively accomplish this objective, you have to offer news and entertainment value, and your approach has to be organized.

CREATE CONNECTIONS TO YOUR EXPERTISE

It's important to broaden your view of the promotional possibilities in connecting subject matter, genre, and/or expertise to current news, holidays, or political, economic, and cultural trends. Your book makes you an expert—even if it's a fiction book—because you've researched the topical ingredients. You should be able to cast yourself in a variety of roles as a quasi-authority, the depth of which should be sufficient for the time and probing radio and TV programs require. The unlimited source of world events and trends awaits your creative connecting ability—you can always weave in your book.

A SUGGESTED PROMOTIONAL APPROACH

Using your radio and TV list of shows and organizations, every 4-6 weeks e-mail and fax promotional pieces in the form of one-page queries. Whatever the pitch, don't focus on your book. Focus on the news connection you've developed. I've included some suggestions, examples, and ideas below:

THE QUERY

The subject line of the query will be the key to getting attention; it will immediately connect you to the news you are inventing. For example, if you are:

- A self-publishing author: "Anybody Can Get Published."
- An expert on parenting: "Parents Can Show Teens They Know What's Happening."
- A fiction author/geologist/volcanologist: "A Mega-Quake is Imminent."
- An author of a gardening book: "It's Almost Spring, so Let's Plant a Vegetable Garden for Maximum Health."
- A metaphysical author: "What We All Want to Know is Where We've Come from."
- A science fiction author: "Waitress Experiences Automatic Writing of the Real Coming."
- An adventure and travel author: "Preoccupation With Competitive Roughing-It Leads to the Ultimate Adventure."
- A fiction author/biologist: "Expert Introduces a Fantastic Cloning Frontier Based on Recent Research."

The body of the query explains the news/entertainment connections to the author, outlines possible directions for discussion of the connections, weaves in the book and invites the media person to a special radio and TV page on the author's website for background. I suggest breaking down the specific support information available to help cement credibility; for example, list the contents of a downloadable media kit and availability of a download of the book, both in PDF.

At the bottom of the query, place your standard attribution-signature.

GENERIC INTERVIEW

It's important to convince show producers and hosts that you will be an entertaining and amiable guest, someone they can feel comfortable working with. To fully support your radio and TV promotional efforts, include a generic interview on your website; it can be written, audio, audio-video, or all three. If you've followed the plan laid out in this book, the interview should be a part of your media kit and available on pages at your website.

NOTES: An audio file can be recorded and added to a website and media kit, just like any other file. The file could be played (opened) on the website and/or downloaded separately or as part of a media kit. Windows 98 (and up) contains a sound-recorder program; with that and a $10 microphone plugged into your PC, you can easily record an interview (Go to Start>Programs> Accessories>Entertainment).

At this writing, the price of digital audio-video/still-shot cameras has come down to around $400. The files produced on discs can be uploaded to most PCs and worked from there into promotional uses on your website and in your media kit. Theoretically, you could stage an audio/video interview with a cohort right at home, as if you were directing a movie.

The generic interview (written, audio, or audio-video) should be based on weaving questions (that you would want to be asked) about you, your book, business, and other works into news and entertainment connections. The book is not the primary focus. Use the frequently asked questions you've developed for your website as a starter.

Information that should come out in the process of presenting news and entertainment:

- Reasons why the book would be of interest to readers (the audience).
- Where the book can be purchased.
- Interesting and intriguing connections to your expertise.
- Plugs for support information at your website.

- Your business-travel-activities/promotion schedule so you sound busy.
- Pitches for writing projects in progress.
- Giveaways at your website.
- A compelling and interesting lifestyle image, created through mention of your activities and interests.

You could consider producing multiple interview files of interviews that are based on different news and entertainment approaches but still weave in the same key information.

EXAMPLE APPROACH

As the final edit of this book was coming to a close, I was starting to work up an approach to David Letterman's Late Show, developing the role of the most unrecognized, non-famous author in the country, and basing it around Dave's love of the top ten concept (Top 10 Reasons an Author Knows He's Unrecognized). Dave seems to like the outrageous and the underdog. The number ten might be: You know you're unrecognized when Letterman has to buy you a bus ticket to get to the show. The Top 10 I'm developing should give him plenty of ammunition to ridicule me further, and I'm ready with additional facetious kudos to feed him if he needs to rib me more. I'll try the back door first, with Biff Henderson, David Calder, or another staff member I can contact easily. Let them take the credit for discovering me as a potential guest. Wish me luck!

TELEPHONE FOLLOW-UP

Follow up your communications to the major radio and TV talk shows, and all the ones in your state of residence, with telephone calls. You have an arsenal of support at your website and delivery options for your book presentation, author media kit, and review-book. Have your 30-second tell-and-sell ready. Your objectives should be:

- To find out if your fax or e-mail communication got through the high-tech jungle.
- To ask if the news and entertainment story is of interest. If given the opportunity, reintroduce the news approach and move through your 30-second tell-and-sell.

- To give the producer/host the option of going to your website to download the book presentation, media kit, interview(s), and review-book, or receiving PDFs of all the files on a CD-R sent by U.S. Postal Service Priority Mail.

If you find it necessary to make another follow-up call, be sure you are prepared to adjust or add something fresh to your news pitch. Try and find an opening you might fill; persistence will win the day.

It may take a while before you have an opportunity to actually talk to a show's producer/host or a key staff member. Be polite and persistent. Record contact information and notes in your contacts record system, and follow-up with thank-yous/reminders—short, postal-mail notes or postcards.

SOURCES FOR STRATEGIES

An excellent source of inspiration and guidance for developing strategies to sell books through radio or TV talk shows is available through Bradley Communications; request their free tape and report. Telephone: 800-989-1400 ext 559. Fax: 610-284-3704.

Advertising in *Radio-TV Interview Report (RTIR)* has proven effective for many authors and small publishers. More than 4,000 producers, hosts, and program directors at radio and television programs nationwide searching for interesting guests read this standard in the industry. Bradley Communications Corp. publishes the magazine. Telephone: 800-553-8002, ext. 125. The magazine will draft your ad copy for review. The last time I checked, the cost was around $348 for a half-page, and multiple-ad discounts applied. Almost every monthly issue of PMA's newsletter contains a full-page ad for *RTIR*. Go to http://www.rtir.com/ for general information.

4. PMA CO-OP MARKETING PROGRAMS

The co-op marketing programs offered by PMA to small publishers and authors place quality promotional information directly in front of media and book-trade market segments appropriate to book genre and/or subject matter. The proven effectiveness of these programs makes the reasonable cost a good investment.

Consider participating in several of the co-op programs over the first year or more of your book's availability in the market. If you're following

Continuing Creative Promotional Plan

the suggestions in this book, you already began participating when you utilized PMA's direct mailing programs to reviewers and libraries.

NOTE: Also see Dan Poynter's special report entitled, "Cooperative Book Promotion," at http://www.parapublishing.com/ for additional information and sources.

PROGRAMS, COSTS AND DELIVERY

Currently, the cost of the PMA marketing programs range from $175-300/mailing, depending on whether the program is a flyer mailing to libraries or a cooperative catalog mailing to reviewers, bookstores, corporate libraries, or one of twelve categories of target markets. The major programs are offered 4-12 times per year with a 45-60-day delivery time after submission deadlines. Go to http://www.pma-online.org/, or check out the PMA monthly newsletter, for program descriptions, advance copy deadlines, and mailing schedules. Knowing months ahead when copy is due will allow you to budget the funds necessary.

NOTE: I will not participate in the programs for bookstores or target markets, because I'm not interested in assuming the risks of producing and maintaining inventory to support consignment selling.

5. PERSONAL PROGRAM

If you want to accomplish writing goals as an author, it will be important to organize a personal promotion program that maximizes sales and is flexible, satisfying, and efficient. I suggest considering the following promotional activities:

- Design, promote, and conduct workshops or classes, and offer consulting services in areas of expertise.
- Design, promote, and offer short peer reviews, critique editing, line editing, and manuscript line proofing.
- Write short stories, columns, and/or articles for publication.
- Register as a speaker at professional websites and organizations like Toastmasters.
- Offer to be a speaker or participate in workshops or panels at major conferences, trade shows, and book fairs.

- Attend local, regional, and major events appropriate to writing, publishing, and your subject or genre.
- Organize a contact program to secure appearances on appropriate radio and TV interview programs.

This is not meant to be an exhaustive list. Out of all the possibilities, choose a mix of activities that satisfies your personal modus operandi. Remember, all the activities you choose need to be supported and facilitated by the credible umbrella of your business website. Outlined below is the mix of activities I've chosen. (For an example of how I support and facilitate an activity, go to my website, http://www.gracepublishing.org/, and examine the "Self-Publishing Workshops" pages.)

WORKSHOPS

This service is my primary personal promotional activity. After wrestling with several workshop ideas, I settled on offering complimentary (a donation bucket is placed at the registration table) self-publishing workshop/signings to writing and arts organizations, libraries, bookstores, colleges, and universities in my state of residence. The workshops are question-and-answer sessions that last 2-4 hours. At the end of a workshop I offer to stay and answer more questions and sell autographed books.

Authors/self-publishers have tons of knowledge to share. If the workshop concept is attractive, you'll think of many organizations to add to a list of potential hosts based on your writing, self-publishing and subject expertise.

To organize workshops, I periodically e-mail invitations to the key program planners or directors of organizations in my state of residence. Fax and postal-mail are alternatives. My objective is to fill out a schedule of committed workshops over the November-May time-period, with consideration to commitments I make to attend or participate in industry events. My website contains pages of information and an e-mail address to facilitate inquiries. In addition, the website provides information for interested workshop participants, including a list of topics to help prepare workshop questions. Some of the elements to consider in organizing workshop/signings are:

- Begin by sending your invitations at least 60 days in advance of when you want to start scheduling commitments. The invitation should direct invitees to specific website pages for information about you, your works, and the workshop, and provide contact alternatives.
- Follow up the invitations promptly with telephone calls.
- Make sure workshop rooms are flexible for last minute adjustments to accommodate at least 20-50 persons, including chairs and a registration table. Schoolroom seats or chairs behind tables work well.
- Request posting of workshop information by local newspapers starting 30 days from workshop dates.
- Post a generic workshop information flyer at your website for host organizations to copy, paste, and customize for their use. An effective flyer is one page, both sides, black-and-white, 8.5 X 11-inch folded once—giving a four-page, booklet/flyer, which saves space. My flyer for self-publishing workshops contains pictures of the front and back covers of this book, purchase information, website and contact information, and the details about the workshop and how to prepare.
- Ask host organizations to make workshop information flyers available to their patrons and/or members by posting them on bulletin boards and/or publishing the information in appropriate schedules, announcements, newsletters, and websites, etc. If there's resistance to producing the flyers, customize and send them to the organization.
- Request public-service announcements from appropriate arts-supporting radio and TV stations on a schedule starting three weeks before workshop dates. If workshops are free, most stations will post and/or announce the workshop.
- Construct an announcement poster and ask permission to have it placed in a prominent location on the organization's premises. Making a display poster is inexpensive; for example, blow up color book cover pictures (front and back), laminate them (estimated cost of lamination is around $20 at Kinkos),

and glue them onto separate pieces of standard poster board. At the top of the poster boards, leave enough space to tape on, or insert under protective plastic, a header for a particular workshop announcement. Hard plastic pockets can be screwed on at the bottom of both sides of a stand-up easel to hold your flyers. The posters are then mounted on both sides of the easel, and the setup is reusable. You will probably have to visit workshop locations about 15 days in advance and place announcement posters in effective locations. Use the trips effectively to build rapport at the workshop location, and schedule visits with media to present timely, compelling news-story tie-ins. You may be able to snag interviews and articles.

CLASSES AND COACHING

I offer individual classes and coaching at the beach-house where I write in Fort Myers Beach, Florida. Locations close to your residence can be chosen for these activities; for instance, public, college, and university libraries usually have free rooms you can sign-up for ad hoc or on a fixed schedule.

I charge $60/person for an all day class of up to three persons and $75 for two-hour individual coaching sessions; sometimes I waive a fee in exchange for a favor or service. I offer these services to serious writers who want to strategically jump-start their perspective on what, why, how, when, and how much it's going to cost to get their self-publishing job done, given decisions regarding their time, energy, and capital resources. I'm very selective providing this helping service, so as not to waste my own precious writing time.

The classes and coaching sessions are organized for participants to field prepared issues and questions concerning the changing field of self-publishing. I provide a topic guide on my website to help participants prepare. The concept of classes and coaching can be applied to any expertise, and in similar fashion to workshops can be fully explained, supported, and facilitated at your website.

CONSULTING SERVICES

I decided I would offer consulting services that revolved around my day-to-day writing and self-publishing activities. I offer authors help in developing important facets of self-publishing expertise. As examples, I have summarized the services I offered at my website at the time of this writing:

- Book review: Review of fiction books after the author has performed the final edit—the author must believe the book is ready for the commercial market. The book review is limited to providing general comments and suggestions on: story development, writing style, character development, front and back covers, front and back pages and formatting. The cost is $150 plus $100/100 pages—or any part thereof—with a $350 minimum.

- Book-promotion planning: Production of a tailored outline of elements and a timetable for implementation, customized to a book's subject and genre and a writer's time, energy, and capital resources. The cost can be as low as $150, and the outline is typically 2-4 pages long.

- Beginning website design: Based on the skill level required to create and maintain my own website, I offer design, planning advice, and hands-on instruction. Savvy authors/self-publishers recognize the tremendous benefits of creating a dynamic Internet information center to support business activities. Over a schedule of 8-10 four-hour sessions, scheduled a week apart, the service consists of studying other author and authors/self-publisher websites, brainstorming the initial design, examining alternative website hosting-services providers, and drafting the website in stages using Microsoft Publisher. The cost of this service is $250 in advance plus $100/four-hour website-drafting session in excess of four. Authors can have credible, business websites in full operation by the end of the service.

SPEAKING AND PARTICIPATING AT EVENTS

To promote your availability as a speaker or event participant, I suggest sending customized e-mail and fax queries to:

- The sponsors/organizers of major national publishing and writing events, for example: PMA, SPAN, SPAWN, BookExpo America (BEA), the Maui Writers Conference, etc. Plug into events well in advance (at least a year ahead). With the majors, you will probably have little success in the beginning, but sooner or later you are bound to find yourself a last-minute substitution or add-in guest if you remain persistent and credibly present yourself. For more information, see the sections below on sources and premiere writing events.

- Major writer, reader, genre, arts, and subject-related organizations, as well as libraries, bookstores, colleges, and universities in your state of residence.

These e-mails and faxes should be one-page sales pieces you design to sell yourself as a speaker. I suggests keeping it concise and to the point. Include a mini-resume, author credentials, and a list of topics. Always include your standard attribution-signature. I also include a headshot in black and white at 75 dpi, and mention that the cost is negotiable. In most cases, I charge a small fee in addition to expenses, or exchange a benefit, for example, a waiver of attendance fees at a major conference or trade show in exchange for speaking or panel participation.

In my state of residence, querying interest in event participation takes place in conjunction with my workshop/signing efforts. Usually, I'm happy to speak or participate in events at my cost as long as my books are readily available for purchase.

If you are interested in seeking quality paying opportunities, I suggest investigating one or more of the major speaker registrars, for example, http://www.guestfinder.com/ ($249/year) and http://www.expertclick.com/ (guest yearbook at $495/year). In addition, it may be wise to join a local chapter of the National Speakers Association, http://www.nsaspeaker.org/, to promote your availability and access training opportunities (about $300/year). Submission forms are available at these sites.

ATTENDING EVENTS

It's positive PR to participate in and/or attend industry events nationally and in your state of residence, such as workshops, conferences, trade shows, and book and art fairs, etc., as well as those related to the genre or subject of your book. Some event sources and premiere industry events are outlined below:

EVENT SCHEDULING SOURCES

- Check the newsletters and websites of PMA, SPAN, and SPAWN. Often these organizations sponsor booths at major trade shows and book fairs for member participation.
- Search the free calendar of events at R. R. Bowker's business-resource website at http://www.bookwire.com/.
- Check out the list of upcoming events at The American Association of Authors and Publishers, http://www.authorsandpublishers.org/.
- Periodically scan the online listings of events that might have a tie-in for you at http://www.shawguides.com/ and http://www.zuzu.com/.
- Track local and regional events through the websites of writer and publisher organizations, libraries, state government, major cities, colleges, and universities. Another tack is to go first to a search engine and search keywords for your state, like Georgia book fair, art fair, bookseller show, library show, book show, book event, art fair, author signings, etc. Then explore keywords related to the genre and subject of your book.

    I consider attending if I'm able to present my books for sale at a table or booth at a reasonable cost. A good idea is to get a few local authors together and attend an event together, sharing the cost of a common presentation booth.

- Trade shows, conferences, and other events involving libraries and the book trade may be important to consider attending. Go directly to the websites of The American Library Association, http://www.ala.org/; the National Association of College Bookstores, http://www.nacs.org/; and the American Booksellers Association, http://www.bookweb.org/, to find listings.

If you plan to attend or participate in an event, the trip can be even more productive if you consider organizing local promotions, for example: library and bookstore signings, media interviews, and workshops, etc.

PREMIERE WRITER AND PUBLISHING EVENTS

- The annual Maui Writers Conference, partially sponsored by *Writer's Digest* and held the week before and during Labor Day weekend, is the place for advice, inspiration, and contacts. The *Writer's Digest* website, http://www.writersdigest.com/, has a link to the conference at its home page, and a special insert for the conference appears in their magazine well in advance.

- Perhaps the most important event in the publishing world happens in October; it's the Frankfurt Book Fair. In recent years more than 8,500 publishers and distributors worldwide have met in Frankfurt, Germany to buy and sell rights and arrange contracts.

- Next in importance internationally would be the London Book Fair, usually held in March; and then the Prague Book Fair held in May.

- In the United States, the largest educational trade show and exhibit for independent publishers is BookExpo America (BEA), held in Chicago annually in the beginning of June. Recent attendance has approached 30,000.

- Just prior to BEA for the last few years, the Publishers Marketing Association (PMA) has held its annual Publishing University, with classes and presentations across the publishing and writing gamut.

- SPAN, Small Publishers Association of North America, held its second annual BookPublish trade show for authors, self-publishers, and independent presses in Los Angeles in October, 2003.

6. INTERNET TESTING PROGRAM

The Internet offers the self-publisher a vast market of open-ended opportunities for testing promotional approaches. I've briefly described some potential candidates below:

TESTING OPT-IN E-MAIL LISTS

Consider contracting an opt-in, bulk e-mailing, or purchase a test list outright. Lists are available for nearly every kind of interest you can

Continuing Creative Promotional Plan

dream up. Prices are usually based on the size of the list. Search the Internet for opt-in lists. Then do your own investigating and deal making; for example, I found consensus recently at around $0.17 per name for a list of 1,000. These contact lists have been compiled of individuals expressing interest in a subject on the Internet by opting in some defined way to receive information by e-mail.

Apply the standards you've developed for managing spam to the design of these e-mail promotions. Responses from small test mailings to interest-based lists having to do with the genre or subject of your book may help you define larger approaches to maximize effectiveness.

TESTING BULK E-MAIL LISTS

I do not recommend experimenting with e-mail promotions using lists on CDs; for example, recently you could pay $99 to purchase 10 million current addresses that included bulk e-mail software with no strings attached. I received similar offers constantly during 2001-2002 through several of my general, business e-mail addresses. During 2003 these spam offers seemed to all but disappear; and then late in the year resurgence began.

7. DIRECT SALES PROGRAM

Within the constraints of your time, energy, and financial resources, the objective of this program is to focus attention on direct sales promotions to your most lucrative target markets. For most of us, this means libraries, potential individual buyers, major book-related organizations (with interest in your book), and selected nontraditional outlets. For the most part, except for nontraditional outlets, these target markets don't return books and don't expect large discounts, making sales you drive and fulfill at or through your website very profitable.

I also recommend selectively placing books in bookstores in your state of residence, if for no other reason than to provide more access to your book close to home and in cities where you are making promotional appearances; in this scenario, the consignment exposure is within your control. If you are using a distributor or wholesalers, direct promotions to bookstores may deserve testing.

SALES OFFERS TO LIBRARIES

Because libraries don't expect discounts, do not return books, pay in advance—or within 30 days—often will pay for shipping, and the cost of e-mail and fax communications is low, I concentrate on winning these sales. The North American market is large, representing a potential sales block as large as 10,000-30,000 books, depending on the subject of the book and its applicability to adults and youth.

Every 4-6 weeks, I suggest sending a fresh sales/announcement to your library lists, first by e-mail and then by fax. Tailor the piece to go to genre-specific selection librarians. Cite your best library testimonials, review kudos, and taglines; and if you offer a discount, make sure it's consistent with your presentation in the PMA co-op flyer program. One of the keys to success with your direct approach to libraries will be communication with a specific selection librarian.

If you have the resources, consider purchasing the CD-ROM of the current edition of the *American Library Directory*. Its new publisher is Info Today, Inc., http://www.infotoday.com/ (previously published by R.R. Bowker). Recently, the cost was $499. Call the customer-service number, 800-300-9868 or 609-654-6266; the directory comes out annually in June. Nearly all the entries have fax and e-mail addresses, and CD facilitates searching and sorting to develop target mailings. The directory covers over 30,000 government, public, and higher-education libraries in North America and Mexico.

Libraries have been reluctant in the past to order books from other than established wholesalers like Baker & Taylor, Quality Books, or Ingram Book Group. But with the onset of the Internet and the number of quality books offered directly by small publishers and self-publishers, libraries are becoming less reluctant to purchase from credible, fulfillment service providers like Book Masters Inc., http://www.bookmasters.com/; Book Clearing House, http://www.bookch.com/; and others who've been in business for decades, have long track records of fulfillment for libraries across the country, and represent hundreds of publishers. The same could be said for the growing number of reputable Internet publisher organizations, for example: http://www.iuniverse.com/, http://www.xlibris.com/, http://www.1stbooks.com/, http://www.unlimitedpublishing.com/, etc.

The plan is: With repetition of quality messages/announcements, using a variety of communication modes, you will be able to convince libraries to order direct from you as the publisher, or from your fulfillment service provider.

In your state of residence, you will be reinforcing your sales efforts through workshop/signings at libraries, and continuing to request reviews as part of developing those library relationships. And remember, your PMA co-op program flyers to libraries should be going out 3-4 times/year.

SALES OFFERS TO BOOKSTORES

If you are using a distributor or wholesalers (consignment selling), I suggest you offer the book by e-mail and fax to bookstores in your state of residence. Use the same approach as suggested for libraries. The discount could be 20%-25% off cover, FOB the bookstore or their client (make sure offers are in line with your distributor/wholesaler pricing and terms to bookstores). Send bookstore owners/managers to the Bookstore Room at your website for a book presentation and author media kit, and to your distributor or wholesalers for fulfillment. A good idea might be to offer bookmarks (free) at the Bookstore Room and through the distributor and wholesalers. You could start out with the 100 bookstores closest to your residence as a test.

Another approach would be to use PMA's co-op program targeting bookstores and PMA's Advance Access program to independent bookstores ($50—see http://www.pma-online.org/; this is a program that offers news and galley or review-books through BookSense, http://www.bookweb.org/, the online presence of the American Bookstore Association, a major organization of independent bookstores). If your tests go well, consider using the *American Book Trade Directory,* published by Information Today, Inc. to compile lists of bookstores (a CD-ROM of this directory is not yet available for purchase). Most major libraries have the book in the reference section. Recent searches on the Internet didn't turn up any other useful sources for bookstores lists, except the bookstore directory of member independent bookstores (of the American Bookstore Association) online at http://www.bookweb.org/.

Several self-publishing authors in Florida have found it worthwhile to visit bookstores in their hometowns and experiment with relationship building as well as placing books on consignment. I see this local consignment activity as productive; it's controllable and provides complimentary opportunities to test displays at counters or entrances, place bookmarks, schedule workshop/signings, and support other local promotions. You could look at the effort as a mini-test-market for applying a variety of promotions to start a word-of-mouth ground swell.

SALES OFFERS TO POTENTIAL INDIVIDUAL BUYERS

Schedule periodic, craftily designed e-mail messages and website postings offering special giveaways to lists you've compiled of potential individual buyers and Internet groups. The objective of these communications is to develop and drive interest to your website for fulfillment. Preparation and formatting of these messages should comply with the guidelines you've developed for avoiding spam.

EXAMPLE GIVEAWAYS

In general, giveaways are something of significant value offered to recipients defined as special—for example, members of a club—for a limited time. To help stimulate creativity, I've listed some examples below of materials and services that could be presented as giveaways:

- Articles that expand on topics in your business, books, or other writing.
- A newsletter that offers benefits for subscribers.
- An archive of your newsletter back issues. In 2003 I posted The Grace Publishing Group's newsletter archive from 2002 through the latest issue as a PDF file for download at a special page accessible to newsletter subscribers; in newsletter issues I reiterated its availability and the special page URL. I kept the archive current by adding the new newsletter issue each month.
- A radio program schedule with topics and expert guests that takes place though the (digital and/or audio) chat room capabilities of your Internet club service provider.
- A complimentary PDF copy of your book.

- PDF booklets, instruction modules, and other multipurposing products derived from your book, works, or other professional activities.

- A one-on-one, half-hour counseling session on any topic within your expertise, scheduled by mutual convenience at a private chat room. For example, you could create a free chat room at Yahoo! Chat prior to a set time and wait for the session recipient to sign on. For information, go to http://www.yahoo.com/ and click on Chat in the list of main topics at the top of the page. Voice communication is also facilitated at Yahoo! Chat. All you need is a $10 microphone plugged into your PC (this giveaway might just be offered to purchasers of your book).

- A mini-edit, critique, or review of an edited short chapter of a novel. It would be necessary to post at your website a detailed explanation of what is acceptable, and an application form for required information and agreement to stated procedures. Keep the process organized, simple, and in your control (this giveaway might just be offered to purchasers of your book).

DELIVERING COMMUNICATIONS TO INDIVIDUALS

Sending e-mail messages to many recipients at the same time is becoming more difficult as Internet-service providers place restrictions on their e-mail services in response to pressures for control of spam. But, it should be worthwhile to invest time sending your messages within the limits. For example, some of the major e-mail service providers allow only 50-100 recipients/e-mail and up to 500 recipients in a 24-hour period, no matter how many accounts you utilize.

On the other hand, if you elect to use an e-mail marketing service (search the Internet for providers.) instead of sending through your e-mail service provider, you eliminate the restrictions, and the risk of complaints going directly to your e-mail service provider. No matter how courteous you try to be or how spam-conscious your communication standards, complaints are inevitable.

SALES OFFERS TO BOOK-RELATED ORGANIZATIONS

Send periodic e-mail and fax invitation/offers to contacts in your list of book-related organizations. You might also want to consider sending the invitation/offers by postal-mail to the majors. The objective is to convince organizations to publish short articles/offers for a limited time to staff and members. I suggest a telephone follow-up to the majors.

THE INVITATION/OFFER

The invitation/offer should:

- Be in formal business-letter format.

- Briefly introduce you, your business, and your book, citing credible references, for example: membership organizations, ISBN, and your major service relationships, such as printer, distributor, wholesalers, vendor of record, etc.

- Offer a complimentary giveaway and/or discounted product to organization members for a specific time.

- Contain taglines and sales hooks.

- Explain the acquisition process for staff and members.

- Invite the organization to call you directly by telephone.

- Cite a special URL (page) on your website for acquisition of a sample article draft to help them construct their own.

- Offer PDF downloads of your book presentation, media kit, and review-book on your website as well as delivery of these files on CD-R by postal-mail.

AN EXAMPLE

Your book is about gardening. The American Gardening Association has a website and a newsletter of around 110,000 subscribers. Your article/offer includes a special member discount on book purchases for a 60-day period. The special offer is to be placed on their website, in their newsletter, and included in periodic listserv announcements to members (assuming they maintain a listserv). Here are some of the main elements of the offer and how it might work:

- 20% off the cover price for association staff and members, plus shipping and handling.

- Donation by the publisher (you) of 10-20% of the cover price (or a dollar amount per book that scales up depending on sales) to support the association.

- Expiration of the offer on a specific date.

- Association members and staff fill out order forms at your website with charge-card information, or postal-mail the order form information and checks to your business. If you don't want to fulfill orders yourself, you could coordinate fulfillment of orders directly through your fulfillment-services provider.

- The article/offer posted on the organization's website contains a hyperlink to a book-presentation and order-form page on your website—or your fulfillment-service provider's website.

- You send e-mail copies of order confirmations to the organization (or your fulfillment-services provider does so), and periodically remit accrued donation amounts.

This kind of promotion can give your book significant free exposure and increased credibility through association with the organization.

SALES TO NONTRADITIONAL MARKETS

Nontraditional markets include everything except bookstores, libraries, and subsidiary rights (foreign deals, TV, film, condensations, serials, merchandise, etc.). The discovery of nontraditional markets for your book and book products is only limited by your imagination.

Dan Poynter, in *Book Marketing A New Approach, A Book Publishing Consultation With Dan Poynter,* indicates that this market is probably larger than 25% of purchased books. Dan says, "Nontraditional markets are where most publishers should spend their energy."

I divide the nontraditional market into general markets and premium sales. If you elect not to enter the consignment business, some of the below markets will not apply.

GENERAL MARKETS

- Non-book specialty shops, for example: gift shops, hospitals, museums, tourist shops, sporting-goods stores, hobby stores and toy stores.
- Mail-order catalogs. You have already sent them galley-book review invitations.
- Warehouse clubs such as Costco, the Office Club, Sam's, etc.
- Academic specialty-book markets such as alternative schooling, reading, or quasi-textbook.
- TV shopping channels.
- Specialty product distribution such as audiotapes, videotapes, and CD-Rs of the book, multipurposing of the book, and audio/video recordings of workshops, classes, seminars, and speeches.

PREMIUM SALES

I don't expect to make significant profits from premium sales. The reasons for my interest are identical to those for generating book-club and catalog sales, that is, to:

- Generate larger, more economical print runs.
- Increase market exposure.
- Initiate a snowball effect from satisfied readers.
- Sell books without financial risk (no returns and no consignment).

Ask yourself if your book can be offered to an organization or group to be given away as an incentive, or sold at a discount, to stimulate membership or provide value to customers or employees, for example:

- A gardening magazine might agree to give away or sell a gardening book at a discount with new subscriptions.
- A book about writing or self-publishing might be sold by a national writing organization at a discount to its members, or given as a gift to stimulate new memberships.

- A book on a healthy-living modus operandi, weight-loss plan, or stress-relief philosophy might be an ideal Christmas present to policy holders of insurance companies as part of a new coverage package.
- A book on investing or finance could be an attractive gift for banks and investment-banking firms to offer their customers.
- If your book's subject or genre is in line with the mission of a major nonprofit organization that actively solicit donations, it might be a candidate for a fundraiser, for example: the Heart Association, M.S. Society, the Girl/Boy Scouts, religious organizations, major trade associations, etc.

PREMIUM IDEAS

I suggest the following sources for stimulating creativity and keeping up with new premium ideas:

- The *Directory of Premium, Incentive and Travel Buyers,* by Salesman's Guide, Inc: 121 Chanlon Road, New Providence, NJ 07947. Telephone: 800-521-8110. Fax: 908-665-3560.
- Specialty magazines such as *Potentials in Marketing, Premium Incentive,* and *Inventive Marketing.*

Most of the big publishers don't concern themselves with this market. Without the big names, the field is open to thinking outside the box.

8. INTERNET ADVERTISING PROGRAM

The Internet offers the self-publishing author a multitude of cost-free and low-cost opportunities for credible exposure on websites of organizations where the bulk of potential buyers for your book, book products, and services go to find information. By investing the time to find these synergistic organizations and groups you can:

- Establish reciprocal links.
- Register with subject directories, web rings and related organizations.
- Develop affiliate/associate relationships with high profile majors to earn commissions from sales by your website visitors.

- Obtain free advertising for you, your books, book products, and business interests by offering articles to magazines, newsletters, and e-zines that have interest in your expertise, subject fields, or business activities.

RECIPROCAL LINKS AND DIRECTORY REGISTRATIONS

Offer to exchange links with important, high-profile organizations on the Internet that have interest in the subject and/or genre of your works. If you've followed the advice in this book, these organizations have been identified in the lists compiled in Chapter IV, for example, book-related organizations and book-presentation and author-posting sites.

Many of these same organizations present author, writer, publisher, or book information in directories on their websites as resources to support and enhance their business activities.

AFFILIATE/ASSOCIATE PROGRAMS

Affiliate/associate programs link sites by placing hyperlinked icons to their organizations on your website. When visitors and surfers to your website use a link and buy something, the process has been tracked and the purchase generates a commission or referral fee for your organization.

Perhaps the largest of affiliate/associate programs for organizations interested in books is Amazon.com.'s associate program. Details and the registration process can be found through links at the bottom of their home page, http://www.amazon.com/. At the end of 2003 Amazon had over 900,000 associate sites in the program.

A Google.com search in early 2003 using the terms, "affiliate programs" and "associate programs," turned up several searchable directories, for example: http://www.affiliatematch.com/, http://www.associateprograms.com/ and http://www.affiliate-program-guide.com/. These sites facilitate finding related programs to consider, and offer free newsletters, articles, and booklets on the affiliate/associate subject to help you climb the learning curve and stay savvy.

POSTING ARTICLES

I suggest organizing an article-writing plan in conjunction with multipurposing your book (or other works). These articles can be offered to high-profile organizations associated with the genre and/or

Continuing Creative Promotional Plan

subject of your book that publish magazines, newsletters, and e-zines—and to news services that post articles for use by the media (see the next section). If you've followed the plan in this book, you've compiled lists of appropriate organizations to sort through. Search the Internet using keywords like "free articles" to find additional posting opportunities.

Articles could be offered in exchange for an eighth of a page ad in several consecutive issues of a publication, or just for the intangible exposure and credibility values the article and attribution-signature may produce.

NEWS DISSEMINATION

Many websites offer services that place your press releases, announcements, articles, interviews, and offers, etc. in front of large blocks of potential media and market interest. The claims of these organizations vary widely. Some of the services are fee-based, and others are free. Typically, they post articles and allow media clients (news organizations, newspapers, radio, TV, magazines, and newsletters) to reprint them in exchange for brief author bios (attribution-signatures) at the end and a link to the author's website. Some experimenting/testing would seem worthwhile. Here's a list of some that have been around for a while and disseminate news announcements to newspapers, radio, TV, magazines, and newsletters:

- Idea Marketers, http://www.ideamarketers.com/, offers a free writer account where your articles are made available to segments of the media.

- PRWeb, http://www.prweb.com/, provides a wire service based on donation. Once approved, your release is posted to their website and submitted to their database of media editors.

- Worldannounce Nework, http://www.worldannounce.com/, posts your news to over 100,000 news channels in 192 countries and to their opt-in subscription list. The basic service costs $20-$55 for 7-60 days of postings.

- Live Press Wire, http://www.livepresswire.com/, distributes press releases and news stories worldwide to targeted media-market segments for a fee based on selected geographic location and number of outlets.

- Ezine Articles, http://www.ezinearticles.com/, is a free posting site for articles, primarily for e-zines looking for content.
- ImediaFax, http://www.imediafax.com/, is a news-release distribution service by fax to specific editors of targeted media; it costs about $0.25 per page.
- Internet News Bureau, http://www.internetnewsbureau.com/, is a fee-based, press-release distribution service to subscribed journalists and business professionals categorized into lists by subject. Fees are based on a charge of $275 for the first list and $80/list thereafter.
- WebProNews, http://www.webpronews.com/, offers a free article-posting service.

9. FOREIGN RIGHTS PROGRAM

I recommend utilizing PMA's Foreign Rights Virtual Bookfair posting at $25/quarter. Your work is professionally displayed at a publisher-oriented website where the marketplace comes to peruse what's happening in the world of small publishers. As soon as your book begins to sell, this posting is likely to catch the attention of quality inquiries; go to http://www.pma-online.org/ for more information.

Begin e-mails and faxes to your foreign rights publishers list, sending them to the Business Page of your website where you've organized links to specific information on the site. Dan Poynter's special report, *Exports/Foreign Rights, Selling U.S. Books Abroad,* covers the subject in depth; it's available at http://www.parapublishing.com/.

E. ASSISTANCE AND SUPPORT TO WRITERS AND READERS

It's always a good feeling to be able to help someone else in this life. If you can't spend the time required to answer all the questions you receive, and you want to provide as much free support as possible to aspiring authors, I suggest considering offering articles, a club, a newsletter, and limited-time access to complimentary, PDF e-book and book products. Access to these aids can be organized on your website, and promotion is through e-mail messages and postings to your lists as outlined previously in this chapter.

ARTICLES

Writing informative how-to articles for the publications of major support organizations in your field is a method for keeping yourself in the networking mainstream.

Consider posting all your articles, along with a schedule of articles in progress or under consideration, on your website for visitors to view and/or download at no cost.

INTERNET CLUB

You can found your own free club to provide a venue for well-thought-out questions, either sent directly to you or posted for member response. For example, I founded the Self-Publishing Club at Lycos Communities, http://www.lycos.com/. If you want to see how it's organized and haven't been to Lycos before, you will have to fill out a registration form. Below is a copy of the founder's message at the club:

> *This club is a professional venue and resource for aspiring writers, college faculty, researchers, journalists... all genres and subjects, to post well-thought-out questions, issues, and give answers to the postings of others.*
>
> *The co-publishers and affiliate author, Marshall Chamberlain, of The Grace Publishing Group (http://www.gracepublishing.org/), monitor the club's postings for appropriateness.*
>
> *The site is organized into permanent discussion topics that appear under boards at the left-hand tool-bar. Choose a discussion topic, then create your own discussion (which becomes a subtopic). You must do that for others to be able to reply to your posting.*
>
> *Use the right-hand tool-bar to start a club chat with one or more members. Just set a time to meet, create the chat room, and conduct your discussion. As soon as you leave the chat, the room is deleted.*

Founding an Internet club is an effective tool for creating buzz and providing a forum for discussion, venting, and posting. It is also a venue for the founder to test new concepts and ideas, provide answers to serious questions, and offer complimentary products. The existence of your club can be included in your e-mail attribution-signature at the end of written works and articles.

Yahoo!, MSN, AOL, Lycos, and other Internet directories and search engines offer free club- and/or group-creation capabilities. The time to monitor and answer questions posted at a club can be well spent. Club members can become important advocates for your activities and endeavors, and a well-run club can keep you up to date on what's on the minds of writers and/or readers of your genre or subject.

CHAT ROOM

Another intriguing idea is to establish a chat room. You might approach the organization of the chat room like you would the creation of a radio program, with scheduled topics and appropriate guests. The radio program could be offered through your club website and at a special page on your business website. The radio program could become another promotional giveaway in your arsenal.

For example, if you're an author/expert on raising teenagers, you might invent the program, *Talking With Teens Live, Sunday Mornings, 8:30-10:00 a.m.* You could make a radio program a permanent part of a club, and include a full presentation on your website with a schedule of guest experts in the field and/or a list of program subjects.

Promotion of the program might include posting at the club URL; e-mails to club members; promotions to appropriate lists; and postings to subject-related groups, clubs, and news-dissemination organizations, explaining how to get to the chat room and how to participate.

Some providers of chat room services, for example Yahoo!, now have both audio and video capabilities, so you can probably figure out a way to go totally live. At the present time, these services are free.

NEWSLETTER

One of the primary purposes of offering a free periodic newsletter is to provide a professional avenue for helping writers and/or readers interested in your genre and subject. It establishes credibility and positive buzz for you, your book, and your business. It can become an important promotional vehicle (giveaway) by affording you worthy reasons (for example citing a particular article or concept) for e-mailing

Continuing Creative Promotional Plan

announcements to your lists of potential individual buyers and postings at appropriate groups, clubs, and organizations. For example:

> Subject: Increasing Book Sales to Libraries
>
> If you're interested in book sales to libraries, the April issue of my monthly newsletter, XXXXXXXXXXXXXXX, introduces a new promotional methodology to the library market. The newsletter is complimentary and comes out around the seventh of each month. Go to http://www.yourwebsite.com/page000000.html to subscribe.

Add your salutation and attribution-signature, and it's done.

My self-publishing newsletter, *Tips Tricks & Scoop*, as an example, was designed as a cutting-edge information piece in the field of self-publishing, and I published it for over two years while I was writing this book. It was free to subscribers who completed a subscription form at my website and I delivered it by e-mail. The flavor of the newsletter can be gleaned from the standard introduction I employed at the top of each issue:

> Keeping it short, keeping it succinct, the objectives of the newsletter are to:
>
> Report significant resources we've discovered...Tips.
>
> Present creative concepts and ideas...Tricks.
>
> Pass on hot, self-publishing news...Scoop.
>
> We will concentrate on originality and timeliness, and cite the source when it does not come directly from us. We want to stir subscriber genius to design new avenues for making a living and selling more books and other book and promotional products. By taking control, and with unwavering determination, we can learn how to get the most out of our computer software, business-communication services, and the Internet. We can all become savvy, dynamic, and successful self-publishers on a pauper's budget.

At the end of the newsletter I included a Notes section for anything short and impacting that has to do with my business as an author and self-publisher, for example:

- Completion of a new article available free at my website.

- A new chapter of a book posted at my website.
- A new booklet available for sale.
- A new t-shirt design for sale.
- Other products or benefits created for subscribers as a special group or for a limited period of time.

Near the top of every issue of the newsletter I presented a hyperlinked, special page URL on my website so subscribers could go and download the PDF files of the current issue and the cumulative archive.

Postscript

You don't have to have a blockbuster to be a successful self-publisher. Speaking for myself, my goal is to make a living through a promotional modus operandi that leaves me fully engaged in enjoyable and fruitful networking, but allows plenty of time to write fiction books. As a self-publisher, if you perform all the publishing functions yourself, your first goal could be a level of sales to enable distancing yourself from the time-consuming mechanics of order fulfillment, paper pushing, dealing with purchasers, and bookkeeping.

YOU CAN MAKE A LIVING SELLING BOOKS

Following the approach laid down in this book, if you only sell 3,000 books/year directly from your website, at workshop/signings, and out of the trunk of your car, you should net about $15/book based on the following assumptions:

- 350-page hardback with a cover price of $28.
- 200-copy print runs at $13/book for printing and shipping to your residence.
- You charge customers for the costs of payment processing, packaging, and shipping (About $0.40 for charge-card

processing, $1 for materials and packaging, $1.75 for up to two pounds at U.S. Postal Service Book Rate).

That's about $45,000/year in gross profit, not including the expenses to run your business, or net income from traditional book-trade sales, or income from workshops, classes, speaking and consulting.

REORGANIZE WITH INCREASING SALES

When your book sales reach a certain level—and when it's no longer a pleasure to process and fulfill orders at home, when you feel bogged down—it will be time to reconfigure the business in order to free more time for you to write and take advantage of other interests.

The next logical step is to develop a business relationship with a reputable, financially stable, printing/fulfillment organization; for example, BookMasters Inc., http://www.bookmasters.com/, takes charge-card orders 24/7 online in their bookstore, or through a toll-free telephone number, or by check and charge-card through postal-mail and fax. Their services include:

- Printing your book at competitive costs for runs of 200 to 15,000 copies, using state-of-the-art equipment that includes the digital technology used by POD and PQN printing organizations.
- Keeping inventory insured and safe and sound.
- Processing sales and returns.
- Taking orders and handling and shipping books according to the terms and conditions you lay down for sales relationships with different segments of the buying market.
- Making monthly reports of income and expenses and remitting proceeds.

In this kind of business relationship, you make no long-term commitments that affect your literary rights or your flexibility to enter into legal agreements with the publishing industry.

DON'T LET SUCCESS CHANGE YOUR MODUS OPERANDI

Even with an adequate level of sales and momentum, you may refrain from opening sales up to the book trade on traditional terms; the risks are still too great. With the marginal success I've mentioned above, distributors and wholesalers will begin contacting you.

Remember, it takes up to 120 days for payments to trickle down to you through the distributor/wholesaler/bookstore-consignment business. The investment in the larger printing runs required will open your business to the potential disasters of over-inventorying, bad debts from segments of a consolidating industry, unexpected book returns, outright loss of books, and returns of damaged books. I suggest retaining the policy of accepting only prepaid orders from bookstores—perhaps experimenting with a major quasi-wholesaler like Amazon.com. (if you can find a way to work around their ability to undercut your sales promotions through their discounting) and granting 30-day terms to libraries where risk of nonpayment is virtually absent.

I have heard that if you sell as few as 10,000 copies of your book as a self-publisher, opportunities from the traditional publishing industry will open up; they will pursue you because you made it happen with next to nothing. You have proven your book will sell in the market, and you have an exact record of just how you attained your degree of success all the way down to the what, how, who, and when.

With distributors, wholesalers, agents, publishers, TV and radio producers, newspapers wanting to review your book, and foreign-rights publishers knocking on your door, a self-publisher is in a position to completely reshape the future. If you get to this point, I strongly suggest legal counsel and reaching out to the individual and organizational relationships you've developed for advice and assistance in handling opportunities one by one.

TALK THE TALK AND WALK THE WALK

If you make the commitment to become a self-publishing expert, then early in the process you must take on the personal attributes and attitudes of the successful professional you know you will become. Be exhilarated in the knowledge that you have taken control and are following a plan. Allow yourself to feel satisfied and confident as you engage and master each step. You are becoming a published author and a self-publishing expert, and you're creating a financially successful business. You can promote your growing expertise as you become vested, allowing you be active in speaking and conducting workshops based on the topics you've mastered.

Use stable industry resources, like those cited in this book, to stay current. You can become the successful, savvy self-publisher you envision in your plan, no matter what the genre or subject of your book, and you can do it in ways that are satisfying and provide an adequate living.

About the only thing you won't be able to do is print your own books. But let's see, maybe we can get the Taiwanese or the Indonesians to build inexpensive book-making machines. Yeah. Or maybe get with Chet Novicki in Hawaii at http://www.gigabooks.net/. He's made a printing machine... I could do it myself, and then...

NOTE

I wanted this journey with me through the jungle of self-publishing to take you to a place of comfort. I've attempted to open you up in multifarious directions, so you could discover your own creative juices. At the same time, I've suggested what must be done and how it can be done with limited resources and minimum risk. Now you should be able to see the forest clearly, understand the trees, and have the confidence to develop your own brand of self-publishing. You can do it!

I wish you a joyful, purposeful adventure, whatever your self-publishing goals. Trust the inspiration that bubbles up from inside, especially when you haven't asked for it, and learn to expect and accept sudden insight.

As you experience your odyssey, please share creative ideas with me. We can all use support from one another. And always take time to help others—it comes back a thousandfold.

Best Regards,

Marshall R. Chamberlain
Author, Publisher, Speaker
author@gracepublishing.org

Index

1

1001 Ways to Market Your Books (2001), by John Kremer 29

A

A Basic Guide to Fee Based Print on Demand Publishing Services, by Dehanna Bailee...13
ABA Book Buyer's Handbook, published by ABA 178
About the Author 132, 134
About.com, writer resources 30
Accounting
   Excel Temporary System.... 199
   Simple Alternative System ... 35
Activities and Availability, posting sites 154
Activity Calendar, Author 137
Advance Book Information Form (ABI) 175
Advance Sales
   Autographed Books 149
   By Internet Posting 153
   Friends and Relatives 152
   Individual 151
   Other Products 149
   Specialty Sectors 148
   Submit to Amazon.com 153
   To Libraries 150
   To Organizations 152
Affiliate Author Program 138
Affiliate/Associate Programs...... 140, 213, 238
Agents 2, 7, 8, 57, 60, 71, 130, 154, 157, 183, 195, 246
Agents, chances of interest...57, 60
ALA Booklist, Up Front
All in One Directory, published by Gebbie Press 58
Amazon.com, online book seller... 9, 110, 153, 174, 193, 204, 238, 246

American Book Trade Directory, published by Information Today, Inc. 56, 62, 231
American Booksellers Association 178, 227
American Booksellers Directory, published by the American Booksellers Association (ABA) 63
American Education 2002, published by Patterson 56
American Society of Journalists and Authors........................... 46
Angela-Adair-Hoy, author 29
Assistance You Provide
   Affiliate Author Program ... 132, 138, 141, 241
   Articles................................ 241
   Chat room 242
   Club 139, 140, 241
   Giveaways 21, 91, 131, 136, 140, 148, 152, 153, 179, 207, 208, 232, 233, 234, 242
   Newsletter........................... 242
Association of Alternative Newsweeklies 63
Attending Events 226
Attribution-Signature... ....77, 78, 108, 126, 159, 209, 212, 218, 226, 239, 242, 243
Auctions .. 32, 39, 40, 88, 111, 148
Audio and Video Interview 39, 131, 218
Author Book Purchases..... 14, 15, 17
Author Media Kit.................... 133
Author Photo Gallery...... 135, 190
AuthorLink.com, author works posting site 71, 154
Authors and Books, page at your website 132
AuthorShowcase.com, author works posting site 46, 154
Autographed Books 149

B

Bad Debt Risk................... 11, 246
Baker & Taylor, wholesaler....... 9, 13, 18, 23, 25, 56, 108, 197, 230
Bar Code 174
Barbara Gaughen, author .. 29, 210
Bio-Sketch 134
Book Business: Publishing Past, Present, Future, by Jason Epstein 26
Book Club and Catalog Deals...... 62, 181
Book Cover Pictures 223
Book Drafting
   Cover Creation 101, 102, 103
   Cover From Scratch 102
   E-Books on CDs 111
   Format and Style 44, 159
   Galley Cover 107
   Headers and Footers.............. 96
   Heading Styles 95
   Indexing......99, 100, 101, 104, 106
   PDF E-Books 104, 105
   PDF Working-Paper Version... 4, 105, 149, 204
   Table of Contents 32, 94, 98, 99, 104, 106, 133, 135, 136, 137, 172
Book Marketing A New Approach, A Book Publishing Consultation

Index

With Dan Poynter, by Dan Poynter 235
Book Operating Plan, 2.5 years .. 3
Book Order Information .. 83, 123, 141, 154, 197, 211
Book Presentation Content 132
Book Presentation Posting Sites
   AuthorLink.com 71, 154
   Authorshowcase.com 46, 154
   JL Books.com 154
   SFF Net 71, 119
Book Products Multipurposing 22, 149, 154, 233, 236, 238
Book Registrations and Listings 173
Book Reviewers 60, 63
Book Reviews and Articles 134, 182
Book Reviews From Prepublication Galleys Through a Continuing Review Program, A Book Publishing Consultation With Dan Poynter, by Dan Poynter 29, 185, 215
Book Selling 101 (2000), by Jean Heine 29
Bookmarks, promotion piece ... 32, 38, 64, 79, 211, 212, 231, 232
BookMasters, printer and fulfillment 93, 94, 245
Books in Print, listing in 175
Books in Print, published by R. R. Bowker .. 20, 128, 174, 175, 279
Books Just Books, POD printer 93, 191
Bookstore Stocking Level Decrease 20

Bookstore Room, page at your website 128
Bookstore Sales Offers 231
Bookwire.com, writer resources 154, 227
Bound Book Date (BBD) 188
Bradley Communications, Media Directories and *Radio & TV Interview Report* 58, 73, 211, 220
Broadcast E-mail 33, 53, 66, 68, 159, 160, 182
   Outlook examples 66, 67, 68, 160
Broadcast Faxes 33, 35, 157, 161, 182
Bulk E-mail 36, 37, 205, 211, 228, 229
Bulk E-mail Software 36, 205
Business Cards 32, 38, 77, 78, 84, 211
Business Forms 32
Business Header 77, 78, 120, 184, 186
Business Inquiries at your website 130
Business Links, page at your website 140
Business Risks 10, 15
Business Room, page at your website 130
Business Services ... 137, 138, 139, 155
Business Services, page at your website 137
Business-Contact Files, using Outlook categories 147, 164, 215

C

Catalog and Book Club Deals 4, 61, 105, 149, 181, 204
Chapters, free 47, 126, 133, 244
Charge-Card Processing 14, 79, 80, 81, 112, 197, 245
Charge-Card Services .. 77, 79, 80, 124, 197, 198, 199
Chat Room, start your own 242
Chat rooms 232, 233, 241, 242
Cheap Labor Compiling Lists ... 70
Classes and Coaching Services .. 7, 85, 86, 88, 136, 139, 154, 221, 224, 228, 236, 245, 270, 271, 277
Collector's Edition 92, 148, 149
Commercial Success 15, 19
Computer File Backup 111
Computer Software
    Adobe Acrobat 4.0+ 32, 104, 136
    Adobe PageMaker 6.5 ... 32, 36, 102, 103, 104, 106
    Adobe Reader 33
    Arcsoft PhotoStudio 2000 .... 35, 36
    Dreamweaver 34, 118
    Intuit QuickBooks 34, 35, 80, 81, 82, 197, 198, 199, 200
    Microsoft Access .... .34, 37, 52, 53, 58, 67, 68, 69, 128, 160, 185, 231, 240
    Microsoft Escel .. 35, 53, 67, 68, 160, 199
    Microsoft FrontPage 34, 118, 120
    Microsoft Outlook ... 32, 35, 36, 37, 39, 52, 53, 54, 66, 67, 68, 78, 85, 87, 89, 141, 147, 148, 157, 158, 159, 160, 161, 163, 185, 196, 205, 206, 207, 209
    Microsoft Publisher 5, 32, 34, 36, 37, 69, 78, 103, 104, 105, 106, 108, 109, 117, 120, 121, 122, 124, 135, 137, 141, 142, 143, 145, 169, 170, 172, 174, 184, 186, 187, 189, 211, 225, 248
    Microsoft Word 32, 33, 44, 78, 94, 95, 96, 97, 98, 99, 103, 104, 105, 106, 109, 111, 125, 158, 161, 171, 172, 209, 211
    TrafficSeeker 144
    Website Development 117
    Windows Notepad 54, 70
    WinFax PRO 10.0 .... 32, 33, 35, 36, 52, 53, 54, 81, 86, 157, 158, 161, 196
Consignment Risk 10, 11, 20, 74, 111, 193, 221, 229, 231, 232, 235, 236, 246
Consulting Services.. ...... 7, 85, 86, 136, 139, 198, 205, 221, 224, 245, 277
Contact Lists
    Compilation 55
    Importance-indicator Data-lines 52, 57, 69, 162, 163, 185
Contact Us, page at your website 141
Contacting Your Business 124, 130, 141
Contemporary Authors, published by Gale Research Company ... 178
Content Files, organization of ....

125
Contracts, publishing.....9, 15, 17, 19, 49, 228
Cooperative Book Promotion, by Dan Poynter........ 221
Cover Price .. 9, 10, 11, 17, 18, 22, 23, 24, 181, 193, 194, 235, 245
Credible Image Building.... 12, 20, 111, 116, 129, 149, 150, 167, 180, 205, 219

D

Damaged Book Risk ... 10, 11, 246
Dan Poynter, author... 2, 29, 30, 31, 61, 74, 117, 165, 171, 173, 176, 196, 197, 200, 201, 210, 215, 221, 235, 240, 279
Danny O. Snow, author......2, 29, 30, 117, 195
Database Management............. 34
Dehanna Bailee, author....... 13, 94
Delivery Confirmation...... 81, 199
Delivery Time.......11, 20, 93, 94, 153
Directories, Internet........ 140, 242
Directory of Premium, Incentive and Travel Buyers, published by Salesman's Guide, Inc. .. 237
Discounts ... 11, 14, 17, 18, 23, 28, 56, 71, 143, 150, 153, 175, 178, 180, 193, 194, 198, 229, 230, 231, 234, 236, 246
Products Bought.................. 220
Products Sold..... 149, 179, 180, 181, 234
Distribution, PMA Trade Distribution Acceptance Program 11

Distributors and Wholesalers
Economic Perspectives ... 10, 11
Financial Risks................ 10, 11
Promotional Lists.................. 62
Valuable Services.................. 11
Drafting and Saving E-mail Messages............................ 159
Dustbooks, publisher............... 177

E

E. B. White, author and self-publisher................................3
Earthlink Website Hosting...... 118
Earthlink, design and test website free.. 119
Ebay.com, auction site..... 32, 111, 148
E-Book
PDF Creation 103, 105, 148
Sellers................................ 110
E-Books on CDs 111
Economics of Making a Living.... 117, 137, 139, 147, 243
Edgar Allen Poe, author and self-publisher................................3
Editing
Author Final Edit. 43, 45, 61, 91, 167, 219, 225, 278
Author First Edit 43
Author Second Edit............... 44
Contacting Editors................ 47
Editor Sources... 46, 47, 92, 220
My Story Metamorphosis Concept........................... 45
Selecting an Editor....45, 48, 92
Edward L. Paulder, author 61
E-mail
Backup Business Addresses.....

88
Drafting and Saving Messages.. 159
Services Providers 88
Subject Line. 151, 157, 158, 160, 161, 179, 206, 209, 217
Three-line Preview.............. 206
Encyclopedia Britannica 36
Equipment Needed...... 38, 39, 111
Ernest Weckbaugh, author........ 29, 210
Events
   Major Writing and Publishing... 228
   Scheduling Sources............. 227
Excerpt... 4, 33, 57, 116, 126, 133, 134, 136, 265

F

Fan Club Concept 130
FAQ to Promote Your Business... 118, 125, 131, 134, 136, 140, 218
FAQ, page at your website 140
Fax Services, free...................... 85
Film Producers and Agents....... 57
Financial Resources ... 2, 3, 12, 21, 38, 51, 127, 183, 212, 229
Foreign Rights 62, 213, 240
Formatting and Styles
   Book Drafting...................... 95
   Promotions............ 79, 188, 234
Forwriters.com, writer resources... 30
Free Chapter 126, 133
Fulfillment System
   Design................................ 196
   Finishing and Labeling 201

Initial Order Handling......... 196
Invoice Processing and Order Processing 197
Packaging.................... 170, 200
Receiving and Storing Books... 200
Record Keeping 199
Shipping 202
Fulfillment-Services..... 17, 23, 24, 93, 94, 245
Fulfillment-Services, cost 22

G

Gale Research Company, media directory publisher 177, 178
Galley-Book
   Cover Drafting 107
   Format Costs and Delivery...... 170
   PDF E-Book........................ 170
Galley-Book Review Presentation
   Content................................ 167
   Costs.................................... 170
   Delivery 168
   Delivery Options 170
   Format Options 170
   On CD-Rs............................ 172
   Packaging Materials and Construction................... 170
   Using CD-Rs....................... 172
Galley-Book Review Promotion... 156
   Review Invitation Broadcast E-mail 159
   Review Invitation Broadcast Faxing 161
   Review Invitation Coding ... 157
   Review Invitation Content .. 158

Index

Review Invitation Purposes... 156
Review Invitation, general.. 157
Review List 162
Review Objectives 157
Telephone Delivery Follow-up.. 173
Galley-Book Reviewers
   Automatic Deliveries List.. 162, 163
   Compiling the Review List... 162
   Local Market Area 163
   Major Authors 57, 163
   Major Publishers 59, 164
   Movers and Shakers 163
   Other Major Organizations...... 164
   Telephone Follow-up Program.. 164
   Telephone Techniques 164
Gebbie Press, media directory publisher 58, 73
General Information Brochure...... 169, 188
Giveaways and Freebies......... 131, 136, 140, 152, 219
Groups and Clubs, list sources and organization 64

H

H. W. Wilson Company, publisher 214
Home, page at your website.... 126
Houghton Mifflin, publisher..... 29
How to Publish and Promote Online, by M.J. Rose and Angela Adair-Hoy 29

I

Indexing 99
Individual Buyers List........ 13, 20, 65, 67, 68, 69, 70, 155, 212, 229, 232, 243
Information Today, Inc., publisher 55, 56, 57, 151, 178, 231
Ingram, wholesaler... 9, 13, 18, 23, 25, 56, 108, 230
International Directory of Little Magazines and Small Presses, published by Dustbooks 177
Internet
   Directories............. 65, 140, 242
   Future of............................... 25
   Internet Club, page at your website 139, 241
   Internet Club/Group, create one 139, 140, 241
   Internet Communications
      Delivering Communications to Individuals...................... 233
      E-mail List Promotion Testing.. 228
      News Dissemination Services... 239
   Internet Groups and Clubs, joining 65
   Internet Listservs, joining 64
   Internet Publishing (POD)
      A Basic Guide to Fee Based Print on Demand Publishing Services, by Dehanna Bailee 13, 94
      Costs...................... 13, 15, 17
      Limited Profits 17
      Perspective 12
      Risks.............................. 15, 18

Services.......................... 11, 13
Test the Market 16
Who Are They? 12
Who Might Use? 13
Internet Search Aid, acquire the
   Google Tool-bar 31
Internet-Service Provider, backup
   .... 87, 89
Internet-Service Providers (ISP)
   .... 58, 77, 86, 87, 142, 211
Interview Suggestions 218
Invoices and Receipts by Fax or
   E-mail 35
ISBN (International Standard
   Book Number) 173
Ivan Hoffman, author and attorney
   31

J

J. I. Rodale, author 29
James Lichtenberg,
   communications consultant 110
James Redfield, author and self-
   publisher 3
Jan Venolia, author 29
Jason Epstein, author .. 26, 76, 110
Jean Heine, author 29
JL Books.com, author works
   posting site 154
John Grisham, author and self-
   publisher 2
John Kremer, author 29, 117
Jump Start Your Book Sales
   (1999), by Marilyn and Tom
   Ross 29

K

Keywords 37, 57, 69, 117, 126,
   143, 145, 146, 227, 239
   Development 145
   Register as Websites 145
   Registration 145
Kirkus Reviews, published by
   VNU eMedia 75

L

L. Ron Hubbard, author and self-
   publisher 3
Laptop Computer 39, 87, 89,
   111, 274, 275
Legal Assistance 31
Legal Information Institute,
   Cornell University 31
Library Journal, published by
   Reed Business Information ......
   75, 168
Library of Congress
   Library of Congress Control
      Number (LCCN) 176, 177,
      187
   Preassigned Control Number
      Program (PCN) 177
Library Promotions
   First Sales Offers 150
   Later Sales Offers 230
   Second Sales Offers 180
   Workshops 222
Library Room, page at your
   website 127
List Creation 52
List Descriptions 55
Listservs
   List Sources and Organization
   64

Index

Managing Messages Received 70
Literary Market Place, published by Information Today, Inc. ... 57, 58, 59, 60, 62, 63, 178
Logos 77, 120, 121

M

M. J. Rose, author 29
Making a Living 117, 147, 243, 245
Marilyn and Tom Ross, authors 29, 30
Mark Twain, author and self-publisher 3
Mary Embree, author 29
Media Databases on CD Rom ... 58
Media Kit Content 133, 134
Media Kit, Master PDF File ... 136
Media Needs 188, 207, 279
Media Room, page at your website 127
Media Sources 58, 59, 63, 73, 211, 220
Midwest Book Review, writer resources 30, 60, 110, 144
Mini-Media Kit 214
Mini-Media Kit, postal-mail test 214
Morris Publishing, printer 93
Movers and Shakers ... 69, 70, 162, 163, 183
My Favorites, Windows folder 39, 64, 70, 72

N

National Directory of Catalogs, published by Oxbridge Communications, Inc. 61
National Union Catalog, published by the Library of Congress 176
Net Zero Premium, ISP 87
News Releases and Book Publicity, A Book Publishing Consultation With Dan Poynter, by Dan Poynter 29
Newsletter
  create one 139, 243
  Mine as an example 242
  page at your website 139
Newsletters in Print, published by Gale Research Company 63
Newsletters, E-zines, Newsgroups 68

O

Official Publication Date (OPD)... 149, 159, 176, 204
Online Bookstores
  Book Submissions 192
  Cost and Profits 194
  E-Books 109, 111, 195
  Intangible Value 194
  Orders 193, 196
  Sales Presentation 193
Opt-in E-mail List Cost 228
Outlook Importing . 33, 52, 53, 67, 157, 158, 159, 160
Over 75 Good Ideas for Promoting Your Book (2000), by Patricia Fry 29

P

Para Publishing and Dan Poynter, writer resources.... 2, 29, 30, 31, 61, 75, 117, 165, 171, 173, 176, 196, 197, 200, 201, 210, 215, 221, 235, 240, 279
Parrot Media Network, media posting service 59
Patricia L. Fry, author 29
Patterson Education Directories, publisher 56
Payment Processing 11, 15
Payments in Advance 20
PayPal, charge-card service provider... 79, 80, 124, 197, 199
PDF E-Book Promotions 4, 91, 103, 105, 106, 129, 137, 148, 149, 152, 204, 214
Peer Review 221
Personal Resources, use of..... 2, 3, 12, 21, 38, 51, 127, 183, 186, 212, 224, 225, 229, 243
Personal Telephone Number... 141, 169
Photographs, useful 102, 103, 135, 168, 170, 171, 187, 190, 215
POD Publishing
   Comparative Guide 13, 94
   Costs 13, 15, 17
   Limited Profits 17
   Perspective 12
   Risks 15, 18
   Services 13
   Test the Market 16
   Who Are They? 12
   Who Might Use? 14
Podwholesale.com, printer 93, 191
Policies of Publishers, A Handbook for Order Librarians, published by Scarecrow Press 178
Policies, page at your website 141, 178
Portable Document Format (PDF) Files, creation of... 32, 104, 105, 136
Postcards, promotion pieces ... 211, 220
Poynter's Secret List of Book Promotion Contacts, by Dan Poytner 74, 173
Premium Sales Ideas 236
Press Releases .. 20, 108, 135, 159, 239
Print On Demand (POD) 1, 13, 14, 18, 19, 21, 23, 25, 26, 93, 94, 191, 194, 245
Print Quantity Needed (PQN) 1, 21, 93, 245
Printer/Fulfillment-Services Providers 93, 94, 245
Printers 92, 93, 94, 191, 245
Printers, selection of 92
Printing
   Costs 15, 17, 18, 61, 62, 191, 194
   Hardback 94
   POD/PQN 93, 191, 192
   Runs . 10, 19, 61, 102, 181, 194, 215, 246
   Sources of Quotes 92
   The Galley-Book 93, 112
Professional Activities
   Classes and Coaching ... 7, 85, 86, 88, 136, 139, 154, 221,

Index

224, 228, 236, 245, 270, 271, 277
Consulting Services ... 7, 85, 86, 136, 139, 198, 205, 221, 224, 245, 277
General....................... 136, 233
Posting your Events and Activities........................ 154
Speaking and Event Participation.... 225, 226, 227
Workshops ... 63, 117, 128, 129, 137, 138, 155, 163, 180, 181, 221, 222, 231, 232, 245
Professional Groups and Associations, join or associate 28
Profits ...10, 11, 13, 14, 15, 16, 17, 18, 19, 22, 23, 24, 49, 61, 71, 193, 194, 229, 236, 245
Promotion Lists
Beginning of List Descriptions 55
Contact Data 51, 52
Corrections........................... 54
Importance-Indicator Data-lines 52, 57, 69, 162, 163, 185
Sorting 53, 161, 185, 230
Using Microsoft Access........ 52
Using Notepad or WordPad.. 54
Promotion Log........ 150, 182, 213
Promotion Piece Ideas ... 4, 21, 32, 35, 36, 72, 126, 129, 152, 159, 211, 213, 214, 217
Promotion Pieces
Bookmarks........32, 38, 64, 79, 211, 212, 231, 232
Business cards.... 32, 38, 77, 78, 79, 84, 211

Postcards.... 184, 189, 211, 212, 215, 220
Prepublication Review Sheet.... 188
Promotion Planning
Advice From the Experts 210
Affiliate/Associate Programs.... 140, 213, 237, 238
Attending Events................. 226
Bulk E-mail Lists 72, 211
Bulk E-mail Software... 36, 205, 229
Chat Room 242
Classes and Coaching.......... 224
Consulting Services.... 139, 221, 224, 277
Core Advice 210
Databases 210
Defining Promotion Programs 212
Developing A Generic Interview 218
Direct Sales Program 229
E-mail Lists 72, 229
Event Sources...................... 227
Foreign Rights Program 240
Galley-Book Review Promotion 156
Giveaway Examples............ 232
Internet Advertising Program... 237
Internet Testing Program ...212, 228
Long-term Strategy 210
Major Writer and Publishing Events............................. 228
Media Kit 133, 136
News Dissemination 239
Newsletter 242

PDF E-Book .. 4, 105, 148, 149, 204
Personal Program 212, 221
PMA Co-op Marketing Programs 150, 174, 212, 220
Posting Articles 238
Premium Sales 236
Print-Media Program 213
Radio and TV Program 73, 216
Radio Program 242
Reciprocal Links and Directory Registrations 238
Review-Book Promotion ... 107, 155, 181, 182, 213
Speaking and Participating at Events 225
Summary of Programs 212
Summary of Promotions Prior to Printing 203
Telephone Follow-up Programs 162, 168, 172, 173, 180, 182, 185, 192, 212, 213, 219, 234
Telephone Techniques 164
Toward Setting Non-Spam Standards 204
Workshops ... 63, 117, 128, 129, 138, 155, 163, 180, 181, 222, 231, 232, 245
Promotion Products 130, 149, 154, 179, 198
Publishers and Agents, chances of interest 7
Publishers Directory, published by Gale Research Company 177

Publishers' International ISBN Directory, published by K. G. Saur Publishing Company (Sub. of R. R. Bowker) 178
Publishers Marketing Association Co-op Marketing Programs 150, 155, 174, 180, 212, 220, 221
Newsletter 29
Trade Distribution Acceptance Program 11
Publishers Marketing Association (PMA), writer resources. 11, 28, 29, 30, 46, 79, 92, 93, 103, 110, 150, 151, 155, 156, 169, 174, 175, 180, 196, 204, 212, 220, 221, 225, 227, 230, 231, 240
Publishers Trade List Annual, published by *R. R. Bowker* .. 177
Publishers Weekly Magazine, published by Reed Business Information 75
Publishers Weekly, published by Reed Business Information .. 28, 75, 103, 196
Publishers, Distributors and Wholesalers of the United States, published by R. R. Bowker 178
Publishing Events 226
Publishing Functions 2, 16, 31, 212, 244
Publishing Industry, future of ... 25
Purchase Confirmations and Receipts 35, 81, 124, 196
Purpose of this Book 3

Q

Quality Books, distributor 75, 230

R

R. R. Bowker, directory publisher 174, 177, 178, 227
Radio and TV
   Developing a Generic Interview 218
   Promotion Program 73, 216
   Promotion Strategies ... 217, 220
Radio and TV Room, page at your website 131
Radio Program, start your own 242
Radio-TV Interview Report, published by Bradley Communications 220
Reader Room, page at your website 129
Reciprocal Links 140, 237, 238
Record Keeping 15, 199
Registered, Autographed Collector's Edition (RACE) . 92, 148, 149
Registrations, of your book 173
Returns 10, 11, 22, 95, 97, 199, 236, 245, 246
Review Quotes 56, 57, 92, 107, 109, 127, 128, 129, 133, 134, 157, 158, 167, 169, 180, 211, 230
Review Sheet, prepublication promotion piece 188
Review-Book Presentation 186
   Alternative Formats and Delivery 183
   Costs Using CD-Rs 191
   Costs Using Hard copy 190
   Costs Using PDF Files on Your Website 192
Review-Book Promotion
   Compiling the Review-Book List 185
   Sending Review Invitations 182
   Telephone Follow-up Program.. 185
Reviews and Articles, organize an archive 189
Richard M. Nixon, author and self-publisher 3
Royalties ... 8, 13, 17, 61, 111, 195

S

Sales Hooks and Taglines .. 47, 73, 79, 108, 127, 128, 129, 130, 131, 136, 140, 143, 145, 152, 158, 166, 168, 169, 186, 188, 189, 211, 215, 230, 234
Sales Offers
   As Premiums 236
   Book-Related Organizations 234
   Bookstores 231
   Libraries 150, 180, 230
   Potential Individual Buyers 151, 179
SAN (Standard Address Number) 173
Scanner 35, 77
Scarecrow Press, publisher 178
School Library Journal, published by Reed Business Information 75
School Lists 56

Sci-Tech-Mystery-Thrillers, Chamberlain's new genre...... 4, 109, 125, 146, 186, 267, 277, 278, 279
Search Engines .. 46, 57, 143, 144, 145, 242
Search-Engine Registration
  Combination Approach....... 144
  Free Services............... 143, 144
  Keywords........................... 145
  Register Yourself................ 144
  Registration Services .. 126, 143
  Software...................... 143, 144
Self-Publishers, examples............ 2
Self-Publishing
  A Practical Publishing Approach 21
  An Alternative Publishing Approach 23
  Dealing with Bookstores....... 20
  Fulfillment System...... 182, 196
  Fulfillment-services Provider... 14, 17, 21, 22, 23, 24, 29, 84, 85, 108, 112, 128, 140, 196, 197, 200, 235, 244, 245
  Publishing Partner Relationships 12, 23, 194
  Who and Why..................... 1, 2
Self-Publishing Manual, by Dan Poynter... 29, 61, 165, 171, 176, 197, 200, 201, 210, 279
SFF Net, author works posting site 71, 119
Shirley MacLaine, author website 117
Signature-Attribution........77, 78, 108, 126, 159, 209, 212, 218, 226, 239, 242, 243

Small Press Record of Books in Print, published by Dustbooks 177
Small Publishers Association of North America (SPAN), writer resources 28, 30, 79, 92, 93, 103, 164, 175, 225, 227, 228
Small Publishers, Artists and Writers Network (SPAWN), writer resources...... .28, 30, 225, 227
Software Books......................... 37
Software Costs 31, 35, 37
Software Needed........... 31, 35, 37
Sol Stein, author...................... 29
Spam Policy, setting non-spam standards 204
Speaking and Participating at Events................................225
Speaking Topics..................... 135
Special Orders .. 94, 128, 197, 246, 279
Stein on Writing (2000), by Sol Stein 29
Stephen King, author 110
Stocking Levels........................ 10
Storage of Books......... 22, 94, 196
Storyline in Writing 42, 92, 166
Synopsis 41, 47, 109, 133, 135, 169, 278

T

Table of Contents ... 32, 94, 98, 99, 104, 106, 133, 135, 136, 137, 172
Telephone Call Program
  Develop a 30-Second Tell-and-Sell 164, 165, 166, 219

Index

Develop Rapport with Reviewer Assistants 166
Follow-up Delivery of Galley Review-Books 173
Follow-up Notes 167
Follow-up to Major Media .. 212
Galley-Book Review Invitation Follow-up 162
Get Through Screeners 165
Grab Attention 165
Major Book-Related Organizations Follow-up 234
Review-Book Delivery Follow-up 215
Review-Book Invitation Follow-up 162, 185
Sign Off Quickly 166
Telephone Techniques 164
Telephone-Services
  Answering Service .. 84, 85, 197
  Call Waiting 83
  Caller ID 82
  Distinctive Ring for Fax-Number 82, 86
  Fax 85
  Long-Distance Providers. 77, 83, 84
  Main Business Number 82
  Toll-free number 84
  Voice-mail. 78, 82, 84, 108, 121, 141, 165, 197
  Voice-mail Message 83
Test Promotion Ideas 56, 63, 211, 214, 228, 231, 232, 241
Test the Book in the Market 15
The American Book of Days, published by H. W. Wilson Company 214

The American Heritage Dictionary of the English Language (2000), published by Houghton Mifflin Company .. 29
The Author's Toolkit, A Step-By-Step Guide to Writing a Book (2000), by Mary Embree 29
The Catalog of Catalogs, by Edward L. Paulder 61
The Concrete Guide to Self-Publishing (2001), by Marilyn and Tom Ross 29
The Elements of Style, by William Strunk Jr. and E. B. White 3
The Encyclopedia of Associations, published by The Gale Research Company 68
The Los Angles Times 76
The New York Times Book Review 76
The Synonym Finder (1978), by J. I. Rodale 29
Theodore A. Rees Cheney, author 29

U

Ubid.com, auction site 32, 111
Unlimited Publishing, LLC (UP), POD publisher 195
U-Publish.com, by Danny O. Snow and Dan Poynter 2, 29
U-Publish.com, writer resources... 2, 30

V

Vanity Press 16

Vendor of Record...... 20, 24, 108, 128, 134, 140, 141, 158, 170, 174, 234, 279
Victoria Strauss, author website 117
Virtual Staff............................ 141

W

Website
   As Keywords 146
   Author and Self-Publisher Examples 117
   Command Buttons 123
   Common Page Features 120
   Control Forms 122, 123, 124
   Copyright Release................ 126
   Developing........................... 115
   Form Type Examples........... 125
   Free Hosting Services 119
   Hosting and Management Services........................... 144
   Hosting Costs...................... 119
   Hosting Services ... 77, 118, 119
   Hyperlinks . 120, 121, 125, 138, 139
   Look and Theme 115, 120
   Major Pages 125
   Master Content Files........... 125
   Master Page. 104, 106, 120, 139, 141
   Navigation Buttons 120, 125, 138, 139
   Objectives 116
   Offering Purchase Options....... 109, 123, 133
   Option Buttons............ 122, 123
   Order Form 123
   Purposes.............................. 116

Registering Keywords......... 145
Single-line Text Box 123
Software 117
Special Form Examples 123
Testing Features 141
Understanding Caveats 126
Uploading............................ 141
Wholesalers.... 7, 9, 10, 11, 13, 18, 19, 20, 22, 23, 24, 25, 40, 62, 108, 111, 128, 129, 134, 140, 141, 149, 156, 158, 162, 170, 174, 183, 188, 197, 229, 230, 231, 234, 246, 279
William Strunk Jr., author and self-publisher...........................3
Windows, Notepad Program....54, 70
WinFax PRO 10.0, software 33, 81, 86, 157, 196
Working-Paper Version, PDF E-Book................ 4, 105, 149, 204
Workshops
   Charging Fees 138
   Organizing...........................222
   Participant Information. 139, 222
   Self-Publishing............ 138, 139
   Workshop/Signings...... 63, 117, 128, 129, 138, 155, 163, 180, 181, 222, 231, 232, 245
Write Right! A Desktop Digest of Punctuation, Grammar, and Style (1995), by Jan Venolia .29
Writer Assistance, offering support 240
Writer Resources.................28, 29
Writer's Guide to Hollywood Producers, Directors and

Screenwriter's Agents,
  published by Skip Press 57
Writerswrite.com, writer resources
  30
Writing
  Articles 241
  Events 226
  Fiction 41
  General Story Folder 41, 42, 43
  Scenizing 42
  Sculpting Process 43
  Story-Writing Elements 43
  Writing Style 48, 225
  Writing Voice 42, 43

Y

Yahoo! Groups 65
Yahoo! Website Hosting Example
  .... 88, 118
YearBook of Experts, writer
  resources 59

Synopsis and Excerpt

Synopsis and Chapter I:

The Mountain and the Place of Knowledge

By Marshall Chamberlain

Coming from The Grace Publishing Group in 2004

Synopsis

Who are we? Why are we here? What is the truth about evolution and man's historic past? Are we alone in the universe? The ANCESTOR SERIES of sci-tech-mystery-thrillers is about these important questions. This is the first installment.

Geologist John Henry Morgan, ex-captain U. S. Marine Corps, is the unorthodox director of a new U.N. agency, the Institute for Study of Universal Phenomena (ISUP). An old friend, the Belizean Minister of Interior, has reached out to John Henry for help. An ancient *Diary*, written by the most revered sorceress in Mayan mythology, has been recovered from the ruins at Caracol. Translation of the Diary by the minister's museum curator leads to the discovery of a *Place of Knowledge* inside a mountain, a place created by unknown powers, wielded by unimaginable intent, a place beyond description.

Mysterious metallic *Scrolls* and a stalk-like *Scepter* were found with the Diary in the burial chamber of the sorceress, Myakka. Partial translation of the Scroll's Sanskrit-related language provides the ISUP scientists with clues to the purpose of the hidden center and operation of arcane high-tech apparatus.

Accessible through a materializing entrance, operated by long-hidden controls outside the mountain's sheer rock-face, John Henry and Mary Ellen Rollins, ISUP's deputy director, gain entrance to the mysteriously carved-out interior, and find themselves directed by bizarre mental prodding into experiencing the most shocking and incomprehensible phenomena of their lives. The protection and study of the *Mountain's* secrets becomes an ISUP project.

In the middle of organizing the project, John Henry is suddenly called upon to bring ISUP scientific resources to bear in the aftermath analysis of a massive earthquake that has severely affected 2,500 miles of the ocean-buried Atlantic Ridge and ripped a fifteen-mile-long *Rift* across the face of Iceland's largest ice cap. As the U.N.'s designated agency, ISUP is given the responsibility for planning and immediately implementing publicly-announced U.N. action responses.

Stretched thin, focused on revamping to deal with these two volatile situations, ISUP unwittingly finds itself engulfed in a hidden war of deceit and death, directed by nations intent on imposing their wills on the human race. CIA friends have compromised ISUP communications. Staff must scramble to protect themselves and the new agency from perceived terrorist actions. Two world powers have discovered the existence of the Mountain, acquired translations of the esoteric documents, and appear poised to take great risks to harvest operant technologies existing inside the *Place of Knowledge*.

ISUP rapidly discovers that its objectives of preservation and scientific study for the Mountain are naïve. But can the fledgling U.N. agency find trustworthy partners with compatible intents and sophisticated resources in time to figure out a way to protect priceless assets left from an ancient time, assets that demonstrate healing and destructive powers beyond the imagination of today's science? Whoever wields these capabilities will be able to drastically alter the course of civilization.

end

Chapter 1
Coming Home

October 10th

I'M GLUED TO THE window, thirty minutes out, watching the early morning light creep over the horizon, embrace the plane, and cast shadows over the landscape. This far out, the building tops around the center of Prague look tiny, peeking out through a layer of soupy fog and flashing like rosy sparklers in the sunlight. This is a beautiful old city, so lucky to escape the devastations of World War II. It feels good to come home. Calcutta's a long haul, with only one quick fuel stop in Johannesburg.

I've been wrestling with my curiosity for a couple of hours now since checking out the voice mail from Mary Ellen, wondering why she didn't just call me direct instead of leaving the message. ISUP's special e-phones let us know who's calling even when we're on the phone, so she knows to wait and I'll come right on. Playing it back several times didn't spark any revelation.

There's a fax waiting from Belize; she doesn't say who sent it or what it's about. It has to be Jacobson; he's the only person I know in Central America. If she didn't want to wake me up, she could have faxed it to the plane. It seems a little out of character ... but maybe it's just a personal note.

I watch more of the city materializing as the morning's fog blanket dissipates, and my mind meanders. It's hard to believe two years have already gone by since we took up our roles in this fledgling U.N. organization. I wouldn't have taken the job if Mary Ellen hadn't agreed to come as my number two.

Neither one of us had the slightest clue we'd find ourselves submerged in a world of strange mysteries and confrontation, filled with one adrenalin rush after another, dealing with the unknown, and fearful of how rational men might react to new definitions of reality.

THE WAY I landed here at the controls of ISUP was bizarre. I was exactly where I wanted to be, doing what I wanted to do. I'd just stepped in as the Chair of the combined Anthropology and Geology Departments at Florida State University when the invitation came out of the clear blue. The U.N. wanted a managing director for a new international organization, The Institute for Study of Universal Phenomena; it was supposed to investigate phenomenological events anywhere in the world. The director general wanted me to come to New York and talk.

I couldn't believe it. I was in the final throes of taking off again with Mary Ellen and a slew of graduate students. It was the third consecutive summer in the Middle East working with oil companies analyzing drilling cores before they were discarded in debris heaps. The invitation cited: ...sterling, uncompromising character; demonstrated ethical standards; administrative and leadership style; and personal magnetism. Incredible. There was a casual reference made to a recommendation by an unnamed, ranking government leader—intriguing stuff. At first the whole thing cracked me up. I didn't know anybody in government outside the military, and that was a long time ago. So what government leader? It felt like a set-up by someone with a devious sense of humor, and I knew several candidates.

It had to be a joke. I mean I used to stay in the field as long as I could to escape the paperwork and politics at the university. Sometimes I wouldn't return at the end of the summer until the week before classes began. And what leadership style could include the example-setting demonstrated by the rag-tag wardrobe I favor? I like old clothing, things with a history and character, and it doesn't matter what anyone thinks about it. People skills, now there's a magnetic attribute I can claim—definitely not a strong point, as my file certainly bears out. Being described behind my back, and even confronted face-to-face, as abrasive in one form or another is something I let roll off my back daily. I'm sure most of my peers believe I have little respect for the system. Yeah, I say what's on my mind, but I take care to be as accurate as I can and let the chips fall where they may, no malice. I don't hold back, and I think people tend to stay at arm's length because they don't want to hear the truth. So, with relationships on the scarce to nonexistent side, I consider myself happily spoiled, not having to listen to the petty problems and coarse humor characteristic of those I observe sharing quality time.

I'm accused of being reclusive. Nobody ever thinks I might simply be introspective, an acceptable philosophical concept.

And the invitation said the right guy had to be a scientist, an administrator, and a decision-maker. Well, that would be a tall order for somebody who's consistently on record going with the flow and using unorthodox methods and a seat-of-the-pants methodology.

So where could the kudos be coming from? The invitation had to be a prank. There was no way I was the responsible people person they were looking for to run that organization. But curiosity got the better of me. After a couple of harmless calls on the pretense of verifying times and dates, I was amazed the invitation proved legitimate. Even more amazing was that even though I knew there couldn't possibly be a match, I accepted, just like that. Very unusual for me. I look at myself as pretty analytical, not prone to jumping into something without a lot of thought. At the time I chalked it up to going with the flow.

By the time I boarded the plane for New York, I wasn't thinking about not making the grade. I had a positive mindset for the trip that made perfect sense. When I settled into first class and sat back with a pre-take-off Bloody Mary, I was preoccupied with ways to graze the island of Manhattan.

But like I say, the whole thing was bizarre. Strange things began happening as soon as I arrived, starting with a series of total submersion classes over the three-day trip, a chronology of world events over the last ten thousand years from a phenomenological point of view. I'd had no idea how much of history was labeled inexplicable, even during the last few hundred years, despite better documentation and the application of scientific methods. I found myself in a constant state of unraveling; my belief system was taking some deep hits.

Right from the first day, I began having bouts with a strange sense of fleeting insecurity; it would rush in, leaving me momentarily feeling vulnerable and disoriented, like a fish out of water. And just as quickly it would be gone.

And then, during the three days of revelation, virtually every U.N. official responsible for bringing ISUP into existence approached me, leading me off in confidence to a secluded corner or vacant room, encouraging me to accept the position, a job that in no way by no means had ever been offered. There had to be dozens of candidates under scrutiny. To say the least, the spontaneous encounters kept me confused. It never seemed appropriate to confront these people; I had no experience with the possible games that might be going on at this level. After about the third time it happened, I decided to take it in stride and just wait and see how it would shake out. But after a while, with so many important people I'd never met constantly drumming at me about taking the job, I actually started believing that maybe it was supposed to happen. As the days unfolded, I remember becoming oddly drawn, interested in what I was learning and stimulated in a mysteriously personal way. And each time I would fight off a bout of the creeping insecurity, a peculiar sense of euphoria took its place.

Stranger still, on my last scheduled day I was among the hundred or so guests at a big reception for the president of Kenya. I was told to get a hands-on feel for diplomatic protocol, see how I fit in, just mill around and be polite. So I rented a tux, boned up on what the protocols all meant, and resigned myself to enjoying another new adventure. I arrived at the reception in a cab, went through the invitation-checking and greeting-line formalities, and found the bar. Ten minutes later, I was trying to look adept at controlling a gooey hors d'oeuvre, when the U.N. Secretary General himself, whom I hadn't met yet, tapped me on the shoulder and asked if I was going to accept the offer. This was the final incongruity. I was polite, but told him in no uncertain terms that an offer hadn't been made, that he was far from the first to ask me the same thing, and that I was genuinely confused. Nonplussed, he pulled out an envelope from the breast pocket of his dress whites, handed it to me, and mumbled something about coming to his office in the morning. Before I could say anything, he turned and left me, at the hail of a waving diplomat setting up the podium. He hadn't said anything about time. So, there I was. I had the tickets in my pocket telling me I was on the return flight to Tallahassee at 8:10 in the morning, but now I was supposed to show up to see the Secretary General sometime the same morning.

I'm sure my mouth was hanging open a little as I watched the Secretary General walk away, but I put thoughts aside and made a beeline for the restroom. In the privacy of a stall I ripped open the envelope. It contained an incredible offer relative to what I'm accustomed to in academia, and at 9:00 the next morning I found myself virtually encased in a leather loveseat outside the anteroom for the U.N. Secretary General. On the one hand, I felt totally out of place in the elegant surroundings, dressed in khaki pants and a worn tweed jacket, at best looking like a park ranger, but on the other hand, I was naturally at ease, seemingly accepted in my obvious nonconformity.

It was simple; I got five minutes with him, said yes, got congratulated, and was sent to personnel for processing. After all the years of dedication to academia, teaching, and research, there was no hesitation. I remember telling myself over and over as I walked away from those plush offices and out into the streaming throng of people on Park Avenue, it was just part of going with the flow. But the elation was extraordinary; the flow had never felt that good before.

Boarding the plane the next morning, I was the new managing director of ISUP, me, John Henry Morgan, ex-U.S. Marine Corps turned college professor, just two days before my thirty-fifth birthday.

To this day, I've never thought about being out of place again. I left the docile gates of academia to be catapulted into a world of astonishing anomalies and phenomenological happenings, events that are defining the present in ways no one could have anticipated, precipitating massive shifts in interpretations of written history, and introducing serious challenges to the theories of evolution. The experience has invigorated my life and riveted it with purpose.

Over these past two years running ISUP, circumstances have brought a diversity of individuals together. We're galvanized by the same challenges and objectives, which require unusual levels of frankness if we're to confront the unexpected and inexplicable and still keep our sanity. The staff has somehow learned that magic. There's never a right way to catch the ball, so nobody feels exposed; every individual's motivated to give input. What we're doing is making a difference in the world we can see, touch, and feel, and for everyone right down the line that translates into fulfillment.

THE AGING 737 hits turbulence, and the panorama of evaporating haze over the city snaps back in focus. As we move over the skyline, the runway comes into view several miles off, glittering with puddles from last night's rain. I shut my eyes to get a handle on what I need to do back at ISUP before leaving for London. The last few months have been relatively quiet, allowing us to make needed adjustments on how we process the growing number of inquiries for assistance, as well as develop contingency plans for dealing with unique situations in the field. But I've learned that just when you think everything's under control, you need to make sure you're packed and ready to go.

I can't imagine what Jacobson could have on his mind in Belize. It's been at least two years since I spoke to the old man. The crusty Brit must be ready to retire about now.

The plane suddenly drops into an air pocket, leaving me detached and jammed against the seat-belt restraints. We level off, and through force of habit I take a quick look around to make sure we're all right and confirm location of the emergency parachute stack.

I lean back. Flashes of Calcutta start up like a newsreel, reminding me how glad I am to leave the place. Teeming millions spewing out over filthy streets like swarms of soldier ants. Everywhere you go, cacophony and claustrophobia disrupt perspective. Sense of smell is confounded around every corner. You're so saturated with sensory input that staying out of the way of bicycles and crazy drivers requires a Herculean effort.

The University of Calcutta is one of ISUP's affiliates. Its renowned international foundation, the Civicenter, supports an anthropological investigation into why life expectancy in many ancient civilizations decreased as cultures peaked—not what you'd expect, and definitely a phenomenon in need of explanation.

The wheels hit the runway unevenly. We fishtail, and the tires screech. Papers fly off the workstation in the midsection of converted passenger spaces, and my laptop slides off the seat next to me and topples into the aisle. I unbuckle from the window seat and gather everything up, piqued, ready to blame Fred for the landing, the air pockets, and my daydreaming.

Synopsis and Excerpt: *The Mountain*

As the plane brakes sharply, I hang on to the upper baggage rail in front of my seat and flip the intercom on the armrest.

"I'm sorry about that," Fred says before I can get the mike up to complain. "A cross-wind hit us at the last second. You okay?"

I was going to say, nice landing, Freddie, but I let it pass. "Yeah. I'm all right. I was daydreaming back here and thought it might have rubbed off. You wanna go for a quick beer? I've got a couple of hours or so before I have to meet Mary Ellen for lunch," I say, not wanting him to get any ideas. Both of us are usually so disoriented from long-distance flying that we go for beers no matter what time it is.

"Thanks, but no can do. Got a pressing engagement, if you know what I mean. So what's next on the agenda?"

"We go to London midday tomorrow—let's make it 1100 hours. Gotta see Shalard at Cambridge. Sorry, old buddy. But I'll make it up to you. You know that." No serious partying for Fred this time.

"Hey, not a problem. Do I ever bitch? We'll drink apple juice and pretend. I'll be there."

He's a good guy, loyal, trustworthy, puts up with a lot of last-minute stuff, even if he is a bit of a hound.

"Just keep your phone handy, Laddie," I add. "I'll ring you if there's a change. Have a good one. Maybe we can grab some time in London."

"Roger that. We'll be ready. Blue only needs turnaround maintenance."

Fred named the ISUP 737 Crystal Blue.

"So what's with Shalard this time?" he asks.

"Don't really know. You know how he is. He wants to show me something. Can't tell me—has to show me. It probably has something to do with his pet volcano project in Indonesia. The whole Cambridge grant is coming up for review in a couple of months, so I have to get up to date. I hope he doesn't have something new. We've got enough on the docket right now. Talk to you later."

I stuff all my paperwork back into folders, stash them in the laptop carrying case, and grab my pack. Saying goodbye to Angie, our do-it-all attendant/technician, I jump down from the open hatch instead of waiting for the boarding stairs to move in place. As I sling on the backpack and hustle past the cockpit, Fred waves and I give him thumbs up. It's probably a good thing he's tied-up. I'll have to put on some speed anyway to clean up and make it to the restaurant on time. Mary Ellen doesn't like to wait.

end

About the Author

Marshall Chamberlain lives in a small, old beach-house he calls The Writing Rock, located on Estero Island, better known as Fort Myers Beach, FL. Typically he spends November through May writing the sci-tech-mystery-thrillers that make up the ANCESTOR SERIES; conducting self-publishing workshops, classes and coaching; giving interviews; and speaking at writing and publishing events. Through his business, The Grace Publishing Group, he offers consulting services to authors by reviewing books and facilitating promotion planning and website creation. The rest of the time he packs up and moves around from one special spot to another in Sgt. Browning, his '84 VW camper, writing and visiting family and friends.

Graduate degrees in earth science and international management and finance provided the backdrop for sixteen years in investment banking and small-business consulting. Training and combat experience in Vietnam as a U.S. Marine Corps officer, and an ongoing search for meaning, are additional life installments that add flavor, depth, and authenticity to his fiction writing.

Prior to 1998, when he was led to locate in Fort Myers Beach, he wrote professional research, metaphysical and inspirational articles and memoirs, and dabbled in novel writing. Literally out of the blue, what has become the ANCESTOR SERIES began spewing from his pen while perusing *USA Today* at the local library. Like automatic writing, it just wouldn't stop.

Creative Self-Publishing in the World Marketplace became a book when Chamberlain began developing the business plan necessary to self-publish the first book of the ANCESTOR SERIES entitled, *The Mountain and the Place of Knowledge*. It ended up taking more than two and a half years to get the book to the printer.

The Mountain was in final edit as this book went to press, scheduled for the printer in late 2004. For your reading curiosity, a synopsis and a draft of Chapter I have been included after the postscript in this book. Chamberlain is already at work on the next two books in the series.

Visit Chamberlain's website, http://www.gracepublishing.org/, to download his media kit. Review copies of *Creative Self-Publishing in the World Marketplace* and chapters of the unfolding ANCESTOR SERIES of sci-tech-mystery-thrillers are available to media and industry professionals. Chamberlain offers self-publishing workshops to libraries, bookstores, writing and arts organizations, colleges, and universities. He encourages speaking invitations. Contact him at author@gracepublishing.org/.

Rapid Book-Order Form*

Individual Orders: Go to the publisher's website, http://www.gracepublishing.org/, and click on *Reader Room* to order direct from the vendor of record; or go to your favorite bookstore and place a *special order;* or send the information in the form below for yourself, or for a gift recipient, with your check payment to: The Grace Publishing Group, P.O. Box 3070, Fort Myers Beach, FL 33931, USA.

Library and Bookstore Orders: See appropriate information in *Books in Print;* or go the publisher's website, http://www.gracepublishing.org/, and click on *Library Room* or *Bookstore Room* for vendor of record and wholesaler information.

Visit Marshall Chamberlain's website, http://www.gracepublishing.org. Download his media kit, and peruse chapters of the unfolding ANCESTOR SERIES of sci-tech-mystery-thrillers. Media editors and publishing-industry professionals, please order review copies of *Creative Self-Publishing in the World Marketplace* (Grace, 2004) online by going to the *Media Room*. Author Dan Poynter says, "It's an indispensable companion to the *Self-Publishing Manual*."

Marshall offers writing and self-publishing *workshops* to libraries, bookstores, writing and arts organizations, colleges, and universities. Contact him at author@gracepublishing.org.

Copies of *Creative Self-Publishing in the World Marketplace* make great gifts! Please send to:*

Name of Sender if Gift: _____

Name of Recipient: _____

Delivery Address: _____

City: _____ State: _____ Zip: _____

Telephone Number: _____ Fax: _____

E-mail Address: _____

Price: $19.95 US, plus 6% sales tax for books shipped to Florida addresses. Delivery in the U.S., add $4.95 shipping and handling; each additional book add $2.50. International delivery, add $10.00 shipping and handling; each additional book add $5.00.

*Confirmations of order receipt and delivery are sent by e-mail, fax or postal mail at the discretion of the publisher or vendor of record.

Printed in the United States
26423LVS00005B/62